Computer Science, Algorithms and Complexity

Computer Science, Algorithms and Complexity

Edited by

Adele Kuzmiakova

www.arclerpress.com

Computer Science, Algorithms and Complexity

Adele Kuzmiakova

Arcler Press

224 Shoreacres Road

Burlington, ON L7L 2H2

Canada

www.arclerpress.com

Email: orders@arclereducation.com

Arcler Press publishes wide variety of books and eBooks. For more information about Arcler Press and its products, visit our website at www.arclerpress.com

ABOUT THE EDITOR

Adele Kuzmiakova is a computational engineer focusing on solving problems in machine learning, deep learning, and computer vision. Adele attended Cornell University in New York, United States for her undergraduate studies. She studied engineering with a focus on applied math. While at Cornell, she developed close relationships with professors, which enabled her to get involved in academic research to get hands-on experience with solving computational problems. She was also selected to be Accel Roundtable on Entrepreneurship Education (REE) Fellow at Stanford University and spent 3 months working on entrepreneurship projects to get a taste of entrepreneurship and high-growth ventures in engineering and life sciences. The program culminated in giving a presentation on the startup technology and was judged by Stanford faculty and entrepreneurship experts in Silicon Valley. After graduating from Cornell, Adele worked as a data scientist at Swiss Federal Institute of Technology in Lausanne, Switzerland where she focused on developing algorithms and graphical models to analyze chemical pathways in the atmosphere. Adele also pursued graduate studies at Stanford University in the United States where she entered as a recipient of American Association of University Women International Fellowship. The Fellowship enabled her to focus on tackling important research problems in machine learning and computer vision. Some research problems she worked on at Stanford include detecting air pollution from outdoor public webcam images. Specifically, she modified and set up a variety of pre-trained architectures, such as DehazeNet, VGG, and ResNet, on public webcam images to evaluate their ability to predict air quality based on the degree of haze on pictures. Other deep learning problems Adele worked on include investigating the promise of second-order optimizers in deep learning and using neural networks to predict sequences of data in energy consumption. Adele also places an emphasis on continual education and served as a Student Leader in PyTorch scholarship challenge organized by Udacity. Her roles as the Student Leader were helping students debug their code to train neural networks with PyTorch and providing mentorship on technical and career aspects. Her hobbies include skiing, playing tennis, cooking, and meeting new people.

TABLE OF CONTENTS

LIST OF FIGURES

LIST OF TABLES

LIST OF TABLES

LIST OF ABBREVIATIONS

BB	branch-and-bound
BFS	breadth-first search
BP	British Petroleum
CIA	confidentiality, integrity, and availability
CSMA/CD	carrier sense multi access/collision detect
DAG	directional acyclic graphs
DFA	determinant finite automaton
DFS	depth-first search
DL	deep learning
DoS	denial of service
DP	dynamic programming
DS	differential search
DSTV	digital satellite television
ETDC	end-tag dense code
GO TV	GO Television
HF	high frequency
IDF	inverse document frequency
LED	light emitting diodes
LSE	London School of Economics
LV	Las Vegas
MST	minimum spanning tree
NLP	natural language processing
PACC	perhaps approximately correct calculation
PPM	prediction via partial match
PRAM	parallel random access mechanism
RAM	random access memory
SAT	satisfiability

SE	search engine
SLS	sentinel linear search
STP	shielded twisted pair
TF	term frequency
TLS/SSL	transport layer security/secure sockets layer
UHF	ultra-high frequency
UTP	unshielded twisted pair
VHF	very high frequency
VSAT	very small aperture terminal

PREFACE

In computer science, an algorithm is described as a process used to solve distinct computational problems. Generally, the invention and study of algorithms are central to all fields of computer science including: artificial intelligence, databanks, graphics, networking, security, and operating systems among others.

However, algorithm development involves more than simply programming. It needs an understanding of various alternatives accessible for solving computational problems, such as firmware, networking, programming language, or output constraints accompanying any given solution. It also needs an understanding of what it entails for algorithms to be "accurate" in a sense that it entirely and proficiently solves the equation at hand.

Another accompanying concept is the development of a given data structure that allows an algorithm to operate smoothly. The significance of data structures comes from the belief that the vital memory of a workstation (where information is kept) is lineal, comprising of a series of memory cells which are serially structured 0, 1, 2…Therefore, the most basic data structure involves a linear array, whereby adjacent components are numbered with sequential number "indexes" and a component's value is retrieved by its special index.

This volume is divided into ten chapters that discuss various aspects of computer science and algorithms. Chapter 1 discusses the basic methods for development and analysis of algorithms, Chapter 2 discusses the computational complexity theory, Chapter 3 discusses the graph and networking algorithms, Chapter 4 discusses the cryptography, Chapter 5 discusses the algebraic algorithms, Chapter 6 discusses the parallel algorithms, Chapter 7 discusses the randomized algorithms, Chapter 8 discusses the pattern correspondence and text compression algorithms, Chapter 9 discusses the genetic algorithms, and Chapter 10 discusses the combinational optimization.

Furthermore, an array may be used, for instance, to keep a catalog of names, and effective methods are required to proficiently search for and recover a given name from the list. For instance, sorting the catalog into alphabetical sequence allows for the so-called binary searching method to be used, whereby the remaining of the list for search at every step is subdivided by half.

The search method is same as searching a phone book for any given name. Noting that the book is arranged in alphabetical order permits one to turn rapidly to the page that's close to a page holding the desired name. Several algorithms have been designed for sorting and searching through data lists efficiently.

While data items are often recorded successively in memory, they can be joined mutually by pointers (basically, memory addresses kept with an object to specify where the next object or items in a structure are located) so that the information can be structured in ways same as those where they'll be accessed.

Besides, the simplest of such a structure is known as the linked list, where non-contiguously stored objects can be retrieved in a pre-specified sequence through following the pointers available from one object in the catalog to the next. This list might be cyclic, with the last object pointing to the initial, or every element may have indicators on both sides to develop a double-linked catalog. Most algorithms have been designed for effectively manipulating these lists through examining, adding, and removing items where necessary. Pointers, such as graphs, furthermore provide the capacity to apply more complicated data structures.

Basic Techniques for Design and Analysis of Algorithms

CONTENTS

1.1. INTRODUCTION

In computing, algorithms represent a group of instructions used to solve certain problems. Considering that algorithm design methods are increasing at a fast rate, it has become crucial for IT specialists to improve their knowledge so as to meet the rising industry demands. Among the ways to achieve this is the learning design and analysis of algorithms. No matter the programming language that you apply for programming, i i's essential to understand algorithm design methods in data structures so as to create scalable systems (Figure 1.1).

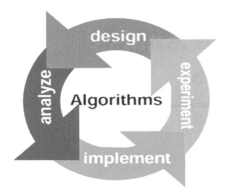

Figure 1.1: Most algorithms pass through a number of stages before application.

Source: https://www.university.youth4work.com/itmgg_institute-of-technology-and-management-gida-gorakhpur/study/4846-design-and-analysis-of-algorithm (accessed on 6 April 2020).

Currently, search, and sort algorithms stand as the most reputed and trusted trails for taking users into the realm of algorithm analysplusand data structure designing. Case in point, the "Google Search Engine (SE) Algorithm" is among the most complex algorithm designs applied by Google to categorize webpage's in their result pages depending on their relevancy (KABAT, 2013).

More recenre's there is been a radical change in how people find d plusand hash tag algorithm is yet another illustration of algorithm design which has been especially common with social media operators. Even though hash tagging comprises of a complicated learning curve, it won't be inappropriate to say that in searching across large lists with multiple of items, hash tag is definitely way faster. One great illustration of the hash tag algorithm is applying "Instagram hash tags" to link particular content, deliberations, conversations, or specific brands.

Choosing a proper designing method for parallel algorithms is a rather tough but essential task. Many of the parallel coding problems might even have several solutions. In this publication, some of the designing techniques that are discussed include; divide and conquer, dynamic programming (DP) and greedy method among others (KABAT, 2013).

1.1.1. Analyzing Algorithms

An algorithm is defined as a series of steps for solving a problem. The design and analysis process of algorithms is crucial for developing algorithms for solving different kinds of issues in computing and information technology. In abstract analysis of algoithms, it i's common to approximate their complexity through the asymptotic sense, which is, estimating the complexity role for arbitrarily massive input. The word "analysis of algorithms" originally was developed by Donald Knuth.

The algorithm analysis consists of an essential aspect of computational complexity concept, which offers theoretical valuation for the needed resources of the algorithm to resolve a particular computational problem. Many algorithms are developed to work with arbitrary length inputs.

The analysis of algorithms refers to determining the aggregate of time or space resources needed to implement it. Typically, the proficiency or running period of an algorithm can be mentioned as a function pertaining to the input length of a number of steps, commonly referred to as time-complexity, memory capacity, or space complexity (KABAT, 2013).

1.1.1.1. Importance of Aalysis

There i's a need for discussing the analysis orithms and, plus how to select an advanced algorithm for solvinutational matters. Through analyarticuar problem, it i's possible to start developing pattern recognition such that same kinds of problems may be solved with help from the algorithm.

Usually, algorithms are different from each other, even though their goal is more or less the samor instance, it'sit is known that a group of numbers may be sorted by applying different algorithms. The amount of comparisons done by a single algorithm can differ from others with regards to the same input. Therefore, time complexity of the algorithms can dianwhile, there's there is need to evaluate the memory space needed by every algorithm (KABAT, 2013).

Evaluation of algorithm is a procedure involving the analysis of problem-solving function of the algorithm, with regards to the duration and size needed (the memory size for storage during implementation). Nevertheless, the primary concern of algorithm analysis is the requisite time or performance. In general, these are the main forms of analysis:

- **Worst-Case:** The total amount of steps covered on any example of scope a.
- **Best-Case:** The number of steps completed on any example of scope a.
- **Average-Case:** The average amount of steps completed on any illustration of scope a.
- **Amortized:** The sequence of operations used for inputting size a, which is averaged across time.

In order toolve a matter, it'sit is important to consider both time and space complexity since the program can run on a structure where memory is narrow, but sufficient space is accessible or rar vice-versa. InForthis context, it i's necessary to compare between bubble sort and merger sort lgorithms.

While tThe bubble sort algorithm doesn't need addiory, the ; however merge sort algorithm needs additional space. Even though the time complexity for bubble sorting is greater compared need for applying bubble sorting is greatin a setting where memory is rather limited (KABAT, 2013).

1.1.2. Some Examples of the Analysis of Algorithms

There are various examples given for measuring the resource intake of an algorithm, various strategies are applied some of which comprise the following:

1. **Asymptotic Analysis:** Asymptotic behaviof the function $f(n)f(n)$ mean developme of $f(n)f(n)$ whilen n gets bier. Normally smalln n values are ignored, considering that most people are usually focused on approximating how sluggish the program shall be on massive inputs. The ideal rule of thumb mentions that the slower an asymptotic growth pattern, the more advancee algorithm but it'sit is not always factual. For illustration, the linear(n) e $*n$+kf(n$f(n)$equals $= d \times n+ + k$ is constantly asymptotically better compared to quadratic one, whis cad $f(n)n)$qualc. $c + (n)$

f) quals $= c.c \times n2n2+ + q$.

2. **Solving Repetitive Equations:** A repetition is the equation or inequality which defines a function in regards to value on minor inputs. Recurrences are normally applied in the divide-andquer model. Take T(n)*T(n)* to act as the run-ti on a matter of sizen. *n.* In case the problem scope is sll noh, let's yn $n \ll c$ *c* wherebyc *c* is the constant, then the direct solution will cover a constant time, normally captured as $\theta(1)$. When the problem division yields an integer of b-issues with scope *nbnb*.

For solving the mtteuration of *a.* $\times$ T(n/b)*T(n/b)* is required. By factoring the time needor subsion is D(n)*D(n)*, plusand the time needed for merging the outc of sub-issues as C(n)*C(n)*, the repetition relation may be symbolized as:

$$T(n) = \theta(1)aT(nb) + D(n) + C(n)$$ if $n < c$ otherwise n)plusC(n), or else.

The recurrence relation may be solved through the following techniques:

*   **Substitution Technique:** In this technique, the operator guesses a bound and applying arithmetic induction is for proving that the assumption was accurate.

*   **Recursion Tree Process:** Here, the recurrence tree is designed where every node signifies the price

*   **Master's Theory:** It i's another crucial technique for finding the weight of a repetitive relation.

3. **Amortized Examination:** Amortized analysis is commonly used for particular algorithms where a series of similar applications are performed. This method provides a bound for the real cost of a whole sequence, rather than bounding the rate of operation sequencing separately.

Moreover, amortized analysis varies from average-case examination; probability isn't involved in this case and guarantees the regular performance of every operation in the least case. The system isn't simply anlysis tool, rather it'sit is a method of thinking around the design, given that planning and analysis are somewhat related.

*   **Aggregate Technique:** The aggregate example provides a global outlook of the problemFor this method, whenn *n* operations rec worst-case period T(n)*T(n)* in total. It means the amortized rate of every ation is generally T(n)*T(n)/n*. Even though different

activities may require different intervals, in this technique varying rate is ignored.

- **Accounting Technique:**   For this method, varying charges are assigned for different operations based on their real cost. In case the amortized rate of operation surpasses its real cost, the variance is allotted to the item as credit. It therefore credits assistance to pay up for later operations where the amortized rate is less compared to the real cost case the real cost plusand the amortized rate of ith procedures are c_i or c_l, then the equation is represented d as $\sum_{i=1} nc_l^\wedge \le \sum_{i=1} nc_i$.

- **Potential Method:** This process represents the pre-paid function as potential energy, rather than considering prepaid effort as credit. The energy can be freed to pay for upcoming erations. By performingn n operations beginning with a primary data system D_0. Then consider, c_i being the real cost while d is the data configuration of ith operation. Here the possible function Φ maps onto the real figure $\Phi(D_i)$, including the related potential which is D_i. Beside amortized rate $c_l c_l^\wedge c_l^\wedge$ may be described as:

  1)$c_l^\wedge = c_i + \Phi(D_i) - \Phi(D_i - 1)$

- **Dynamic Schedule:** If the allocated space for the table is not enough, we must copy the table into larger size table. Likewise, if massive amounts of members areoved from the table, it'sit is a great idea to re-assign a table using a smaller size. Thr amortized analysis, it'sit is possible to determine that the amortized rate of insertion or deletion is continuous and vacant space in the dynamic table doesn't surpass a constant portion of the overall space.

1.2. DIVIDE-AND-CONQUER ALGORITHMS

When the scope of the input sequence is large, sometimes the algorithms may take a rather long period to run. The divide-and-conquer algorithm provides a solution in such situations. ParticularoperateTheta(n\lg n) $\Theta(n\lg n)$\Thet icling left sequence,n, n\lgn,n, right sece time in every case, plusruns inTheta(n\lg n) $\Theta(gn$\Tta, left sequence,n, n\lgn,n, right sequence rval in the ideal case plusand on average, even when the worst-situapertis \Theta$\Theta(n^2)\Theta$ (n2n)\Theta, left sequence, n, squared, right sequence (Mandloi, 2018) (Figure 1.2).

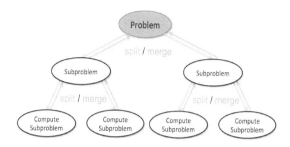

Figure 1.2: This algorithm divides problems into sub-problems *oblems for easier solving.*

Source: https://medium.com/cracking-the-data-science-interview/divide-and-conquer-algorithms-b135681d08fc (accessed on 6 April 2020).

In divide-and-conquer, merging sort and quicksort applies a regular algorithmic paradigm depending on recursion. The model, divide-and-conquer, subdivides a problem into mini-problems which are the same as the primary problem, which recursivesolves the subproblems, plusand finally merges the answers to each subproblems for solving the primary problem. Since divide-and-conquer resolves subproblems recursively, every subproblem should be smaller compared to the original case, and there should be a base example for subproblems.

Consider this algorithm as consisting of three sections: First divide the issue into multiple subproblems which are smaller cases of the similar problem. Proceed to conquer these subproblems by resolving them recursively. But in case they're insignificant enough, consider solving these subproblems in form of base cases. Merge the solutions to subproblems within the solution for an original problem.

Additionally, you can effortlessly remember the phases of divide-and-conquer algorithms in form of division, conquering, and combination. Assuming that every division step forms two sub-problems (but some divide-and-conquering algorlop ore than two), : In case it i's then possible to stretch out to ddititwo separate subproblems, the divide-and-conquer algorithms constitute several recursive calls (Mandloi, 2018).

1.2.1. Merge Sort Review

Since the system uses divide-and-nquer for sorting, there is a's need for determining exactly what the subproblems shall look like. The whole problem involves sorting an entire array. Consider if the subproblem is sorting a subarray for instance.

Particularly, the consideration would be sorting a sub-array beginning with index *ppp*, then moving over index *rrr*. This shall be appropriate for having a subarray notation, for instance, array[p. r] signifies this subsequence of array (Mandloi, 2018).

Remember that this "double-dot" notation isn't legal JavaScript; instead, the goal is using the program to define the algorithm, instead of any specific application of the code algorithm. With regards to this notation, considering an array of *nnn* components, it can be said that the primary problem is sorting array[0.*n*–1].

Below is an example of how merge sort utilizes the divide-and-cer method:

- **Division:** This isIt's done by determining the amount *qqq* at the position midpoint between the points *ppp* and *rrr*. The step can be repeated in a similar way as the mid-space in binary search: include *ppp* and *rrr*, subdivide by 2 then proceed to round down.
- **Conquer:** Recursively sort the sub-arrays found in every one of the dual subproblems developed by the divide stage. Meaning, to recursively categorize the sub-array array[*p.q*], then recursivelycategorize the sub-array array[*q*+ + 1.*r*].
- **Combine:** This involves merging the dual sorted subarrays reverse into the solitaed sub-array array[*p.r*].

There's here is also need for base case. This refers to a sub-array comprising of lesser than toments, which is, where $p \geq rp \geq rp$, is larger than or equivalent to, *r*, given that a subarray having no components or merely one component is already sorted. Therefore, the divide-conquer-combneocess applies only where $p << rp < rp$, is lower than, *r*.

Consider this example. Let's begin with an array comprising of [14, 7, 3, 12, 9, 11, 6, 2], su the original subarray is really actually the whole array, then it means the array0.7] ould ed as ($p = 0p = 0p = 0$ or $r = = 7r = = 7r$, is equals, = 7).

The subarray consists of rly two comtherefore it'sit is not actually the base case. In this exe, the sub-arrays array[0.0] plusand array[1.1] are fundamental cases, considering that each contains lesser than two components (Mandloi, 2018).

Many of the stages in merge phase are basic. Consider checking the base case effortlessly. Detecting the mid-focus *qqq* within the division stage is also quite simple. You must make at least two recursive contacts in the conquer stage. This is the combine stage, whereby you must merge a pair of sorted subarrays, whereby the actual work happens (Mandloi, 2018).

1.2.2. Merge Sort Analysis

She md operates in \Tta$\Theta(n)\Theta$ (n)\Theta, left sequence,n, n, right sequence interval when merging nnn components, therefore getting w tht mrgeS\ Theta$\Theta(n \log\_2 n)\Theta$ log2n)\Theta, or left parenthesisn, n, gin, start base, dual, final basen, n, right sequence time.

The goal is to begin by thinking on the three elements that make up divide-and-conquer, including how over for their running periods. It'sIt is assumed that the case involves sorting an overall amount of nnn components within the entire array.

1.2.2.1. The Tree Diagram

Computer researchers map trees upside-down, which is different from how real trees develop. The tree basically is a graph having no cycles (routes that begin and end within the same venue). The rule is calling vertices within a tree from its nodes. Here, root node is found on top, whereas the root is marked with the nnn sub-array scope for the unique nnn-element array.

Beneath the root are a pair of child noery one identified as $n/2n/2nn/2n/2n$, slash, where 2 represents subarray scopes for t subproblems of scope $n/2n/2nn/2n/2n$, with slash 2. Every one of the miniproblems of scope $n/2n/2n$, and slash 2 recursively classifies two subaays of scope $(n/2)/2$ left sequencen, n, slash 2, right sequence, slash 2, and $n/4n/4n$, with slash 4 (Mandloi, 2018).

Since there is a pair of subproblems of scope $n/2n/2n$, with slash 2, there exist 4 subproblems of scope $n/4n/4n$, with slash 4. Every one of these 4 subproombines an average of $n/4n/4nn/4n/4n$, with slash, 4 compounds, and therefore the merging period for every one of the 4 subproems can be described as $cn/4cn/4c,n, n$ with slash 4. Calculated over the 4 subproblems, it can be seen that the whole merging time for every subproblem of scope nn, and 4 is basic \cdot$\times$ cn/equs= $cn4 \times cn/4$ equals= $cn4$, d,c,,n, n, slash, 4, is equal to,c, c,n. n.

Normally, the firsthase of the tree displays one noden and matching merging durations ofc $c \times n$. The next phase of the tr res two nodes, every one of ½n,n, plusd a merging terval of $2 \times c \times$ ½nn,, similar asc $c \times n$.

Meanwhile, the 3rd phase of the treereveals 4 nodevery one of the ¼nn sequence plusand merging interval of 4 c 1/4n, n, which Is similar toc $c×n$. n. The tree is identified as "sSubproblem size," while the right alternative is considered the "Total merging duration for every subproblem of the scope."

In comparison to Dynamic Programming (DP), Divide and Conquer (D and C), and DP section the given issue into subproblems before solving these subproblems. On how to select one of these for solng a given problem, normally d andC c is used when similar subproblems aren't assessed multiple times (Puntambekar, 2010).

Anyway, Memoization and DP must be used. For instance, Binary Srch has been identifis a d andC c algorithm, though it'sit is impossible to assess these same subproblems successively. Otherwise, for computing nth Fibonaci figure, DP must be consid.

1.3 DYNAMIC PROGRAMMING

DP Mostly, DP is concerned with optimization rather than mere recursion. Whenever a recursive solution is identified that hasetitive calls for similar inputs, it'sit is possible to optimize the system through DP. Basically, the idea is storing tmes of subproblems, such that there's there is no need for having to re-compute these when required later. Generally, this basic optimization procedure reduces time complexities from simply exponential to polynomial. Case in point, by writing arecursiveer for Fibonacci Numbersnumbers, it's it is possible t get exponentinterval complexity., Addiy,plus through optimizing it byttoring answers of subprobleeans time complexity is reducedlessens to linear (Puntambekar, 2010). Ugly numbers are commonly used for DP; they consist of integers whose single prime factors include 2, 3 and 5. he serie 6, 8, 9, 10, 12 and 15, containreveals the original 11 ugly digits. Conventionally, 1 is covered. Considering the number(n),the duty of k would be finng n'th uUgeger.

For instance,in s 1 which is also known as the (Simplesimple) technique. It involves looping all positive integers up to when the ugly integer count is lesser than (, in cases where the ugly numeral ist t the incremental ugly number would count. In order to check whether an integer is ugly or not, consider dividing the digit by its highest divisible integers of 2, 3 or 5, and if the integer is 1 then it means the figure is an ugly integer otherwise not.

Case in point, to dete how to look for 300 and whether it's it is ugly or otherwise. The highest divisible factor of 2 is the number 4, following the sion of 300 by 4 you will get 75. PlusAnd the greatest divisible factor of 3 is also 3, and after subdividing 75 by 3 the answer is 25 (BASU, 2013). Furthermore, the highest divisible factor of 5 remains to be 25, so after subdividing 25 with 25 we finally get 1. dering that, we reach 1 finally, then 300 is then considered to be ugly integer. This technique is n't not time sufficient since it checks up for every integer up tohe point the ugly number sum becomesn, *n,* however space complexity of the method remains to be $O(1)$

1.3.1. Using Dynamic Programming

It's It is a time effective solution consisting of an $O(n)$ extra distance. The ugly-number arrangement is 1 to 6, 8, 9, 10, 12, 15, since every number must be divided by 2, 3 or 5, one way in order to look up the sequence or split therdero 3 oupss shown her

1.	1.	2 2	2 2	2 2	4×2 2	5
2.	3 3	3 3	3 3	4×3 3	5×3	
3.	1×5 5		2×5 5	3×5 5	4×5 5	5×5

You will find that all subsequences consist of the ugly-sequence by themselves (1, 2, 3, 4, 5, ...)tiplied by 2, 3 and 5. Thereafter, it'sit is possible to apply a similar merge technique as the merge sort, in order to get nearly every ugly integer from the available triple subsequence. Each step chosen highlights the smallest integer, and then moves one step thereafter (BASU, 2013).

- **Reducing the Rate of Subdividing the Array intSets:** Considering the array arr[], plusand the integer K, it means the work involves partitioning the data array into equal *k* non-empty sets, whereby every group exists a sub-array of the provided array and every component of the array consists of part of just one group. Every element in any particugroup should have a similar value. It'sIt is possible to perform this operation any amount of times. Simply pick a component from any of the array or alter its value to another quotient. Thereafter, print the least number of these operations needed to subdivide the rray.

1.3.2. Illustrations

- In case *k* = = 1, it means then that the set is a whole array by itself. For minimizing the amount of operations required the most natural activity to take is changing all the foundations of the array, and makes them similar to the array mode (component with the greatest frequency).

- As for *k* groups, mostly the last component of the array shall always be among the Kth group, whereas the 1st component shall be among the 1st group.

- In case the Kth group is found accurately then the issue will subsidize to partitioning the remainder array into $K - 1$ sets using the minimum operations.

Approach: The problem can be resolved through DP.

- Allow DP(i,j) to represent the basic operationrequired to divide the array [1.i] intoj j sets.

- Now, the work involves finding DP(N, K) where the minimum operations required to divide the array[1.N] are partitioned into *k*rous.

- The basic cases DP(i, j) in whichj $j == 1$ may be easily answered. Given that the whole array array[1.i] must be subdivided into one group only. Going by observations, detect the module of array[1.i] then convert all the components in array[1.] for the mode. In case the mode happened$x$ x times, it means then that $i-x$ components must be changed, that is, $i-x$ operations.

- Considering that the Kth group terminates at the final element. Nevertheless, it might begin at different possible positions. Considering that the K-th set begins at a given index, it then array[it. N] must be subdivided into one main group while array[1. ($it-1$)] should be subdivided into K−1 sets. The rate of dividing array[1.($it-1$)] up into K−1 sets is DP($it-1$, K−1) including the rate of subdividing array[it.N] into one group may be calculated through a given mode, including its frequency observation.

- In order to locate the frequency of aisting component in the range [$it.i$], it'sit is possible to utilize a hashmap or an integer variable. Besides, the integer variable signifies the present highest frequency. The diagram stores all components seen until now together with their frequenc In case an element is perceived then it'sit is frequency is arose in the map, in case the element's frequency is greatern the present highest frequency, then it'sit is important to update the present top frequency to the rate of the only seen element.

- Thus DP(i, j)ers the least aspect of DP($it-1, j-1$) plusand cost of subdividing array[*it.i*] within group 1 for every conceivable value of it.

1.4. GREEDY HEURISTICS

The greedy heuristics is any algorithm which covers the problem-solving calculations of making the naturally optimal choice at every stage, with the goal of detecting a global optimum. For many problems, the greedy strategy doesn't typically produce the most optimal solution, though still a greedy heuristic might yield locally optimum solutions which approximate a universally optimal answer in a reasonable duration of time (Figure 1.).

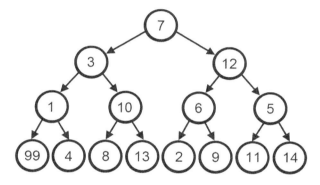

Figure 1.3: Greedy heuristics follows the most natural pattern for problem solving.

Source: https://brilliant.org/wiki/greedy-algorithm/ (accessed on 6 April 2020).

For instance,a greedy technique for the traveling sales-man problem (that's of great computational complexity) follows this heuristic: On each stage of the trip, visit the closest unvisited city. The heuristic doesn't intend to discover a best solution; however it ends in a reasonable amount of steps; getting an optimal answer to an otherwise complex problem normally requires unreasonably numerous steps. For arithmetic optimization, greedy algorithms normally solve combinatorial issues having the elements of matroids, while providing constant-factor estimates to optimization challenges with submodular arrangement (Dave, 2007).

Generally, greedy algorithms consist of five parts: (i) The candidate set, where a solution is formulated; (ii) Selection function, which selects the most ideal candidate for addition to the solution; (iii) Feasibility function, this is applied to determine whether a candidate called upon to contribute towards a solution; (iv) Objective function, which allocates a v for the solution, or partial solution, plusand finally; and (v) Solution function, indicating when a complete solution, has been detected.

The greedy gorithms generate ideal solutions only foron a few mathematical prers. Many problems for prty is constitute two properties: First isgice element.

Here, the user makes whhoice that seems ideal at that timee period, and then resolves the subproblems which come up later. Besides, the choice made through a greedy algorithm might depend on choices which have been carried out so far, however not on impending choices or every answer to the sub-problem (Dave, 2007).

Basically, it iteratively makes a greedy selection after another, limiting every given matter into a lesser one. For other cases, the greedorithm doesn't reconsider its choices. It's It is the primary difference that separates it from DP, that's more exhaustive and definite for finding the solution. Following each stage, the DP will make decisions depending on the decisions whicve been made during the previous phase, plusand also may reconsider the preceding stage's mathematical route to the solution (Dave, 2007).

1.4.1. The FastDP Algorithm

This is an example of a greedy heuhich can produce slightly fastr and g. , plus is a sequence of magnitude quicker. P algorithm covers four key methods:which are universap, vertical swapping, local reorde and single-segment gathering. The stream of FatDP stream is also provided in the primary aAlgorithm.

Global swapping is a technique which gives the highest wire length reduction. It insects all cells individually. For every cell ii, the objective is moving it to the optimal point. In any ven placement, the optimum location of celli i can described as the area so that in case celli i is established in it, then the wire length would be optimal (Dave, 2007).

Besides, it may also be determined from the context of a median notion. AlloEi to be the group of nets attached to celli. i. Meanwhile for everyet (e) $\in Ei$, the bound box discounting celli i would be calculated. Allow xLe and xUe tothe x-sequence of left/right boundaries, plusand yLe and yUe are the y-coordinates denoting lower and top boundaries, respectively.

Additially, the optimum x-coordinate for the celli i is provided by a median of th group of bounry coordinates reading $\{xLe:e\ e \in Ei\}\cup\{xUe:e\ e \in Ei\}$. Gerally, the optimum coordinate for the celli i is an area rather than one point a the amount ofcomponents in the group $\{xLe:e\ e \in Ei\}\cup\{xUe:e\ e \in Ei\}$ is even. Liwise, the optimum y-coordinate for the celli i is provided by the average of the groupof boundary coordinates represented as $\{yeL:e\ e \in Ei\}$ (Dave, 2007).or instance, thoptimum region of the i attached to 3 ths would be A equals = { 1, B equals i, l asC C equals = $\{i, 6, 7\}$. }, Constiting constitutin optimal parts of celli. i. Even though it's it is desirle in regards to wirelength for moving celli i to the optimal area, this optimal region might not have adequate space to fully accommate the cell. Thus in global swap, the celli i seeks to swap with a different cell or space within an optimal region. The advge function is calculated for every cell plusand each space within the optimal region.

In case there exists the cell or some space with progressive benefit, the matter with the grtest benefit shall be swapped with the celli. i. The advantage function comprises of two main components. The first element covers improvements in the total wire-length in cas swap is done.

As for the second phase, it's it is known as the penalty. It involves swapping up cells of varying sizes or exchanging a large cell with a lesser space to create an overlap. This overlap is resolved through shifting of adjacent cells. This penalty is a feature of the least quantity of shifting needed to resolve this overlap. The vertical swap is more or less the same as global swap. But the main difference is that the cell tries to switch with a few adjacent cells a row above or below its present position (Dave, 2007).

In some cases, the cell get moved through global swap, since there's there is no cell or distance in the optimum region with a progressive benefit. Vertical swap permits the cell to transfer toward its optimum region to lessen the vertical wirelength. Furthermore, vertical swap is way quicker than global swap, since the amount of candidates who are to be regarded for swapping is way less.

The locare-ordering considers every possible set ofn n successive cells in a line. For every group, all poial left-right cell orderings are tried, plusand the one having the most ideal wire-length is chosen. Limited reordering is a rather inexpensive method for locally mimizing horizontalelength. Practically,n n is fixeto 3. It'ss not required to use a biggern, n, since it'sit is more efficient for fixing nonlocal faults through global swap.

Meanwhile, single-segment clustering is another technique used for minimizing the horizontal wire-size by moving the cells in segments without altering the cell order. For FastDP, the segment refers to a maximal uninterrupted segment of a typical cell row. The single-segment clustering inspects every segment individually. Once a segment is marked, the cell locations in other sections are fixed. An effective algorithm based on the clustering concept is provided to discover the optimum non-overlapping allotment of cells in the segment (Dave, 2007).

1.5. SENTINEL LINEAR SEARCH

The sentinel linear search (SLS) as its name shows is a form of Linear Search whereby the amount ofuses fewer comparisons becomes reduced, in comparison to when compared to a conventional linear search. Once a linear search has been done on a variety of size (N), then for the unlikely scenario an average of N n comparisons would be made once the search element is compared to every element in the array. plusAnd then (N + + 1) contrasts are done for the element index to be compared, such that the index isn't completely out of bounds for the array that can be abridged in a typical SLS (Mandloi, 2018).InFor this search, the final component of the ay can be replaced usingthe element which is for searched for. Then the, nhe linear search would be done on the arrayminus checking whether the present index is within the index magnitude of the array, or otherwise since the element for search will certainly be found within the array-even when it wasn't existing in the primary array because the last comppped with fore, the index for checking nveron't ever be boundlesshe number of comparisons amoutats he worst scenario here isshall be (N+ + plus 2).

1.5.1. Linear Search Essentials

The notion behind linear search involves comparing the search object with the componentsthe list individually (using a loop). It willplus stop immediately when the first copy is obtained for the search component in the list. Consider the worst situation where the search coonentdoesn't exist within the catalog of scopeN. n. Tthen th Basic Linear Seal take an average of 2N+ + 1 comparisons , where (N comparisons aainst each component in the searching list and N+ + 1 contrasts are for stihe finish he loop status).

ForSLS,the idea is minimizeszing the amount of comparisons needed to detect an element within a list. Here, the goal is replacing the final component of the list using the search component itself then operate a while loop, in order to find out whether there exists a copy of the searching component in the record and leave the loop immediately the search element is found (Mandloi, 2018).

In this situation, it can be seen that while loop cane just one comparison in every iteration and it'sit is definite that it will end since the final component of the list consists of the search component itself. Thus, in the worst situation (in case the search constituent doesn't occur in te list) it means there sha be at the highest N+ + 2 comparisons (total ofN *n* comparisons for while loop and 2 contrasts for th 'if' condition). This is better compared to (2N+ + 1) comparisons which are also present in the Simple Linear Search. This algorithm contains a time complexity raof O(n) (Mandloi, 2018).

1.6. BACKTRACKING

It's Backtracking is an algorithmic-technique used to solve problems recursively through trying to create a solution incrementally, or one bit per time, eliminating those solutions which fail to fulfill theproblm constraints at any given point (with time, here, refers to the duration elapsed until reaching a particular level on the search tree).

Case in point, consider the SudoKo solution finder, where the goal is trying to fill digits individually. Upon findhe current digit can't lead to any solution, it's it is ideal to eliminate it (backtrack) then attempt the nexit. This formulation is much better than the naiveNaïve technique (creating all likely combinations of numbers and then attempting every combination individually) while dropping a group of permutations upon backtracking (Mandloi, 2018).

For Sudoku backtracking, considering a partially occupied 9×9 2D sequence 'grid [9][9],' the objective is assigning numbers (from 1-to-9) to the unfilled cells such that all rows, columns, and sub-grids of scope 3×3 eatures exactly one example of the numbers from 1- up to 9. Consider solving the matter on "PRACTICE" initi before commencing to the next solution. The NaiveNaïve algorithm similarly is applied to create all probable configurations of figures, from 1 up to 9, for filling the empty cells. Consider every possible configuration individually, until the most accurate configuration is discovered.

Backtracking algorithm is the best for solving Sudoku problems by exclusively assigning dito empty cells. Prior to allg a number, it's it is important to check if it's it is safe to allocate. Basically, check that a similar number isn't present in the present row, column, and 3X3 sub-grid (Mandloi, 2018).

Following a safety checkup, a number is consequently assigned, before the operator recursively checks if this assignment provides a solution or otherwise. In case assignment doesn't provide any solution, then it'sit is possible to try the subsequent number for the present empty cell.

PlusAnd, if none of this number (1–9)o any solution, it returns false. In case there's there is no conflict for numbers at any given row, then col assign a number to row, or col and recursively attempt to fill up the remainder of the grid). However, if recursion is successful, then return true) otherwise, remove a number and attempt another step. When all digits have successfully been attempted and nothing seems to work, then return false (Mandloi, 2018).

- **The Knight's Tour Challenge:** Problems that are normally solved through backtracking method have certain properties in common. Like, they can just be solved through attempting every likely configuration al configurations are attempted only once. One NaiveNaïve solution to these problems is attempting all alignments and output the configuration which follows considering problem constraints. backtracking functions in increm manner, plusand is an optimization above the NaiveNaïve solution whereby every likely configuration is being produced and tried.

Case in point, consider the below Knight's Tour illustration:

The knight is located on the original block of the empty board while, movement based on the guidelines of chess, shoisit every square exactly once.

- **Knight's Tour NaiveNaïve Algorithm:** Thisorithm is used to produce all tours one by one, plusand to check whether the produced tour fulfills the constraints. The Backtracking works incrementally to attack problems. Normallhe model begins from an empty resolution vector plusand one-by-one adds objects. (The meaning of items also differs from one problem to another. For the case of Knight's tour problems, the item ise of a Knight's transfer). By adding an object, it'sit is possible to check whether adding the present item violates any problem constraint, if so then remove the object and attempt other alternatives.

But if these alternatives don't work then visit the previous stage then remove the object include in the preceding stage. Upon reachinitial phase back then it can be said that there's there is no solution existing. In casding an object doesn't violate any constraints, it'sit is possible to then recursively include items individually. But if the solutions vector is complete then proceed to print the answer.

Remember that Backtracking isn't the moseal solution for executing a Knight's tour, but it'sit is still applicable. Among the applications for Knight's tour problem is that it can print one of the potential answers in 2D matrix context. Essentially, the output consists of a 2D 8*8 matrix having numbers ranging from 0-to-63 and the numbers display steps completed by Knight.

Additionally, the Magnet Puzzle uses Backtracking as its fundamental approach. This puzzle game entails placing a group of domino-design magnets (even electrets or other similar plarized items) in a subclass of slots within a board, in order tll a group of constraints. Every slot conistsmprises of a blank inclusion (secified by 'x's), comprising a "magnet both + + VE and –VE ends. The integers alogbboth the top and left sides reveal the amounts of '+ + ' squares present in given r or columns (Mandloi, 2018).

The ones found acrossthe right and lowermost sections revealf '–' symbols in given rows or colum either end is uncontrained concernig the amount ofdon't have to have '++' and '–' signs, with regard to which number is missing. Apart from fulfilling these mathematical constraints, the puzzle solution should also fulfill the constraint that there are no two orthogonally close squares which can have a similar sign (diagonally combined squares aren't constrained) (Mandloi, 2018).

1.7. BRUTE FORCE/EXHAUSTIVE SEARCH

Brute Force algorithm is designed to develop and evaluate nearly ible solutions. As for discrete matters where there's there is no proficient solution technique known, it could be appropriate to test evpossibility chronologically so as to find whether it'sit is the answer. This exhaustive assessment of every possibility is reo as exhaustive examination, direct search, orand een the "brute force" technique. Unless it is revealeds that NP-problems are equal to P-problems, something that seems unlikely though hasn't yet been verified, NP-problems may only be solved through exhaustive search for the worst situation (KABAT, 2013).

In computer science studies, exhaustive or brute-force search is commoferred as the generate-and-test process. This is, it's a comprehensive problem-solving method and algorithmic paradigm which methodically enumerates all potential candidates to get the solution, apart from checking whether every candidate satisfies a given problem's statement. This algorithm is commonly used to discover the divisors that encompass a natural digitn,' erating each integer ranging from point 1 ton, n, lusand checking whether every one of them subdividesn *n* without leaving a remainder.

The brute-force technique for the 8 queens puzzle will assess every possibonfguration of 8 sets on a 64-squared chessboard, plusand, for every arrangement, determine whether every (queen) piece may attack another.n though brute-force search is basic to implement, plusand will always get a solution wherever it exists, still its cost is relative to the amount of candidate solutions-and this in many practical cases tends to increase quite fast as the magnitude of the problem rises (§Combinatorial explosion) (KABAT, 2013).

Hence, brute-force search normally is applied when the problem scope is limited, or where there are problem-exact heuristics which can be applied to minimize the group of candidate solutions up to a manageable scope. The technique is also applied when the of implementation is way more crucial than speed. It'sIt is the case, for instance, in crucial applications whereby any faults in the algorithm may have serious ramifications, alternatively when using the computer to prove some mathematical theory.

The brute-force search can further be useful when applied as a baseline technique for benchmarking other codes or metaheuristics. Certainly, brute-force search may be seen as the most basic metaheuristic. This search however must not be mistaken for backtracking, where massive sets of solutions may be rejected without being explicitly numbered. The brute-force technique for discovering an object in a table-specifically, check every entry for the latter, sequentially, this is known as linear search (KABAT, 2013).

1.7.1. Applying the Brute-Force Search

For effective application rute-Force search in a particular group of problems, it'sit is necessary to apply four main procedures, which are first, next, validated, and output. The procedures must consider as a standard the file P for the ific example of the problem which is to be resolved, plusand must follow this protocol: first (P): formulate a primary candidate answer for P. Then (P, *c*): produce the succding candidate r P following the presenone which isc. *c*, valid(P, *c*):).

To check ifandidatec *c* is the answer for P,. output (P, *c*): applyc *c* of P answer as suitable to the program. The next process should also tell if there aren't any more cdidates available for case P, following the present onec. *c*.

One convenient way for achieving this is returning a "null candidate," or a typical data value Λ which is different from most real candidates. Similarly, the original procedure must return Λ in case there aren't any candidates for the case P. Thebrute-force technique is thenisplayed by the algorithmc equation ← first(P) mewhilec $c \neq \Lambda$ ismplemented if valid(P, c) leads to then n output (P, c)c $c \leftarrow$ next(P, c) end while.

For instan, when searching for the divisors that detmine integern, n, the example data P becomes the inter. n. The original (n) must return the value 1 in casen $n \geq \geq 1$, or even or lse; the ca foling (n, c) must return the valuec $c ++ 1$ in casec $c <<n$, n, or otherwise; and integ (n, c) must return true only whenc c is the divisor n.n (As a matter fact, chosinit n e ken ton $n++1$, whil the testsn $n \geq\geq 1$ plusandc $c<<n$ n become unnecessary.). This Brute-Force search algorithm will call output on all candidates which is the solution to a particular case P. It can also be modified to cease after determining the first solution, or any specifiedmoun solutions; or following the testing of a given amthe ountnumber of candidates, or following the spending of a particular quantity of CPU duration (KABAT, 2013).

1.7.2. Combinatorial Explosion

The khniq that typically , for various real-life problems, the amountnumber of regular candidates is excessively large. For example, by cg for the numerical divisors of any given number, the amountmber of caidates tested can be the represented as numbern. n. So, ifn n has 16 decimal numbers, for instance, the search shall need to execute around 1015 computer instructions, and this will take multiple days on any standard PC. In case (n) is the random 64-bit regular number, which contains around 19 decimal numbers on average, it means the search shall on average tughly 10 years (Dave, 2007).

This sharp growth in the amountnumber of candidates, with increase in the scope of the data surges, happens in all kinds of problems. For example when seeking a given reordering of 10 letters, we get 10! = = 3,628,800 potential candidates to check, something that a common PC can produce and test in lower than a second.

Nevertheless, adding one extra letteh is just a 10% surge in data size-shall multiply the amountnumber of candidates by roughly 1approximate 1000% rise. For 20 letters, averagely the amountnumber of potential candidates is 20! This is roughly 2.4× 1018 or just about 2.4 quintillion in figures; while the search takes roughly 10 years. Typically, this unwelcome phenomenon is known as combinatorial explosion, or dimensionality flaw. An example of this is, when combinatorial complexity causes a solvability restriction in solving chess problems.

Chess isn't a solved game but rather depends on the players' moves. From the year 2005, chess game endings having 6 pieces or lower were solved, displaying the result of every position if played seamlessly. It took ars to finish the tablebase having one more chess componentscomponent added, therefore finishing a 7-set tablebase. Including one extra piece to the chess ending (therefore producing an 8-set tablebase) is regarded intractable because of increased combinatorial complexity (Dave, 2007).

1.t-Tracking Brute-Force Searches

An effectivuicken make brute-force algorter is by lessening decreasing th search space (, which is, the group of candidate solutions), through implementing heuristics unique to the problem range. For instance, in the 8-queens problem the issue is to add 8 queens on the standard chessboard such that no queen unknowingly attacks another. Since every queen can easily be set up vailable 64 squares, generally there are roughly 648 (equals= 281,474,976,710,656 possibilities that can be considered.

Nevertheless, since all the queens are similar, and no two queens are replaceable on one square, it means the candidates are every possible means of selecting a sequenceares from a lisquares; meaning 64 choose 8 is equals= 64!/(56!*8!) is equals= 4,426,165,368 and the candidate solution 's'-roughly 1/60,000 of the preceding estimate. Furthermore, no arrangement with a pair of queens found on the scolumn or row can provide a solution (Dave, 2007).

Thus, it'sit is possible to further limit the group of candidates to these particular arrangements. Like some examples show, a tiny bit of analysis shall typically lead rastic limitations in the amount of candidate solutions, plusand may convert an otherwise complex problem into a small one.

For some circumstances, the analysis might lessen the candidates to a group of valid solutions; which is, it might yield an algorithm which directly enumerates every desired answer (or determines one solution, as suitable), without having to waste time with unnecessary tests and the production of invalid candidates. Case in point, for the problem "locate all integers lying bn 1 to 1,000,000 which are evenly dividable by 417" the naiveNaïve brute-force answer shall produce all numerals within the range, testing every one of these for divisibility. Nevertheless, that problem can be solved more easily by beginning with 417 then repeatedlyadding 417 up to a point thatumber surpa00,000—, which will take just 2398 (equals= 1,000,000divided /417) stages, with no tests (Dave, 2007).

1.8. BRANCH-AND-BOUND ALGORITHM

The branch-and-bound algorithm has been designed for solving combinatorial various optimization problems. The typical optimization problemnormally exponentwith regs to time complexity and, plus the solution mayneed exploreing all ntal permutations in worst example. The branch-and-bound This aAlgorithm solves problems rather faster. Take, fo the 0–1 Knapsack problemhe for undersbranch-and-bound algorithmtanding Branch and Bound. Generally, there are multiple algorithms through which the knapsack equation can be solved (Figure 1.4).

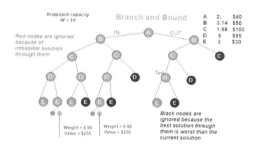

Figure 1.4: The algorithm works by comparing the best and worst solutions for a path.

Source: https://www.geeksforgeeks.oranch-and-bond-agoithm/ (accessd on 6 April 2020).

In For this problem, thea bBacktracking sSolution may be optimized in case of a bound for best possible answer sub-tree rooted with each node. In case thae best in a subtree is worse compared to the current best, it'sit is possible to simply ignore the node as well as its subtrees. Therefore, the goal is computing the bound (best answer) for each node and comparing the bound with present best answer before examining the node (Puntambekar, 2010).

Branch-and-bound (BnB, BB or B&B) is a special algorithm dsigngram for distinct and combinatorial optimizing probleplus mathematical optimization. The BB procedure consistsmprises of a methodical enumeration of candidate answers by way of state space searching: the group of candidate solutions can be considered as establishing a rooted tree having a complee set at the base.

This algorithm examines branches of the tree, representing subsets of a given solution set. Prior to computing the candidate solutions for a branch, this branch is examined agt upper and lesser projected bounds on the optimum solution, plusand is eliminated if it can't create a better solution compared to the best discovered so far thanks to the algorithm.

Additionally, the algorithm relies on effective estimations of the lesser and maximum bounds of locations/branches of the searching space. In case no bounds are accessible, it means the algorithm disintegrates to an extensive search. The Aon Doig and Ailsa Land , where theonol of Economics (LSE) backed by (BP) British eum inthe year 1960 for distinct programming. The algorithm, plus has become one of the widely applied tools for resolving NP-tough optimization problems (Puntambekar, 2010).

18.1. Function

The obje BB algorithm is finding the value x x which maxim or lessens decreases the value of the actual-valued $)$, known as goal function, amidst some group S of permissible, or candidate answers. The group S is known as search space, he feasible area. The remainder of this section presumes that $f(x)f(x)$ minimization is required; the assumption comes without any of generality, because one can determinhe hte $ox)f(x)$ dtermining the of $g(x)(x)$ is equals$=-f(x)f(x)$.

Te B&B algorithm furthermore operates based on two key principles.: First, it recursively sub-divithe search interval into smallr paces, apart from minimizing $f(x)f(x)$ from these lesser spaces.; Tthis splitting is known as branching. By itself, branching can't cover brute-force listing of candidate solutions or testingmall. In order to enhance the output of brute-force searches, the algorithm normally keeps check of bounds for the minimum which it'sit is attempting to find, while using these bounds to "trim" the search space, removing candidate solutions which it can prove won't have the optimal solution (Puntambekar, 2010).

Converting these values into a solid algorithm for a prticular omization problem needs some form of data structure to, representing groups of candidate solutions. This representation is referred to as a problem instance. Symbolize the group of candidate answers of an example I with SI. Thse representation must come up with certain operations. First, it'sit isproducing two or more cases where each represents a subgroup of SI. (Normally, the subsets are detached to prevent algorithms from visiting a similar candidate solution twice, however, this isn't necessary).

1.9. RANDOMIZED ALGORITHM

As the name suggests, randomized algorithm applies a certain a level of randomness as an aspect of its logic. Besides, the algorithm normally uses consistently random bits in form of auxiliary inputs for guiding its behavior, with the hope of attaining positive performance in the "ordinary case" over every conceivable choice of random elements. Officially, the algorithm's performance shall be a randomized variable decided by the random elements; therefore, either the run time, or output (or even both) become random variables.

Users must differentiate between algorithms which apply the random input such that they constantly terminate with the accurate answer, also, where the anticipated running period is finite (the Las Vegas (LV) algorithms, such as Quick sort, or algorithms with a chance of generating the accurate results) or don't produce the best outcomes either by indicating a failure or not terminating (Puntambekar, 2010).

For some situations, probabilistic algorithms become the only feasible way of solving the problem. As a common practice, the randomized algorithms usually are approximated through a pseudorandom numeral generator instead of an accurate source of random parts; this application may diverge from the anticipated theoretical behavior.

r a model, consider the issue of finding th 'a' within a group ofn n compounds. The Input is: A sequence of n$\geq \geq 2$ components, where half of them are 'a's while the remaining half is made of 'b's. Output: Involves finding 'a' within an array. Where there are two editions of the algorithm, a single LV algorithm, and another Monte Carlo one.

In LV algorithm, when an 'a' has been found, it means that the algorithm succeeds, otherwise the algorithm fails. Following k iterations, it thrm $\{\text{find~a}\}]=1-(\text{half})^{k}\}\Pr[\{\mathrm{find~a}\}] =1-(\text{half})^{k}. 1-(1/2)$ k.

The algorithm doesn't guarantee any success, instead the running duration is bounded (Puntambekar, 2010).

The amount of iterations is often less than or equivalent to k. With $k$ard e (anticipated and complete) is $\{\displaystyle\Theta\Theta(1)\}\ \Theta(1)$. Most randomized algorithms are especially useful when facing malicious "adversaries," or an attacker who intentionally attempts to feed some erratic input into the algorithm (consider worst-case complexity or competie analysis (virtual algorithm)) like in the Prisoner's problem.

It'sIt is for this purpose that randomness is pervasive in cryptography. For cryptographic implementations, pseudo-random figures can't be used, considering that the adversary may predict them, therefore making the algorithm efficiently deterministic. Thus, either a resource of really random integers or a cryptographically safe pseudo-random numeral generator is needed (BASU, 2013).Yet another aspect where randomness is applicable is with quantum computing. In this example, the LV algorithm continuously outputs the precise answer; however, its running period is an arbitrary variable. For Monte Carlo aithms (associated with the Monte Carlo technique for simulation) it'sit is guaranteed to finish in a given period of time which may be bounded through an aspect the input scope including its parameter k, though lows a negligible probability of error (BASU, 2013).

1.10. BRANCH-H AND-BOUND

Branch-and-Bound ined to explore the nodes found in the exponential search tree, rather specifically it examines more promising nodes primarily andnificant nodes. For every node, the Branch-and-Bound Branch and Bound program calculates the positive bound: the most ideal likely score to whichhe node lads to.In case the positive bound of the node is less thaner or equals the universal pessimistic bound,prunes away th (comprisingof the whole branch of subnodes). AForacademic papers, normally use the phrase lower bound rather than optimistic bound (plusand the phrase upper bound rather than pessimistic bound), since they lessen the score (BASU, 2013).OptaPlanner is aprotocol that intensifies the score (since it supports combination of ++VE and –VE constraints). Thus, for transparency, OptaPlanner uses various terms, since it shall be confusing to utilize the term lower-bound for the bound rmally higher. For instance, it can trim away every unvisited solutionssolution using queen A from row 0, since none shall be better compared to the answer with an average sore of-1.

Most of you have probably heard of mixed integer programming, or discrete optimization that is a bit more general. In this article we are going to talk about the algorihm that is th propelling the force behind diverse integer programming, as well as B&B algorithm (BASU, 2013).An optimization problem may be summarized in a rather simple way. General, we are considering a situation where the goal isinimizing functionf f (commonly referred to as cost function) through$x$ x which originates from the group X. The group X may be a group of all actual numbers, or a group of integers it could be as well a set comprising of vectors of actual numbers and numbers (which is largely the situation with mixed numeral programming). goal is remembering that X constitutes the feasible set. Therefore, it'sit is important to only show concern with the solutions coming from this set (BASU, 2013).

Computational
Complexity Theory

CONTENTS

2.1. INTRODUCTION

To efficiently make use of the computing resources which is inclusive of time and space, it is important to understand algorithms and how they process data. An algorithm can be defined as a process or a group of steps to be followed when performing mathematical calculations or problem-solving operations using a computer. If we have an efficient algorithm, we can minimize the amount of resources used in the computation. The amount of the resources needed to compute a solution depends on different variables, such as the data volume. For example, fewer resources will be required to analyze a mathematical function for finding the sum of 21 and 62 in comparison to solving more complex function such as multiplication of these numbers.

The ability to analyze whether an algorithm can compute a set of data answers the question of how well the algorithm will scale when volumes of data are thrown at it. For example, considering a company that deals with a number of clients offering insurance or banking services and as the client numbers grows they will require more resources to process the data and the number of resources required will be determined by the analysis of the algorithm processing the data.

When talking about the complexity of an algorithm, we tend to relate it to the worst possible scenario, problems which are encountered by an algorithm provided with the worst set of data for processing. The worst case run time of an algorithm is given the notation O or as it is commonly referred to as the big O and in contrast, the best-case scenario is given the notation Ω or big omega. When measuring an algorithm based on how it analyzes a data set which can be string of data, tuples or files we can call the measure f (n) where the number of the set of data is a representative of n and f of n denotes the number of resources required to solve or process the set of data. The theory of computation in computer science that deals with how efficiently problems can solved using model of computation using an algorithm and considering the amount of resources. This theory has got three divisions that are the automata theory and language, computability, and finally the complexity theory which I will discuss in this article in reasonable detail. The construed difference between the computability and complexity theory is that the former explains what can be computed with the use of algorithms or resources but the latter refers to or more commonly determines more to the run time of data processing or computation.

2.2. BRIEF HISTORY

In 1960s, the world of computer science was graced with the evolution of the computational complexity theory. It all started in 1930s when Turing, a well-known scientist in the field of computer science, developed his computational model. Later scientists began to develop digital computers in 1940s and 50s and Turing machines validated itself as the right theoretical model for computing. The discovery of Turing machine intruduced the inability to rationalize the quantity of time and space or recollection needed for computing. The idea to measure and account for time and space as function of the level of computing was brought up by Hartmann and Stearns in early 60s and thus the theory of computational complexity was born (Calude, 2011).The theory of complex computability among other models led to the understanding of resolvable and unresolvable problems which further lead to the evolution of computers (Calude, 2011). In the early days of research on complexity of computability, scientists mostly tried to gain clarity on these newly discovered measures and their relation to each other. From the research done during this period the first step towards the achievement, efficiency in the process of computation was by the use polynomial time and this steered complexity theory's most significant ideology, NP completeness and its most vital question whether P is equivalent to NP. During the 70s growth of complexity classes was seen by with the application of different computation models and this which led to the evolution of probabilistic complexity classes. Going forward in time in the 80s finite models like circuits which captured computing in a dissimilar way were developed. The 90s scientists progressed to the study of newer representation of computation such as quantum computation and proposed proof systems and this has since then seen the continuation of in-depth research in computational complexity which has seen many computational problems proved as solvable yet some of the concepts like p=NP still remain unsolved.

Computational complexity theory has time after time been defined as a branch of computation in conceptual computer science whose focal point is to classify computational problems based on how difficult they are two solve, defining these problems into complexity classes and relating them to each other is simply to study whether a feasible solution to a problem exists. A computational difficulty is known to be a task that's in theory is tractable to being resolved by a computer which is like stating that the matter maybe solvable by mechanical application of mathematical steps such as the use of an algorithm (Calude, 2011).

A problem is considered as complex if its solution needs a momentous amount of resources regardless of the algorithm applied while computing the problem. The computational complexity theory validates these findings or instincts rather by bringing forward the different mathematical models of computation relevant when studying these computational problems, the theory further quantifies time, space, and memory resources in amounts needed to solve them such as. It is also thought to be an approach used to measure how much effort it would take to correctly solve a computing hurdle or to achieve a particular result. Different computer scientists or analysts use the computational complexity research to determine which tasks maybe most difficult to solve using a computing system. Although computational complexity may show similarities to the normal analysis of logarithms, it is essentially its own branch of mathematics (Calude, 2011).

What is the significance complexity theory? One of the roles of the computational complexity theory is to determine the empirical limits to the capabilities of a computer. The P and NP problem which is one of the seven millennium prize problems that is dedicated to the field of computational complexity yet to be solved. The complexity theory has real life applications particularly in the design and analysis of an algorithm. An algorithm can be analyzed in terms of their complexities which are often described as the big O notation. Often scientists or programmers aim at writing efficient algorithms and the ability to tell if an algorithm runs in polynomial time versus exponential time determines the suitability of the algorithm. "What makes some problems in computability hard and other problems easy?" the answer or explanation can be simplified using examples in our everyday life; examples of easy problems include performing simple mathematical problems such as addition or subtraction or searching for a name in a telephone directory. A problem is called hard if it cannot be solved efficiently, factoring a 300-digit integer into its prime factors, developing an algorithm that can solved puzzles (Calude, 2011).Despite there being gaps of knowledge in this subject computer scientists have to date made progress in relation to complexity classes by developing theoretical proof of the existence of a relationship between complexity classes hence bringing forth the concept of reducibility, which may not be as good as completing gaps and collapsing the hierarchy of complexity classes which will make computing easier.

The most fundamental question in complexity theory remains to be whether we can classify problems as hard or simple and that there is proof to this classification that the problems deemed as hard cannot be solved by computing.

2.3. COMPUTATION MODELS

A computer is device that accepts, stores, and processes data to generate information. There are two types of computers: the analogue and digital computers. In digital computers, the finite sets draw inputs, outputs, and external values while analogue computers parameters assume real values. The models we examine will mostly include the digital computers. In theoretical science to compute any set of data with the use of an algorithm for example, we require a good computation model. Turing, Post, Church, and Kleene in 1930s and 1940s investigated the research on computation models which has greatly improved in depth since then. However, programming languages, language translators, and operating systems were still under-development and therefore became both the subject and basis for a great deal of theoretical work.

The performance of computers during this period was limited and theories related to computational models, algorithms, and analysis were then created to try investigating the efficient use of computers as well as the complexity of their problems and the theory today is referred to as the computational complexity theory. The 1970s and 1980s has seen the development of computation models and methods of analysis which was directed to understanding the functional limits on the performance of computers.

Theoretical computer science stems from development of a variety of computation models for mathematical computation. The goal computer scientists had in mind while exploring this field was to find a universally accepted model that could solve all practical computations. By definition, models of computation describe how an input of mathematical function is computed given an output.

They require extensive computational resources to study the behavior of a complex system by computer simulation. What is computation as used in the complex computability theory? It is any form of calculation that follows a well-defined model encompassing both arithmetic and non-arithmetic steps. Models of computation have been used to measure algorithms when determining their complexity.

The models of computation fall into two broad classes that are circuit models and machine-based models. Within the broad class of machine-based modes, random access machines and Turing machines are the most commonly referred to models (Goldreich, 2010).

2.4. TURING MACHINES

The Turing machines were an invention of Alan Turing that resulted from studying and exploring algorithmic processes. According to the Church-Turing thesis, any math like problem can be modeled by a Turing model when described by an algorithm. Turing machines are very powerful models used in computation. The control unit of Turing machines is a finite state machine. A Turing machine has the ability to simulate an arithmetic logic given an algorithm despite being a simple model A Turing machine is made up of an infinite length tape broken into cells on which the computation input is provided as a finite sequence of symbols. The definition of a Turing machine consists of an 8 tuple $(Q, \sum, \delta, \Gamma B, q0, F)$ where the alphabet; Q is the state space of the finite-state controller which is the initial state, $q0$ is the initial state; and δ is partial function of transition function. B is the blank symbol; Γ is the finite set of tape symbols. $\sum$ is the finite set of input symbols (Goldreich, 2010).

Machine operations associated with Turing machines include the move operation which entails motion of tape head one cell to the right and then followed by a shift to a new state.

The second operation is the write operation in which the symbol is replaced on the tape by another symbol. It is then followed by a shift to a new state and the last operation is the halt operation occurs when the transition of the state and input symbol are not defined and in this case a machine can continue running forever but does not solve the computation. They are designed to be accepting to different computer languages and compute functions.

Turing machines are one of the most commonly used in the determination of the complexity of an algorithm. Different kinds of Turing machines are used when defining complexity classes. And these include deterministic and non-deterministic Turing machines, alternating Turing machines, symmetric Turing machines, and quantum Turing machines. These machines can be termed as being of equal power but differ in relation to space and time bounds (Goldreich, 2010).

2.4.1. Deterministic Turing Machines

The basic form of a Turing machine has a single tape which is used for the input, computing, and output and a single head on the tape. Future set of actions by this type of machine are determined by a given set of rules.

2.4.2. Non-Deterministic Turing Machines

They are able to provide several applicable transition states for the input symbol. It is a deterministic Turing machine with an extra attribute of non-determinism that allows the machine to have future actions with multiple possibilities from a given state. At each step, a non-deterministic Turing machine sprouts out into different paths during each step of computation, and if it is able to solve computational steps in using one of the paths then it is said to have solved the problem. In reality, the model is not practical but in theory, it gives rise to interesting complexity classes.

2.4.3. Probabilistic Turing Machines

A probabilistic machine is a little bit different from a deterministic machine since it has an extra set of bits; these problems are solved more efficiently since a probabilistic machine has the ability to make probabilistic decisions with the assistance of algorithms.

2.4.4. Alternating Turing Machines

It is defined as a non-deterministic Turing machine with two sets of state, a universal state and existential state in which there is acceptance if transition leads to an accepting state. It encompasses languages in NP and Co NP in a way that brings them together. A universal state accepts even without transitions but the latter does not. An alternating Turing machine is a five tuple. The functionality of the alternating Turing machine can be compared to a tree starting from the root nodes, if the machine reaches a deterministic state while alternating between the two states then there is only one move it can make following a set of rules into a transition state.

2.4.5. Random Access Machines

A machine contains the following; it has to have some programming capabilities, memory, input, and output capabilities. The memory is used for input output function and for programming. The random-access machine is a basic computation model that consists of a memory with unbounded sequence of registers of which each may hold an integer value. A random-access machine is able to oversee fetch and executive command cycle and has a minimal set of steps and potentially a number of words not bounded. The program is held by a control unit for example it can be a list of statements, the order sequence of executed of statement to be executed is determined by the program counter. There are rules to the execution of a RAM program for each work cycle only one statement is executed; the number of statements that is to be executed is determined by the program counter. The program ends when an invalid value is taken by the program counter. For a program to run in the RAM the program, starting values for the register and the program counter need to be defined. The instruction from RAM is in the finite portion of the machine. The RAM's equivalent of the Turing machine is called the random-access stored program machine and together with other types of random access machine, they are used in the analysis of the complexity of computation (Kozen, 2006).

2.4.6. Oracle Turing Machines

Oracle Turing machine play a significant role in the complexity theory and it's relevant in the study decision problems but falls in the halting problem. It has multiple tapes with infinite length. An oracle machine has a profound impact on tractability and decidability of computation languages but it is also characterized by undecidability. In simple terms, an oracle machine in theory can be compared to a black box which can tell whether a machine will halt given an input; it can answer questions like if there are problems harder in comparison to the halting problem. What is their significance to the world of computer science? Oracle machines can be used to express the relative difficulty between computational problems. In the complexity theory they are helpful in identifying obstacles to establishing the proof of example the N=NP question. Oracle machines can also have optimization algorithms formulated for their use.

2.5. COMPUTATIONAL PROBLEMS

A computational problem can be defined a collection of continuous situations provided with a solution for each situation. In computational complexity theory, we try to find proof whether the problems encountered in computation are solvable. For example, the instance or situation can be a number 5 and the solution can be to find out whether five is an odd number so yes if it is and no if it is not. To shed light on this further is an example of the decision version of traveling salesman whether there is a route of a maximum of 2000 km going through the 15 cities in Germany? In this problem, the theory will address the problem in trying to find a solution but not the problem instance. Some of the problems solved in the complexity theory include function problems and decision problems. The answer to decision problems is a yes or a no. The objective is to make a decision with the help of an algorithm. From Function problems, we expect a single output unlike the decision problems which have two possible outputs; the other difference is that the output itself is also complex in comparison. Examples can be carrying out mathematical calculations like the factorization of a number or solving the problem instance of the travelling salesman. Although the concept of functional problems seems to carry greater weight than that of decision problems functional problems can be recast as decision problems as this is not the case (Kozen, 2006).

2.5.1. Decidable vs. Undecidable Problems

A decidable problem in theory of computation is one which an algorithm can always be constructed to solve the problem if we are asked to find prime numbers between 200 and 300 it can be easily answered when computing by the use of an algorithm. When referring to decidability in relation to Turing machines, a problem is termed as decidable if it fulfills the halting concept by giving a yes or no answer in the presence of a corresponding Turing machine. The machines halt on every input either accepting or rejecting the output. Problems for which cannot create an algorithm cannot be created are referred to undecidable problem, they are partially decidable but will never be decidable therefore creating a halting problem where the Turing machine goes through an infinite loop without solving the problem examples include language learning,

2.5.2. Measurement of Instances

As explained earlier on computational complexity theory, we analyze computational problems and we also determine the amount of resources an algorithm will require such as time that will be required in finding a solution to a computation problem. This problem can be measured and even assigned classes. The type of instance will determine the amount of resources required. A small instance such as solving simple mathematical problems will require fewer resources while large instances such as determining whether a horse which horse wins a race or completing a puzzle or other probability functions will take more resources. In the complexity theory, the amount of resources required by an algorithm to solve a problem is calculated as a function of the instance since complexity in computing increases with the amount of input or data to be processed. If T is time and n is the size of the input, then the worst-case time complexity is T(n) which is the maximum amount of time taken on all inputs of n sizes. If it is a polynomial in n then it will be referred to an algorithm for polynomial time. If an algorithm admits a polynomial, time algorithm it can be solved with a reasonable amount of resources this is according to Cobham's thesis (Kozen, 2006).

2.5.3. Measures of Complexity

Deterministic Turing machine is a computation model that will be used in the determination of the amount of time and space it takes to solve an algorithmic problem. The total amount of time taken together with the input will be the total number of steps the Turing machine will make before halting and generates a yes or no answer.

Since the theory is interested in classifying problems in relation to their difficulty then a set of problems solvable within time f(n) on a deterministic Turing machine will be defined or rather denoted as DTIME(f(n)). Computational resource can be drawn from computational measures. Circuit, communication, and decision tree are some of the other complexity measures some of which will be discussed in measurable detail as we progress further into the discussion on the computational complexity theory. The big O notation is often used to express the complexity in the analysis of an algorithm.

There are three different ways of measuring time complexity of inputs of similar quantity that is the best-case complexity, average case and worst case complexity each which have the best input, an average and the worst input in that order.

2.5.4. Upper and Lower Bounds of Complexity Problems

The worst-case complexity is the most fundamental complexity when analyzing the performance of an algorithm. Proving upper and lower bounds on the maximum length of time needed by the most efficient algorithm solving a problem is critical when evaluating resources, such as processors or space.

To demonstrate the upper bound, one only has to show the running time which is the amount time an algorithm takes to solve a problem but getting the lower bounds of an algorithm may prove to be hard as they as it entails showing all possible algorithms that can solve a computing problem. This does not only include present algorithms but also those yet to be discovered. The big O nation is also used to state the upper and lower bounds.

2.6. COMPLEXITY CLASSES

2.6.1. Resources and Complexity Classes

Complexity classes are a way of grouping problems together. A complexity class consists of a group of all the computational problems solved considering an amount of resources. Space and time complexity is basis on which complexity of computational problems can be grouped by. The classes are a collection of languages that can be determined and defined by the following three factors which include:

- A model of computation that majorly falls into two classes that is; machine and circuit-based models. Turing and random-access machines are the two of the essential families of machine models discussed and relevant to the complexity theory. Deterministic machines are the connection to reality if we have the intentions to replicate tangible computations. Other models of computation are considered because of two things one which comes from the computational problems whose difficulty we are trying to decipher and these examples are the hundreds of the real-life NP problems that are as result from non-deterministic Turing machines which replicate tangible computational problems and the second reason which is associated with the first that is the aspiration to understand this real life computational problems.

- The sort of computational difficulty. Most of the computational problems in the field of computer are decision problems, however computational problems can either be function problems which is a computational problem where a single product is expected for each input is and it is more complex than that of a decision problem, counting problems, optimization problems and promise problems among others.

- Resources such as time, space or number of processors that are being unbounded and the bound.

Some of these classes have complex word definitions which do not fit into the above framework. Thus a typical complexity class has a definition as the set of decision problems solvable by a deterministic Turing machine within time f(n) this complexity class is known as DTIME f(n). If we allow polynomial variations in running time, Cobham-Edmonds thesis states that "the time complexities in any two reasonable and general models of computation are polynomially related" a (Goldreich, 2008). This forms the basis for the complexity class P, which is a set of decision problems solvable by deterministic Turing machine within polynomial time. The corresponding set of function problems is FP (Table 2.1).

Table 2.1: Most complexity classes are resource-bound. They are defined by time or space bounds used by an algorithm

Complexity Class	Model of Computation	Resource Constraint	Complexity Class	Model of Computation	Resource Constraint
Deterministic Time			**Deterministic Time**		
DTIME	Deterministic Turing machine	Time	L	Non-deterministic Turing machine	Space
P	DT Machine	Time	PSPACE	NDT machine	Space
EXPTIME	DT Machine	Time	EXPSPACE	NDT machine	Space
Non-Deterministic Time			**Non-Deterministic Time**		
N TIME	DT Machine	Time	NSPACE	NDT machine	Space
/NP	DT Machine	Time	NL	NDT machine	Space
NEXPTIME	DT Machine	Time	NPSPACE	NDT machine	Space

The complexity theory was developed in relation to space and time constraints. Time can be fined as the number of steps executed during computation. In relation to Turing, machine space can be defined as the number of tapes used during computation. Space can also be considered as undefined if an operation does not come to a halt (Lolli, 2011).

1. **Time Complexity:** It is the time taken by a computer to run an algorithm. It is calculated by estimation of the number of operations performed by an algorithm given that each operation takes a certain amount of time to perform. Worst-case and average case measures are measured as a function of the input sizes. An algorithm can run in different times such as linear time, exponential, polynomial, logarithmic time, factorial time, cubic time but the most relevant to the complexity theory is polynomial

time. Problems that exist in a deterministic polynomial time belong to the class p of complexity problems which is central to the complexity theory. Polynomial time algorithms include mathematical operations, matching in graphs, and sorting algorithms. One can make the difference between strong and weak polynomial time when in the optimization of logarithmic functions and the relevance to which is present if integers are of concern. In computation basic mathematical operations only take a unit time step to perform irrespective of the size of inputs. In polynomial time algorithms run strongly if the number of operational is bounded by a polynomial in the numerical size of values in the input stance and space used is also bound by polynomial time. If the two conditions are not met, then this is no longer true. The idea of polynomial has led to the generation of complexity classes in this theory. The relevant classes include class p, NP, ZPP, RP, BPP, and BQP.

2.   **The Complexity Class P:** It is a compact class producible by a deterministic Turing machine; it is a collection of decision problems with the possibility of being solved by a deterministic machine in polynomial time. It is built on the intuition that worst case scenarios can be solved. P computation problems are therefore often solvable with efficiency. Problems solvable in the theoretical sense but not in the practical sense are commonly referred to as intractable. There exist problems in P which are intractable in practical terms and may require a number of operations in order to be solved. P encompasses many natural problems, including some versions of linear programming, shortest path problem, and finding a maximum matching in a string. For P problems O (ny), the algorithm solves an instance of size n for the integer y.

3.   **The Complexity Class NP:** In computational complexity theory, NP stands for non-deterministically polynomial and is a set of decision problems solvable in polynomial time on a non-deterministic Turing machine. It brings forth the ideology of non-deterministic algorithms. They are problems verifiable by a deterministic Turing machine in the worst-case polynomial time. All the problems in this class have the property that their solutions can be checked effectively. This class contains many problems that scientists would like to solve, they including The Boolean satisfiability problem, and the Hamiltonian path problem, the vertex cover problem. These decision problem or

instances are computed using an algorithm by a nondeterministic turning machine in the following way. It begins with a guess about the solution produced in a non-deterministic way, in the second part a deterministic algorithm verifies if the guess is a solution to the problem. Decision problems therefore have the probability of changing classes if fast solving algorithms are discovered given that complexity classes are assign on the time performance of an algorithm (Lolli, 2011).

In complexity theory, the NP complete problems are the most difficult problems in NP to solve in the sense that they are the one not likely to be in P but all P problems are contained in NP. At present all known algorithms for NP-complete problems require time that is super polynomial in the input size. The following approaches can be used to solve an NP-complete problem for any size, they include heuristic, approximation, and probabilistic.

4. **CO-NP Complexity Class:** It a complexity class that is opposite to or complements the NP class. NP class problems are able to verify only those which gave answers as "yes"; meaning only "yes" answers are polynomial time verifiable. If we have to verify all "no" answers in polynomial time, then all these all these set of problems that are giving no answers verified in polynomial time lie in the CO-NP class.

5. **NP-Hard Complexity Class:** It is described as the hardest problem in NP. If these problems can be solved in polynomial time, then all NP problems can be solved in polynomial time that is less likely as most of these problems are termed as hard to solve.

6. **NP Complete Complexity Class:** NP-complete means that the problem is at least as hard as any NP problem. An algorithm that can solve NP complete problems computed in polynomial time can solve all NP related problems. Some decision problems can be NP hard rather than complete this is inclusive of the halting problem. It is easy to prove that the halting problem in the former rather than the later. For instance, the satisfiability (SAT) problem can be reduced to a halting problem which attempts the assignment of truth values and after matching with one satisfying the steps it goes into a never-ending loop.

2.6.2. Space Complexity Classes

These complexity classes are bounded by space or memory; it is the amount needed by an algorithm for computation or the function running to completion. In space complexity, the amount of memory or working storage required to efficiently run a program is measured without considering the input and output. The amount of storage required varies with the problem size. Occupied space is generally by a varying measure of space covered by the component variable whose size is dependent on the problem size and by a set of memory occupied by the space for the program algorithm. Space complexity is expressed as O (n2) based on size/magnitude. If the input double let's say by 10 will require more memory or working storage to perform a computation. For a deciding space bound Turing machine DSPACE (f (n)) is the class of language and NSPACE (f (n)) for a non-deterministic Turing machine. The big O notation in this case requires a non-deterministic Turing machine to halt on every input and use tape cells every computation path. An algorithm can run in polynomial space, exponential space, logarithmic space, and non-deterministic exponential, logarithmic, and exponential space. Space can be reused and therefore expresses more power than the use of time.

1. **PSPACE:** Deterministic Turing machines can solve space decision problems, with respect to size in a polynomial amount of space. It has context sensitive language. There is no extra power in not allowing a machine to be deterministic therefore making NPSPACE equal to PSPACE. All complements in PSPACE are equal.

2. **NPSPACE:** They are a group of decision problems with the probability of being solved in a polynomial space in relation to input size. Its problems are solved by a non-deterministic Turing machine. NL, CS, REG are encompassed by NPSPACE.

3. **EXPSPACE:** In EXPSPACE are solved by Turing machines in an exponential amount of space. According to the Savitch theorem the relationship of the space complexity classes can be expressed using the following equation that is PSPACE=NPSPACE while EXPSPACE= NEXPSPACE. His theory creates the proof there is no significant power attributed to non-determinism in space complexity, it also proves that a problem requiring exponential space cannot be solved in polynomial space for deterministic Turing machines (Figure 2.1).

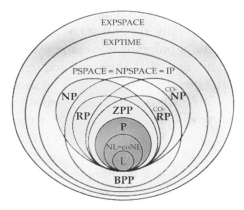

Figure 2.1: Complexity theory.

Source: https://brilliant.org/wiki/complexity-theory/ (accessed on 6 April 2020).

2.7. RELATIONSHIPS BETWEEN COMPLEXITY CLASSES

In this section, our major interest is to compare complexities of space and time specified by deterministic and non-deterministic machines. PSPACE encompasses NP and P but whether the two are equal is still yet to be determined. The key relationships that we need understanding between the complexity classes is PSPACE is equal to NPSPACE, NEXPSPACE is equal to EXPSPACE, P is a subset of NP and NP is a subset of PSPACE and finally PSPACE is a subset of EXP some of these relationships are yet to be proved. There are many complexities that fall between P and PSPACE these classes include the PP Class, BPP, BQP, and RP among others. If P is proven to be equal to PSPACE the polynomial, hierarchy will collapse and each the problems can be used to solve the other through concepts such as reduction this will be a major breakthrough in the field of computer science. The class with containing complementing decision problems is the Co-NP class and NP is not equal to this class however, this ideology is yet to have verifiable proof. If these two classes are unequal, then there is no way we can insinuate that P is equal to NP since problems in Co NP are dual to those in NP likewise it is not known whether problems solved in logarithmic space are encompassed in P and equivalent to P. There is also the question of whether BBP is equal to NEXP and if BPP equal to P (Kozen, 2006).

2.7.1. Hierarchy Theorems

There are two hierarchy theorems time and space. They induce a hierarchy on the complexity classes that are defined by resources constraints. For some complexity classes, where one is a subset of the other as seen above. After the classifications of the sets have been made, we can go forward and make quantitative statements on how much time or space is required to solve a problem.

The theorem of time states that DTIME is a subset of DTIME raised to log squared but the two classes are not equal. In the theorem of space states, that DSPACE is a subset of but is not equal to D SPACE. The basis of result separation is based on time and space hierarchy. The theory further explains and provides the proof that P is encompassed in EXPTIME and the space explains that L is contained PSPACE.

2.8. REDUCIBILITY AND COMPLETENESS

The concepts of reduction and completeness were introduced to computer science with respect to the computability theory. Reduction has been defined differently but the simplest definition is that it is transformation of a single problem into another problem and using algorithm to solve the problem. Having discussed some of the complexity classes studied in complexity theory, we can ask the question of their inherent structure of these classes.

This question can be answered by studying the concept of reducibility can be studied in which one problem is transformed to another and of a problem being complete for a class.

A problem can be classified or mentioned as reducible if using A and B as two complexity problems problem A can be termed as reducible to problem B if a method or steps used in solving B would yield a method for solving problem B.

The reduction of problem A to problem B therefore means and can be construed as being as difficult as solving A (Wegener, 2005).

When referring to the concept of completeness, a computation problem is complete for a class if in practical sense it is the hardest to solve. Give a complexity class K and H, a hurdle K is said to be complete for a complexity class H in case K is a subset of H and all hurdles in H and all hurdles in K are reducible to H. The completeness of K for H will be perceived as showing that K is characteristic of the most challenging hurdles in H.

2.9. RELATIVIZATION OF P VS. NP PROBLEM

Is P equal to NP? Having gone through the complexity classes we understand that P can be referred to as a subset of the NP class and all P problems are considered as efficiently solvable and are commonly simple problems falling at the bottom of the polynomial hierarchy. In class NP, the problems are said to be verifiable in polynomial time. If P is unequal to NP it means that there a lot of problems found in the NP class that are not efficiently solvable vs. NP has often been called the biggest unsolved in computer science. Our big O analysis of algorithms is pessimistic, but real life problems may actually be pretty simple. For example, generalize Sudoku is challenging, but computers can solve the standard N by N grid, very quickly. Beyond that, we often have very efficient approximation algorithms that are good enough, even if they aren't perfect. We know chess is hard, but we already have computers that can beat humans and chess. Analyzing problems in this way, allows us to connect the theoretical with the practical, helping us know what is easy and what is hard, and how we can get around hard problems. But to me, the appeal of P versus NP cuts deeper than that. This type of analysis allows us to see the underlying nature of problems it strips them down to their core unveiling the two problems that seemed very different on the surface are really two sides of the same coin. An answer to this question would be if questions can be confirmed in polynomial time can they also be solved in this time. This means that computing problems in the NP class that are harder to solve than to verify. It means the can only be verifiable in polynomial time. Aside from being a problem to computation, solving the P vs. NP problem could be of great significance to the field of computer science since it would be able to solve some of natural and theoretical problems termed as difficult, solved in polynomial time. In the relativization of the P vs. NP problem, a theoretical approach is used which suggest solving the hard problems with use of an oracle machine which can give answers to a predetermined collection of questions, then it would be able to solve problems a bunch of question such as finding the shortest route. In the first step, the oracle is not counted against the running time of the sequence. In a world containing oracles proofs are theoretically applied in uniform regardless of what it does and thus the proofs are called relativizing. Baker, Gill, and Solvay in 1975 demonstrated with the use of oracles that P=NP and in others P was not equal to NP and since relativization of proofs can only prove notions that are uniform then in respect to all possible oracle, the relativization of the P vs. NP problem does not solve the problem (Wegener, 2005).

2.10. POLYNOMIAL HIERARCHY

Polynomial hierarchy is a concept provided by Meyer and stock Meyer as an extended classification of the complexity classes and it is sometimes referred to as the polynomial-time hierarchy. The two scientists referred to this hierarchy as collection of classes between P and P space which includes P, NP, and Co-NP the hierarchy generalizes these classes to oracle machines. As much as many hard decision problems have been proved as NP-complete, a small number of classes outside NP have escaped this classification. The mathematical logic, arithmetic hierarchy, and analytical hierarchy are its resource bounded counterparts (Calude, 2011).

The polynomial hierarchy consists of an infinite sequence of complexity classes within it, with the P complexity classes at the bottom of the hierarchy. The first level in the hierarchy is the NP complexity class and the second level is problems in NP relative to an NP problems augmented by an oracle. Each class at each level encompasses classes of the previous level. We require proof to ascertain that these classes belong to a certain level in the polynomial hierarchy and that they are indeed subsets of each other or equal to each other. The polynomial hierarchy tends to explain and sum up the problems that surround the P and NP Relationship. We could have P being equal to NP but also it is equal co-NP, the resulting hierarchy collapses onto NP. The complexity of classes PH is the union of all classes in polynomial hierarchy.

2.11. ALTERNATING COMPLEX CLASSES

Deterministic Turing machine with general guidelines for accepting computations that generalizes guidelines used in defined complexity classes P and NP are referred to as alternating Turing machines a concept presented by stockmeyer, Chandra, and kozen. co-NP class can use the model of computation if it meets the condition that all choices result to an accepting state does the computation accept. An alternating Turing machine keeps changing between the states. The states are divided into two universal and existential states. An existential state results into an accepting state if it is led by some transition while a universal state that has nonexistent transitions accepts without condition. The entire machine is accepting if the initial state accepts. It is 5-tuple unlike the deterministic Turing machines. The following classes are relevant to alternating Turing machines. For example, AP is equal ATIME of which these are languages decidable in polynomial time. AP SPACE is equal to ASPACE languages which are decidable in polynomial time and finally AEXPTIME is equal to ATIME are decidable in exponential time. Considering resources used by an alternating Turing machine, these classes are similar to the description of P, PSPACE, and EXPTIME. Scientists like stockmeyer have been able to provide proof on the above theorems. The comparisons include AP is equivalent to PSPACE, ALOGSPACE is equal to P, APSPACE is equal to EXPTIME, AEXPTIME is equal to EXPSPACE, ATIME is a subset of DSPACE, NSPACE is a subset of ATIME. The parallel computation thesis explains a more general form of the relationship between the classes (Calude, 2011).

2.12. CIRCUIT COMPLEXITY

It contains Boolean functions which are grouped according to the measures of their sizes and hollowness. We refer to this as the complexity of a Boolean circuit. Complexity circuit identifying in relation to Boolean circuits include AC0, AC, TC0, NC they are defined in terms of hierarchies for each positive integer a class NC I-is present. There are two major speculations in circuit complexity, the first is that a Boolean function in the smallest size of any computing circuit and also minimal depth of any computing circuit is as a result of the depth of the of a Boolean function. The ideology generalizes when one considers circuit complexity of infinite formal languages. Boolean circuits only allow a fixed number of input bits. Such that no single one is able to decide on such a language, circuit complexity is also meaningful in non-recursive languages. NC that consists of polynomial size circuits of depth, held fan in, AND, OR or NOT gates. We construct AC and AC when we consider unbounded fan in gates. By allowing different gate sets, we may end up building many circuit complexity classes with the same size and depth. It relation to time complexity considering a language W belonging to a time complexity class denoted as TIME (t(n)) for a given function N then W has a circuit complexity of O (t2 (n)) (Calude, 2011).

2.13. PROBABILISTIC COMPLEXITY CLASSES

Probabilistic Turing machines solve PP problems. PP in full is probabilistic polynomial time. It is a complexity call that was defined in the 1970s. If a decision problem falls within the class PP, an algorithm is allowed to unbiasedly toss a coin for it determining the course of action therefore making a random decision this is done in polynomial time. This method can be used to solve computational problems that maybe be difficult or infeasible to solving by deterministic models of computation can be efficient to solving with the use of probabilistic algorithms. Other probabilistic classes include BPP, RP, and ZPP and can be referred to as randomized complexity classes.

- ZPP-zero-error probabilistic polynomial time are decision problems solvable with a 50% chance that an answer will not be provided by an algorithm and therefore a rerun is done to produce a correct answer.
- RP-randomized polynomial time-in this case when a NO answer during computation the output produces a NO and vice versa but a 50% probability.
- CoRP-in this class the algorithm outputs YES and NO at 50% probability.

BPP and NP are subsets of PP to prove this it is shown that the NP complete satisfiability problem belongs to the PP class. MA, BQP are subsets of PP but BQP is a problem solved by quantum computers in polynomial time. A PP machine gains nothing from being able to perform or solve a BQP problem. A PP oracle solves problems in PH and the whole polynomial hierarchy a result determined by Toda in the late 1980s and is referred to as Toda's theorem and provides the proof that it is hard to solve PP problems. Class PP is encompassed in PSPACE and can be demonstrated by the use of a polynomial space algorithm. For MAJSAT, MAJSAT, PP has complete problems and lastly there is lasting proof that shows PP is tied beneath complement.

2.14. INTERACTIVE MODELS AND COMPLEXITY CLASSES

Interactive systems model computation as the exchange of information between two entities. The verifier and the prover which are the two entities engage by the transfer of messages to each other in order to confirm whether a string belongs to a language or does not. Unlimited computational resources are possessed by the prover but are not to be trusted while the later has bounded power of computation. Information is exchanged between the two until the verifier has an answer to our problem and has satisfied that it is a fact. These systems have requirements which are two that is completeness given that this is true then the honest verifier can be satisfied of this by an untrusted verifier, the second requirement is soundness if a statement is untrue no prover can satisfy the honest verifier that the statement is indeed true by exception of a small chance.

An assumption has been made in relation to the verifier and that it is always honest. The abilities as well as the set of bounds imposed on a verifier determine the complexity class of languages a proof system can recognize. It is also dependent upon the characterization of the messages transferred between the two. They have an effect on complexity classes defined by use of a single machine and this complexity classes include AM and IP. The NP class can be seen as a basic proof system; in this system, the verifier is a deterministic machine running in polynomial time. The protocol is prover views the inputs and processes the answer using power with no bounds and provides a polynomial-size proof certificate. The verifier the goes further and confirms that the certification is sound in polynomial time that is deterministic. If it is sound, it accepts and vice versa. If a sound proof certificate exists, the prover makes the verifier accepting by certifying it when the latter happens it can still convince the verifier because a proof or certification is nonexistent (Calude, 2011).

The concept of computation through interaction was brought forth by two different research groups in the 1980s. The NP class has been seen to adopt interaction. The Arthur-Merlin class also known as AM was defined in relation to its randomness based on the Trading group theory. In this explanation, Arthur is the verifier while Merlin is the prover considering the use of a probabilistic Turing machine in the case of the verifier and unlimited resources for the prover. For the MA class the different in comparison the NP class is the use of a probabilistic system instead of determinism and when it comes to accepting the validity of certificates, it is more lenient. In conclusion, the machine is therefore more powerful than the normal NP interaction protocol. The concept of the public coin protocol versus the private coin protocol is the public remains public and the private. Rounds of interactions for the IP class are helpful as the private coins may not be helpful. We get a class of IP problems if we allow the interaction of probabilistic a powerful prover and probabilistic machine in polynomial time. These IP problems are equal to PSPACE problems thus can be solved in polynomial time. QIP is equal to PSPACE which is a result of interaction of quantum interactive proofs system from quantum computation (Kozen, 2006).

2.15. KOLMOGOROV COMPLEXITY

How can randomness be defined? It is a concept developed on the basis Kolmogorov complexity which was developed by the Russian scientist Andrey Kolmogrov and the Argentinian scientist Gregory. By definition, it is the complexity measure of sequence denoted by k(S) which is the shortest length possible description of S. Our description in this case can be a Turing machine or even a programming language as long as it is able to run an algorithm. A sequence can be defined as random if the shortest way to describe the sequence is the length of the sequence plus a constant. K(S) =/s/+ c. If there is no short program that can describe the sequence, then the sequence is random which means there is no way to understand the sequence other than seeing the whole sequence. For a given sequence, s is there any path where we can compute the Kolmogorov complexity of sequence s. The common ideology of Kolmogorov complexity is that it can be used to prove how impossible results can be and is a kin to Gödel's incompleteness and Cantor's diagonal theorem. In computation with the use a program, for example the result can be larger than the input (Kozen, 2006).

CHAPTER
3

Graph and Network Algorithms

CONTENTS

3.1. INTRODUCTION

Generally, in graphs model, the attachments in a network are widely used in a range of physical, natural, and information systems. It is possible to apply graphs for modeling the brain neurons, flight path of airlines, among other functions. The makeup of a graph consists of "nodes" as well as "edges." Every node represents a unique feature, while the edges represent a link between a pair of nodes (Figure 3.1).

Figure 3.1: Graph algorithms are elaborate and interconnected from the nodes.

Source: https://www.mathworks.com/help/matlab/graph-and-network-algorithms.html (accessed on 6 April 2020).

The graphs offer a powerful tool for modeling objects and finding relationships among items. Originally, graphs study dates back to the 18th century, when Euler described the Königsberg bridge issue, and ever since the technology has widely been adopted by many researchers. Particularly, graphs may be applied to fashion problems in various aspects like scheduling, networks, software engineering, and robotics, among others.

Various optimization matters from the ones mentioned above and many other may be phrased through graph-theory terms, initiating algorithmic questions concerning graphs. The graphs are described through a number of vertices as well as number of edges, whereby every edge links a pair of its vertices. Furthermore, graphs are categorized into directed and uncontrolled graphs, based on whether the graph's edges are directed. A crucial sub-class of directed graphs which arises in different applications, like precedence-constrained programming problems, is directional acyclic graphs (DAG) (Jungnickel, 2013).

IIt is often said that "a photo speaks 1000 words," but indeed a graph says a lot more than that. The visual depiction of data, as a graph, helps people to gain practical insights and promote better data-based decisions depending on them. However, to really comprehend what graphs are and why they're used, there is need for understanding a concept called *graph theory*. Grasping this concept makes users better programmers (and better data science experts).

Additionally, graphs can be defined as mathematical systems used for studying pair-wise connections between items and entities in the field known as discrete mathematics.

The study has found different applications in chemistry, linguistics, computer science, and operations research among others. Data science as well as analytics make use of graphs to create different structures and problems. Being a Data Scientist, it is easier to solve issues in an efficient way and graphs offer a mechanism for doing that in situations where the information is organized in a particular way (Jungnickel, 2013).

For the case of di-graphs, there is a difference between what '(u, v)' means in comparison to '(v, u).' Typically, the edges are known as arcs used to show a perception of direction. Different packages exist in form of R and Python for analyzing data through graph theory models.

For marketing analytics, graphs may be applied to determine the most influential elements in social network. And advertisers and marketers may estimate the largest bang for the advertising buck by steering their message through various influential individuals in the social network. Additionally, in banking transactions graphs may be used to detect unusual patterns that help in preventing fraudulent transactions.

Similarly, supply-chain graphs assist in detecting ideal routes for product delivery trucks, and in detecting locations for warehouses as well as delivery stations. Big pharma companies may also help in optimizing the routes of their salespersons using Graph theory. It helps in reducing costs and decreasing the salespersons overall travel time (Jungnickel, 2013).

3.2. TREE TRAVERSALS

In computer science, the tree traversal refers to a kind of graph traversal including the procedure of visiting (reviewing or updating) every node in the tree data structure, just once. These traversals are ranked based on the order whereby the computer nodes are visited. This definition is more or less self-explanatory to comprehend.

The tree traversal algorithms may be classified widely into two main categories by the structure in which these nodes are visited:

The first option is depth-first search or (DFS) Algorithm. It begins with the root-node then visits every node on the branch as intensely as possible for a given Node, and prior to back-tracking, and it visits every other branch in rather a similar way. Besides, there are a total of three other sub-groups under this particular category. The second option is Breadth-First Search (BFS) Algorithm. This also begins from the root-node and traverses all nodes of present depth before transferring to the subsequent depth within the tree (Valiente, 2013).

In-order traversal is among the widely used variations of Depth First Search (DFS) tree traversal. The preorder traversal is yet another variation of DFS, whereby atomic processes in a recursive operate, are as similar as in-order traversal even though with a totally different order.

To understand the model, first there is need to visit the present node first before going to the successive sub-tree. Following the covering of every node found on the side sub-tree, it is then necessary to look at the right-hand sub-tree then visit it in the same way (Valiente, 2013).

3.3. DEPTH-FIRST SEARCH

The DFS is an algorithm that begins with the original graph G node, before going deeper up to the goal node, or the branchless node. The algorithm, thereafter, backtracks from the stuck end towards the more recent node which is still to be fully unexplored. Currently, the data structure being applied for DFS is the stack. This process resembles the BFS algorithm. For DFS, the edges which lead to the unvisited node are known as discovery edges, whereas the edges which lead to a pre-visited node are known as block edges (Figure 3.2).

Figure 3.2: DFS has a triangular structure that cascades downwards.

Source: https://www.hackerearth.com/practice/algorithms/graphs/depth-first-search/tutorial/ (accessed on 6 April 2020).

DFS as an algorithm is commonly used for searching through the graphs and tree data systems. Besides, the algorithm begins from the tree's root (top) node and moves as far as the program can move down a particular branch (path), before backtracking until it reaches an unexplored path, before exploring it. This algorithm performs the entire role until the whole graph is fully explored (Valiente, 2013).

Different problems in computing may be reasoned out and understood in terms of graphs, for example, evaluating networks, mapping routes, planning, and defining spanning trees. In order to examine these issues, graph-search algorithms such as depth-first research are helpful.

Besides, depth-first searches are typically applied as sub-routines in other highly complex algorithms. Case in point, Hopcroft-Karp algorithm utilizes the DFS program to assist in identifying equivalence for the graph. Additionally, DFS is widely used in understanding tree-traversal algorithms, commonly referred to as the tree searches. These have uses in comprehending the traveling-salesman issue as well as the Ford-Fulkerson code (Valiente, 2013).

3.4. ALGORITHM

The DFS algorithm refers to a recursive process that implements the concept of backtracking. It includes exhaustive searches covering all the nodes through going ahead. If this is not feasible, it performs backtracking. In this context, the term backtracking means you need to travel backwards to detect nodes to traverse because you cannot go forward anymore. Afterwards, the nodes shall be visited while on the current trail until all the unattended nodes have been covered, thereafter the following path would be chosen (Erciyes, 2018).

The recursive style of DFS may be implemented through stacks. The fundamental concept is shown here. The first step is to choose a starting node then push all the neighboring nodes into the stack. Next, pop a node directly from the stack in order to choose the ensuing node to call and push its adjacent nodes directly into the stack. This process may then be repeated until the stack becomes empty.

Nevertheless, ensure the nodes which are visited have been marked. This shall prevent you from going back to a similar node multiple times. In case you don't mark nodes which are visited but you visit a similar node many times, you may ultimate end up within an infinite loop. The graph is believed to be disconnected in case it is not connected, that is, if a pair of nodes is found in the graph so that there is no edge amid those nodes. For the undirected chart, a connected component refers to a group of vertices found in the graph which are linked together through distinct paths.

DFS has been defined as a common method that people naturally handle when solving problems such as mazes. Originally, you choose a path within the maze then it is followed up to the very end, or upon reaching the final stage of the maze. In case a particular path doesn't work, then the alternative is to backtrack then follow another route from a previous junction, before trying out that particular path. In most cases, only edges covering unexplored vertices would be explored. Once all the ss's edges have completely been explored, next the search will backtrack up to the point it finally reaches an unmapped neighbor (Erciyes, 2018).

This procedure continues until every vector that is accessible from the primary source vertex is identified. In case there are some unvisited vertices, then depth-first search chooses one of them being a fresh source and replicates the search directly from that vertex. DFS represents a great means of solving mazes, as well as other puzzles which have one solution.

The key strategy for depth-first searches is exploring further into the graph as much as possible. Generally, the algorithm replicates this whole process until all vertexes have been discovered. The algorithm is keen not to replicate vertices, such that every vertex is discovered once. In addition, DFS applies a stack data system to put a check on vertices (Erciyes, 2018).

3.4.1. Applying Depth-First Search

IIt is common to adjust the algorithm to keep path of the edges rather than the vertices, since each edge defines the nodes at every end. This is practical when one is seeking to restructure the traversed tree following the processing of each node. For the case of network forests or a set of trees, the algorithm may be extended to cover an outer loop which iterates over every tree so as to process each particular node.

In addition, there are three unique strategies for applying DFS: these are pre-order, in-order, as well as post-order. The pre-order DFS functions by visiting the present node and consequently traversing to the left up to a point where the leaf is reached, meanwhile visiting every node towards the path there (Erciyes, 2018).

When there are no other children present on the node's left, and then children found on the right would be visited. It is the most typical DFS algorithm currently available. Rather than visiting every node while traversing down the tree, the in-order algorithm detects the leftmost node present in the tree, tours that node, and consequently visits the node's parent.

Thereafter it goes to the offspring on the right then detects the subsequent leftmost node present in the tree for visiting. The post-order strategy functions by visiting the left-side leaf within the tree, before moving up to the parental source and down the secondary leftmost leaf found in the particular branch, and so forth until the parental source is the final node to be traversed within a branch (Erciyes, 2018).

Moreover, this kind of algorithm highlights the leaf processing before roots just in case the goal rests at the conclusion of the tree. Besides, DFS has the potential of visiting each vertex once then checks each edge in the diagram once. Thus, DFS complexity can be calculated as O (V + E). The example assumes that the table is characterized as an adjacency catalog.

In comparing DFS vs. BFS, the BFS can be considered as less space-efficient compared to DFS since BFS places a priority queue for the whole frontier whereas DFS maintains just a few pointers on every level. In case it is found that the answer will certainly be found away into a tree, then DFS is an ideal option compared to BFS. Also, BFS is great to use when a tree depth varies or if one particular answer is required—for instance, the briefest journey in a tree.Nevertheless, if the whole tree is to be traversed, then DFS is considered a much better option. The BFS system almost always gives an optimal answer, though this isn't necessary for DFS. As for application, the DFS can be applied in topological sorting, arrangement problems, cycle discovery in graphs, and resolving puzzles using just one solution, like a maze or even Sudoku puzzle. Different other applications include exploring networks, for instance, checking if the graph is bipartite (Erciyes, 2018).

The DFS additionally is applied as a sub-routine in structural flow algorithms, like the Ford-Fulkerson code. Furthermore, DFS is commonly applied as a sub-routine for matching algorithms present in graph theory like the Hopcroft-Karp code. Furthermore, depth-first searches may be applied in mapping paths, scheduling, and discovering spanning trees.

3.4.1.1. Breadth-First Search

BFS refers to a graph traversal code that begins navigating the graph directly from the root node and discovers all the adjacent nodes. Then, it chooses the closest node and discovers all the unidentified nodes. The algorithm covers the same technique for every adjacent node until it discovers the objective.

This algorithm begins with examination of the terminal A and every one of its neighbors. For the next phase, the adjacent code's neighbors are discovered and the process persists in the subsequent steps. Additionally, the algorithm explores every neighbor across the nodes and ensures that every node is toured exactly once and no node is toured twice.

- **Basics of the BFS Code:** BFS code is a graph navigating technique, where you choose a random primary node and begin navigating the graph layer-style in such a means that every node and their individual children nodes are toured and explored. Before going further and comprehending BFS, it is first important to understand two key terms concerning graph traversal. (i) Visiting a node. Just as the name implicates, visiting a node translates to visiting or choosing a node. (ii) Exploring the node. Exploring adjacent nodes (children nodes) of a chosen node (Erciyes, 2018).

The Breadth-First Searching algorithm follows a basic, level-style approach to resolve the problem. The goal is traversing the entire graph through using a Breadth-First Searching Algorithm. You must also be aware of the primary data structure constituting the Breadth-First Searching algorithm. The queue refers to an abstract data structure which marks the First-In and First-Out methodology (where data implanted first will be retrieved first). It is accessible on both ends, whereby one end would constantly be applied for inserting data (enqueue) while the other side is used for removing data (dequeue).

You also need to recognize the breadth-first system as a unidirectional graph. Every vertex resembles a square which isn't an aspect of the wall, and every edge is reliant on adjacent squares.

The path found by the mentioned procedure has a significant property: there is no other path from the main character and the objective passes through lesser squares. That's since the BFS algorithm is the one applied to find it. The BFS, commonly known as BFS, determines the shortest route from a particular source vertex over to other vertices, with regards to the amount of edges present in the paths (Erciyes, 2018).

- **Applications of Breadth-First Searching Algorithm:** The BFS refers to a basic graph traversal technique that has an incredible variety of applications. Below are a few fascinating ways in which the (BFS) Bread-First Search system is being used:
- **Search Engines Crawlers:** The BFS ranks among the top algorithms applied for indexing internet pages. The algorithm

begins traversing from the original page and tracks all the links related to the page. And, every web page shall be regarded as a node within the graph.

- **GPS Navigating Style:** BFS is considered among the best algorithms applied to detect neighboring locations through the GPS unit.

- **Determine the Briefest Path and Least Spanning Tree for the Unweighted Graph:** In terms of unweighted graph, determining the shortest route is rather easy, considering that the notion behind shortest path involves selecting a path having the least amount of edges. Besides, BFS can permit this by navigating a minimum number of nodes beginning from the primary source node. Likewise, for the spanning tree, it is possible to use the BFS or Depth-first traversing methods to detect a spanning tree.

- **Broadcasting:** Networking utilizes what is known as communication packets. The packets take cognizance of a traversal technique to access different networking nodes. Among the most widely used traversal techniques is BFS. It is widely applied as an algorithm which is applied for communicating broadcasted packets along all network nodes.

- **Peer-to-Peer Networking:** BFS may be applied as a traversal technique for determining every neighboring node in a Peer-based Network. Case in point, BitTorrent utilizes BFS for peer-based communication.

The BFS provides two unique values for ever vertex vvv. First is distance, which provides the slightest amount of edges within any path from a source vertex to the vertex vvv (Erciyes, 2018).

Second, there is the predecessor vertex that covers vvv, following the shortest route from the main source vertex. And, the source vertex's precursor is of a unique value, like null, showing that the predecessor doesn't exist.

In case there is no definite path coming from the main source vertex up to vertex vvv, it means that vvv's distance for the most part is infinite, and its predecessor equally has the same unique value in comparison to the source's precursor.

In BFS algorithms, originally the distance is set while the predecessor of every vertex is adjusted to a special value which is (null). The search is begun at the source then assigned a range of 0. Afterwards, there is need to visit every neighboring node of the source, and provide every neighbor a single distance and establish its predecessor so as to act as the source (Erciyes, 2013).Then the user visits every adjacent neighbor whose breadth is 1 and which haven't been toured before, and each of the vertices has an expanse of 2 and establish the predecessor to be a vertex from where it is visited. This continues until every angle that's accessible from the main source vertex are visited, continually visiting the vertices at space *kkk* from the primary source, prior to visiting whichever vertex at an expanse of *k* + 1*k*.A number of questions arise. One is exactly how to decide whether a vertex is already visited. This is rather easy: the vertex's distance will read null until it is been visited, during which time it acquires a numeric integer for its distance. Thus, upon examining the vertex neighbors, the user only visits neighbor whose breadth is presently null (Erciyes, 2013).

When there is no path for instance between vertex 3 and 7, then the search won't visit vertex 7. The distance and predecessor will remain unaffected from their original figure of null.

Another concern is how to checkup which vertices have presently been visited, though they haven't yet been toured from a specific point. In such cases, a queue is used, referring to a data structure which allows users to input and remove objects, where the object removed is often the one which has stayed in line the longest. This network behavior is known as first-in, first out. And, the queue has 3 main operations:

- Enqueue(obj) inputs an item into the queue;
- Dequeue() eliminates from the queue any object that has stayed within it the longest, taking back this object; and
- isEmpty() returns true in case the queue presently has no objects, and false in case the queue has at least a single object.

Upon visiting any vertex, it will be enqueued. From the beginning, users enqueue the original vertex since that's always the first vertex that's visited. In order to determine which vertex should be visited next, users pick the vertex which has stayed in the line the longest before removing it from the column—meaning, the vertex is returned back from dequeuer ().

Note that at every instant, the queue either comprises of vertices which have roughly the same expanse, or containing vertices with range *kkk* followed by apexes with spaces *k* + 1*k*, and, 1. This is how to ensure that the vertices are ideally visited at space *kkk* before touring any vertices at space *k* + 1*k*, and 1.

3.4.2. Single-Source Shortest Paths

In the graph model, the shortest route problem refers to the concern of finding the route between two nodes (or vertices) in a graph so that the quantity of the masses of its integral edges is limited. The issue of finding the briefest path between a pair of intersections on the road map can be fashioned as a unique case of the briefest path concern in graphs, whereby the vertices match to connections and the edges equally match to road sections, with every segment weighted across the object's length.

In other words, the briefest path problem may be described for graphs no matter if it is directed, undirected, or even mixed. It is described in this case for undirected graphs; or directed graphs the description of path needs that successive vertices be linked by a suitable directed edge. A pair of vertices are said to be adjacent when both of them are considered incident to the common edge. The track in an undirected chart is a classification of vertices (Lau, 2006).

Once each edge within the graph is fitted with a unit weight or an arrow equation, it is equal to finding a path having the least edges. But the issue is also sometimes known as the single-pair briefest path problem, in order to differentiate it from other variations. Besides, the single-source briefest path concern, in which the user finds the briefest paths from the source vertex v and connecting to other vertices within the graph.

Meanwhile, the single-destination briefest path problem, whereby it is necessary to find the briefest paths from available vertices in the focused graph to one destination vertex which is v. It can be limited to the one-source shortest path issue by retreating the arcs within a single directed graph. As for the all-pairs briefest path problem, it involves find the briefest paths between two pairs of vertices that are v, v' for the graph. The generalizations have considerably more effective algorithms compared to the basic approach of running the single-pair briefest path algorithm on every relevant set of vertices (Lau, 2006).

- **Common Applications:** Shortest path algorithms are used to automatically get directions between real locations, like driving directions on internet mapping sites, such as Google Maps or MapQuest. The application also has quick specialized algorithms on ready. In case one represents non-deterministic abstract equipment as a graph, whereby vertices define states and edges define possible transitions, then the shortest path algorithms may be applied to determine an optimal series of choices for achieving a particular goal state, or establishing lesser bounds on the period needed to achieve a particular state. For instance, if vertices signify the conditions of a puzzle such as the Rubik's Cube, with each directed edge corresponding to one move or turn, then the shortest route algorithms may be applied to determine a solution which utilizes the least possible number of moves (Lau, 2006).

For a networking or telecommunicating mindset, the briefest path problem is oftentimes known as the min-delay route problem and typically tied with a broad path problem. For instance, the algorithm might seek the briefest (min-delay) broadest path, or broadest shortest (min-delay) route. A rather lighthearted application involves the popular game of "6 degrees of separation" which seeks to find the briefest path in graphs. Different other applications, typically studied in operations studies, include plant or facility outline, robotics, transportation, as well as VLSI framework.

- **Road Networks:** The road network may be regarded as a graph having positive weights. These nodes represent road intersections and every border of the graph can be linked with a path segment between a pair of junctions. Besides, the average weight of the edge may relate to the distance of the related road section, the time required to cross the segment, and the rate of navigating the segment. By using directed edges, it is also feasible to model single-way streets.

These graphs are unique in a sense that a couple of edges are more significant than others, especially for long-distance travelling (example, highways). The property has largely been formalized employing the concept of highway dimension. Additionally, there are a wide number of algorithms which exploit this property, and are thus able to calculate the briefest path much faster than would be conceivable on typical graphs. Every one of these algorithms works in two phases. For the initial phase, the graph would be pre-processed without determining the source or primary node (Lau, 2006).

The next phase is known as query phase. For this stage, the source and target nodules are known. The impression is that the path network is static; therefore, the pre-processing stage can be completed once and applied for a massive number of queries present on the same path network. Generally, the algorithm having the quickest known query period is known as hub labeling, which is capable of calculating the briefest route on the path networks of USA or Europe in just a tiny section of a micro-second. Other methods that have been applied include: ALT meaning (A* searching, landmarks, and triangular inequality) and Arc flags (Lau, 2006).

- **Strategic Briefest-Paths:** Oftentimes, the boundaries in a graph feature certain unique personalities: every edge features its own unique aspect. One good example is the communication network, whereby every edge is the computer which probably belongs to another person.

Various computers have their own unique transmission speeds, meaning every edge within the network contains a numeric weight that's same to the number of milliseconds required to transfer a message. The objective is sending a message while using the shortest time imaginable between a pair of points within the network (Lau, 2006).

ithin the briefest, time possible. Upon determining the average transmission-period of every computer (the mass of each edge), it is possible to use a typical shortest-paths algorithm. In case you don't know the actual transmission duration, then it is possible to ask every computer to determine its transmission-rate. However, the workstations might be selfish: a processor may tell us its broadcasting time is rather long, such that we won't have to bother it using individualized messages. A probable solution to this matter is using a variant to the VCG system, which provides the computers a good incentive for displaying their actual weights (Lau, 2006).

3.4.3. Linear Programming Formulation

There is a natural successive programming formula for the briefest path problem, as described. It is rather simple compared to other applications in discrete optimization, nevertheless it demonstrates connections to different other concepts. If we consider a directed graph or (V, A) together with the source node s, and target node t, it is easier to understand how linear programming formulation works (Lau, 2006).

Generally, the intuition covering this is that the program xij serves as an indication variable for if edge (i, j) constitutes the shortest path:

The number 1 means positive, and 0 means negative. It is possible to choose the number of edges with reduced weight, which is subject to the restraint that this set creates a route from s over to t (signified by the equality restraint: for all vertices apart from s and t, the amount of incoming as well as outcoming edges which form part of the route must be more or less the same (meaning, it must be a route from s to t). The LP also has the unique property which is integral; particularly, every fundamental optimal solution (where one exists) features all variables equivalent to 0 or 1, and the number of edges whose general variables equaling to 1 comprise of an s–t dual path.

he duality for this lineal program is maximizing $yt - ys$ that's subject to vertices ij, $yj - yi \leq wij$, and feasible duals also match to the notion of a stable heuristic for A* algorithm covering the shortest paths. Besides, for any practicable dual y the lessened costs are non-negative and A* fundamentally controls Dijkstra's algorithm on the reduced costs (Lau, 2006).

- **Standard Algebraic Structures on Semi-Rings:** A number of problems may be framed in form of the briefest path for some appropriately substituted notions of inclusions along a given route and carrying the minimum objects. A general approach for this is considering the pair of operations to represent a semi-ring. The semiring multiplication would be carried out along the path, and the addition works between paths. This overall framework is referred to as algebraic route problem.

Many of the original shortest-path algorithms (including new ones) may be devised as solving linear equations over some algebraic systems. Much recently, there is an even much easier structure for solving these (and much less obviously connected problems) which has been created under the context of valuation algebras. Least route in stochastic time-reliant networks as shown in real-life circumstances (Lau, 2006).

For the most part, transportation networks are typically stochastic and time-reliant. As a matter of fact, the traveler traversing the link daily might experience diverse travel times along that link because of not just the variations in travel request (origin-destination matrix), though also because of such incidents like work zones, poor weather conditions, car breakdowns and accidents.

Consequently, a stochastic time-reliant network can be developed as a more accurate depiction of the real road network as compared to the deterministic one. Irrespective of considerable advancements during the past few decades, the system still remains divisive and the question is how an optimal route must be described and identified in terms of stochastic path networks (Lau, 2006).

Generally, there is no single definition of the optimal route under uncertainty. A possible and typical answer to the question is finding a path having the least expected travel time.

One key benefit of using this technique is that usually the most efficient and shortest route algorithms applied for the deterministic systems can be effortlessly be used, particularly to detect the path having the least expected travel time for a stochastic network.

Nevertheless, the resulting optimal path defined by this technique may not be dependable, since this approach doesn't address travel time inconsistency. In order to address this issue, some scholars use travel time distribution rather than the anticipated value of the object, so as to determine the best probability dispersal of overall travelling time through different optimization techniques like dynamic encoding and Dijkstra's algorithm (Lau, 2006).

These techniques use stochastic optimization, particularly stochastic DP for finding the shortest route in networks having probabilistic arc length. Besides, the notion of travel time consistency is applied inter-changeably with travel time flexibility in the transportation study literature, such that, generally, one may say that the greater the inconsistency in travel time, then the lower the consistency would be, and vice versa.

So as to account for the travel duration more reliability and precisely, some common alternative descriptions for the optimal route under ambiguity have been recommended by researchers. A few have even been introduced the idea of the most suitable path, seeking to maximize the likelihood of reaching on time or much earlier, compared to a particular travel-time budget. Others, furthermore, have presented the notion of α-reliable route, depending on what exactly they planned to minimize on the travel duration budget needed to ensure a pre-defined on-time arrival possibility (Lau, 2006).

3.5. MINIMUM SPANNING TREES

iven a networked and undirected graph, the spanning tree is subgraph, which is the tree, connecting together different vertices. One graph may have multiple different spanning trees. The minimum spanning tree (MST) refers to the spanning tree that weighs less than and even equal to densities of different other spanning trees in the network. Additionally, the spanning tree's weight refers to the amount of weights provided to every spanning tree edge. The edge-weighted graph refers to a graph that associates weights and costs with every edge (Sirmacek, 2018) (Figure 3.3).

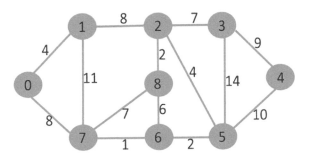

Figure 3.3: Kruskal's algorithm is a popular minimum-spanning tree algorithm.

Source: https://www.geeksforgeeks.org/kruskals-minimum-spanning-tree-algo-rithm-greedy-algo-2/ (accessed on 6 April 2020).

3.5.1. Assumptions

There are several important adoptions that must be considered. First, the graph is interconnected. Second, as the name suggests, the graph should be some form of MST. In case a graph isn't connected, it is possible to adapt the algorithms to calculate the MSTs of every connected component, commonly referred to as the minimum spanning forest. Besides, the edge weights do not necessarily correspond to distance because they can take another different form.

Geometric intuition is also sometimes beneficial although the edge weights may be random. The edge weights might be a zero or negative. In case the edge weights read positive, then it suffices to describe the MST as a subgraph having minimal average weight which connects different vertices.

All edge weights are different in their own perspective. In case edges have equal weights, then MST might not be special after all. Making this assumption supports some of the already established proofs, even though every algorithm works efficiently even in the existence of equivalent weights (Sirmacek, 2018).

3.5.2. Basic Principles

There are two defining aspects of the tree. Providing an edge which connects a pair of vertices in the tree which creates a special cycle, and removing the edge from the tree subdivides it into a pair of sub-trees. In addition, certain properties often lead to a given amount of MST algorithms. The first is Proposition or (Cut property). Considering any cut in the edge-weighted graph (where all edge weights are distinct), it means the crossing-edge of least weight can be found in the graph's MST.

IIt is also important to consider the cut property. This forms the context for the algorithms which are considered for the MST matter. Particularly, they are unique examples of greedy algorithm. To understand this model, consider coloring black all edges within the MST of whichever connected edge-weighted diagram with v vertices: Beginning with all edges shaded gray, locate a cut without any black edges, shade its minimum-mass edge black, then continue until the V−1 edges have fully been shaded black.

3.5.3. Prim's Algorithm

Prim's algorithm functions by attaching a fresh edge to one growing tree at every step: Begin with any vertex acting as one single-vertex tree; thereafter add V−1 edges onto it, regularly taking next (shading black) the average-weight edge which attaches a vertex found on the tree onto a vertex that's not yet based on the tree (the crossing verge for the cut described by tree vertices). The single-sentence definition of Prim's algorithm still leaves unattended a key question, which is: How to (effectively) detect the crossing-edge of least weight (Sirmacek, 2018).

Lazy implementation is an aspect of MSTs, using a unique priority queue for holding the crossing edges and finding a particular minimal weight. Every time an edge is added onto the tree, there is a vertex added to the tree as well.

In order to preserve the number of crossing edges, it is important to add onto the priority queue every edge from that vertex onto any non-tree vertex.

Though there is need to do even more: whichever edge that connects the vertex just adds to the tree vertex which is found on the primary queue and will become ineligible (it is no longer a crossing-edge since it attaches two tree vertices). Oftentimes, lazy implementation leaves these edges on a priority queue, extending the ineligibility exam to when it is removed.

LazyPrimMST.java has been identified as one of the practical applications of the lazy approach; this also depends on the popular MinPQ.java urgency queue. To enhance the lazy implementation model of Prim's algorithm, it will be appropriate to try and remove ineligible edges from a priority queue, such that the primary queue will contain just the crossing edges (Sirmacek, 2018).

Though it is possible to remove even more edges. One goal is to remember that the only attention is in the least edge from every non-tree vertex onto the tree vertex. Upon adding a vertex v onto the tree, then the only likely change with regard to every non-tree vertex w would be that adding v draws w closer compared to previously on the tree.

Generally, there is no need for keeping up on the priority line every edge from the w onto vertices tree—there is only one need which is to keep up with the basic-weight edge, and check if the adding of v onto the tree requires that minimum updates should be done. This minimum (due to the edge v-w which has lower weight), can be achieved by processing every edge in s adjacent list. Meanwhile, it is preserved on the precedence queue just a single edge for every non-tree vertex: which is the briefest edge that attaches it to the primary tree.

Prim's algorithm (keen implementation) for the lowest spanning tree problem or PrimMST.java, is an application of this eager technique. It depends on the system IndexMinPQ.java indexed urgency queue to implement the decrease-key process. Additionally, Prim's algorithm calculates the MST of whichever connected edge-weighted chart. The lazy edition of Prim's algorithm applies space relative to e as well as time comparative to e and log e (for the worst scenario) to calculate the MST of any connected edge-weighted chart with e edges or v vertices; meanwhile the eager version makes use of space relative to v and time equivalent to e and log v (for the worst scenario) (Sirmacek, 2018).

3.5.4. Kruskal's Algorithm

The Kruskal's algorithm activates the edges in accordance to their weight ratios (least to largest), providing for the MST (shading black) every edge that doesn't develop a sequence with edges formerly added, ceasing after addition of V1 edges. Additionally, the black edges constitute a number of trees that grows gradually one tree, which is the MST.

To apply Kruskal's algorithm, it is important to use a precedence queue to understand the edges by weight, union-find data system to detect those which cause cycles, and a queue for collecting the MST edges. The program KruskalMST.java executes Kruskal's algorithm across these lines. It applies the helper MinPQ.java, Queue.java and UF.java data types. The algorithm further calculates the MST of whichever connected edge-weighted chart with e edges as well as v vertices, using additional space that's proportional to e and time proportional to the e Log e (for the worst scenario). A basic spanning tree contains (V–1) edges in which v is the number of vertices present in the particular graph (Sirmacek, 2018).

- **Matching's and Network Flows:** In network flows and matching's, the max flow issue is among the simplest problems of the algorithm design. Instinctively, one can think of the flow network in form of a directed graph whereby the fluid is moving across the graph edges. Every edge has a given maximum capacity which it can transmit. The concept is determining how much flow can be pushed from a particular point to another. The maximum flow problem has uses in areas such as transportation, network routing and so on. This is the easiest problem in a group of many crucial problems doing with the transmission of commodities across a network. They are typically learned in business schools, as well as operations research.

There are two unique vertices in this program which are: a sources, as well as sink t. In case (u, v) isn't a solid edge then it can be modeled by establishing $c(u, v) = 0$. It is assumed that each vertex rests on some track from the object source to sink (or else the vertex really is of no practical use). The flow is an actual valued function on groups of vertices, the $f: V \times V$ R fulfils three properties which are: (i) capacity constraint, (ii) skew symmetry (it can be thought of as backwards flow or negative flow, which is basically for making algebraic calculations easier), and (iii) flow conservation (for skew symmetry, it is equal to mentioning, flow in equals flow out) (Jungnickel, 2013).Nevertheless, it should be noted that flow conservation doesn't apply in any way to the sink and source, considering that we consider ourselves as a pumping flow streaming from s-to-t. Besides, flow conservation also means that there is no flow missing anywhere else within the network, therefore the flow from s will be equated to the drift into t.

Moreover, the magnitude $f(u, v)$ is known as the net flow going from u up to v. And the overall rate of the course f is described as, i.e., which is the flow away of s. Eventually, it turns out this is same as the flow moving into t. For the maximum-flow problem, this is a flow network, source, and even sink vertices which are s and t, finding the current of top value from angle s to t.

Various flow problems have cases whereby different source vertices are connected such as $s1, s2, \ldots, sk$, including various sink vertices like $t1, t2, \ldots, tl$. The program can also be modeled by simply adding a unique supersource s' or supersink t', or attaching s' onto every si and attaching tj

onto *t*.' These edges are left to have infinite capacity, and by driving the top flow from vertex s' to t' and effectively generating the highest flow from every *si*'s to *tj*'s (Jungnickel, 2013).

3.5.5. Augmenting Paths

An augmentation path refers to short route from *s* up to *t* for Gf. Additionally; the residual volume of the route is the MINIMUM volume of any path edge and is symbolized as *cf* (*p*). Observations should also be done by driving *cf* (*p*) flow units along every edge across the path, where a flow of Gf can be attained, and thus this augment can be applied for the current in G. Keep in mind that when describing this flow whenever *cf* (*p*) units found in the flow are pushed across angle (*u, v*) of *p*, then it is a must to drive − *cf* (*p*) flow units across the (*v, u*) reverse edge in order to preserve skew-symmetry (Jungnickel, 2013).

Considering that every residual network edge features a firmly positive weight, and then the resultant flow is usually larger compared to the G current flow. Checking if there is an augmenting route from *s* up to *t* is a simple problem. The first thing is constructing the residual network, apart from run DFS and BFS directly on the remaining network beginning from *s*.

In case the search hits *t* then you know that indeed a path exists (and can follow the precursor pointers rearwards to reconstruct it). Given that both BFS and DFS require (n + e) time, then it can be revealed that the residual setup has, (*n* + *e*) dimension, the operating period of Ford-Fulkerson is generally, ((*n* + *e*) and (amount of augmenting stages)). To establish the accuracy of a Ford-Fulkerson algorithm it is needed to probe more acutely into the model of flows and network cuts.

The cut, (S, T), found in the flow network refers to a vertex set partition subdivided into a pair of disjoint subgroups S and *t* so that *s* translates to □ S and *t* translates to □T. It is defined as the flow along the cut asf (S, T), and this can be described also as the cut capacity which is *c* (S, T). (Remember that in calculating f(S, T) movements from *t* up to S are calculated negatively (through skew-symmetry), and in calculating c(S, T) it is only counted as constraints on edges moving from S up to *t* disregarding those from *t* up to S.) Besides, the volume of flow across whichever cut in the system is same as |f (Jungnickel, 2013).

IIt is not a must to gauge the flow from a particular source to another different sink. In case you need that the movement from source I streams ONLY to the sink I, it means that there is a much tougher problem known as the multi-product flow problem. At times, instead of discussing the vertex flow from the vertex u up to vertex v, which involves talking about the movement from a group of vertices X over to another SET consisting of vertices Y.

In order to achieve this, the description of f is extended by including the notation that it can define movement balance for the vertex u more concisely by simply adding $f(u, v) = 0$. A unique special case of the concept is where X and Y describe a cut (example, a vertex partition of the system into two separate subsets which are X $\subseteq v$ as well as Y = $v - X$). For this scenario, f (X, Y) may be considered as the overall amount of flow moving over the cut (Jungnickel, 2013).

3.5.6. The Ford-Fulkerson Technique

The most fundamental concept here is augmenting flows. The idea is to start with a size 0 flow, then steadily making the flow bigger and bigger by determining a path through which additional flow can be pushed. The network path for the network ranging from s to t through which additional flow may be pushed is known as the augmenting path. This idea is provided by the most basic technique for computing network movements, referred as Ford-Fulkerson technique.

Nearly every such algorithms is centered on this basic idea. But they only differ based on how they determine which path or routes along which to drive flow. This may be considered as proof that when it is impractical to "push" any further flow across the network, then the greatest possible flow is achieved (that is, a locally top flow is universally maximum).

3.5.7. Network Flows and (Supplementary) Matching

The maximum flow issue is among the fundamental aspects of algorithm design. Instinctively, this can be thought of as a flow network being a directed graph whereby fluid is moving across the graph edges. Every edge has given maximum capacity which it can transmit. The impression is determining how much flow is capable of pushing from one stage to another, besides the maximum flow problem has usage in fields like transportation, and network routing.

This is the easiest problem in a series of multiple important problems which involve the movement of objects through a network. They are typically studied in business colleges, and operations research institutes. Remember that flow conservation doesn't relate to the source or sink, considering that scholars think of themselves as pumping movement from s point to t. Moreover, flow conservation translates to mean that no flow gets lost anywhere else within the network; therefore, the outflow s shall be equal to the t flow (Jungnickel, 2013).

The ratio $f(u, v)$ is known as the standard flow from point u to v. Besides, the overall f flow value is described as the movement out of s. This turns out to be the same as flow into t. Besides, the maximum-flow issue is, provided a flow network, and source and sink angles s and t, determine the maximum flow from s up to t.

For multi-source and multi-sink flows, sometimes it may seem excessively restrictive to demand that there is just one source, and one sink vertex. Different flow problems have circumstances in which different source vertices including $s1$, $s2$..., sk are captured, and multiple sink vertices vary from $t1$, $t2$,..., tl. It can also be modeled by simply including a unique supersource s' or supersink t,' then attaching s' onto all the si or attaching every tj to t.' These edges comprise of an infinite volume.

Then by moving the highest flow from point s' to t' it is possible to effectively produce the maximum drift from every si' to tj' points. It should be noted that the concern isn't on which source flow moves to another sink. In case you need that the movement from source i transfers exclusively to sink i, it means you encounter a tougher challenge known as the multi-object flow problem.

Sometimes, rather than discussing the movement from the vertex u up to vertex v, it is important to talk concerning the movement from the SET of X vertices to another vertices Y SET. In order to perform this, it is important to extend the description of f to units by definition.

Using this system, it is possible to describe stream balance for the vertex u more concisely by simply scripting $f(u, v) =$ zero. An important unique case of the concept is generally when (x) and (y) describe a cut (that is, a separation of the vertex pair into two disjoint subgroups which are $X \subseteq v$ as well as $Y = V-X$).

Network algorithms also use this proof. Generally, the residual network determines how much extra flow can propel through G. It means that $f + f$' doesn't ever surpass the complete edge dimensions of G. There are different other flow rules which are simple to verify, but Proof remains to be the most widely used. Yet another model is the Min-Cut theory. It fundamentally mentions that for any flow structure the minimum size cut functions like a bottleneck for limiting the maximum volume of flow.

- **Tour and Traversal Problems:** This algorithm is also referred to as Knight's tour problem, or Backtracking-1. It is a coding paradigm that attempts different solutions up to the time a solution is found which "works." Problems that are normally solved through backtracking methods have certain properties in common. The problems may only be resolved by attempting every possible arrangement and every configuration is attempted only once.

The Naïve answer for these setbacks is attempting all configurations, including outputting a configuration which follows particular problem restraints. Backtracking functions in incremental manner and is a configuration over the Naïve answer where all potential configurations are produced and tried.

Generally, tour and traversal back-tracking is applied when it is needed to check every possibility to get a solution and as a result, it is quite costly. Regarding N-Queen or Knight's tour problems, certain approaches can be used because they need less time compared to backtracking. However, given a limited size input, such as 4x4 chessboard, backtracking still offers the best solution.

3.5.8. Naïve Algorithm

NNaïve algorithm is used to produce all transits individually and determine if the produced transit fulfills the constraints. Even though there are various untried tours, back-tracking works in a rather incremental way to solve problems in this algorithm. Normally, the program begins from a void solution vector, and one-by-one includes more objects (Lau, 2006).

Upon adding an object, next the user checks whether adding the present item disrupts the problem restriction, if it works then the item in removed and other alternatives attempted. In case none of the substitutes work out, then it is ideal to move to the previous stage and eliminate the item required in the past stage.

After the initial stage has been reached, then it can be said that no solution actually exists. In case adding an object doesn't disrupt constraints then it is possible to recursively include objects one-by-one. Besides, in case the solution vector is complete then it is important to present the solution.

The backtracking algorithm that underpins Knight's tour is very efficient. Once every square has been visited, then proceed to present the solution. Otherwise, you can add any of the following moves to the solution path and then check whether the move provides a solution. The code can make a maximum of 8 moves, you can choose 1 out of the total of 8 moves available in this step (Lau, 2006).

But if the move presented in the mentioned step doesn't provide a solution, consider removing this process from the solutions vector, then attempt other alternative processes. Moreover, if no alternative works then consider returning false. This will eliminate the previously included object in recursion, but if a false reading is given by the first recursion call then it means "no practical solution is available."

Nevertheless, following the successful implementation of tours and traversal problems. It is possible to print one of the available resolutions in 2D matrix context. Fundamentally, the output can be defined as a two-dimension 8×8 matrix, having the numbers 0 to 63 and these numbers demonstrate steps made by the algorithm (Lau, 2006).

3.5.9. Greedy Algorithm

As the name shows, Greedy algorithm greedily chooses the ideal choice at every step and expects that these choices may lead users to the ideal answer of the problem. Certainly, the greedy algorithm does not continually provide the best solution, though in some cases it does.

Furthermore, the fraction knapsack may also be resolved through greedy algorithm strategy, that is, through taking the objects with the greatest value-weight ratio first.

Therefore, checking whether the greedy algorithm shall provide the optimal answer or otherwise is the next task, which depends on some basic properties.

The first one is optimal sub-structure. In case the optimal answers of the sub-problems cause an optimal solution for the problem, it means then that the problem displays the ultimate sub-structure property. There is also the greedy choice property, which is the ideal solution at every step that leads to the ideal solution globally, the property is known as the greedy-choice property. Application of this algorithm is a rather simple task, since it is only necessary to select the ideal option at every step, and thus its analysis as compared to other algorithms is also practical.

In an example where the ratio of y ranges from 0-to-4 (in case it becomes bigger than or equivalent to 5, it would be covered as a $5x$ part) and it is possible to check that whichever value between 0 and 4 is made just by applying all value 1 coins. Thus, it is known that the optimal answer for the fraction y will comprise of value coins of just 1. For discussion purposes, it is important to consider the algorithm as an optimal $5x$ solution. When the problem displays an optimal substructure, then the optimal answer to both the sub-problems shall lead to an optimal resolution to the matter.

Considering that $5x$ has been derived from a multiplication of 5, it can easily be produced through the integers 5, 10, and 20 (since they are all multiples of 5). Likewise, in 5, 10 and 20, the greater value is a multiple of other lower values. For instance, 20 is derived from a multiple of 5 or 10 while 10 is considered a 5 multiple.

herefore, it is possible to replace the several occurrences of the lesser numbers with the numbers having greater values and thus, can limit the overall number. Case in point, if 5 is repeating more than once, then it may be replaced by either 10, and if 10 is arising more than once then it can be exchanged by 20. Generally, it is possible to choose the numbers with highest value first in order to limit the overall amount of coins.

- **Verifying the Greedy Algorithm:** There is a need for accurate information concerning the activities of this code to get started. Therefore, it is worth to begin by transiting the arrays featuring the beginning times and end times of the function. The greedy algorithm works with the array which stores the activities s, and f. These arrays denote the start and finishing times correspondingly.

These arrays are generally sorted based on the finishing period of the activities. Then, the next step involves scheduling the activities through prioritizing the opening activity first. When making an array, all the activities covering the optimal solution must be covered and the first activity added onto it (Lau, 2006).TWe also need to keep track of various elements in the solution in order to determine which element will begin next following the activity finishes. Therefore, it is possible to record the activity's index in form of a variable. Again, there is need to repeat over the activities and choose the succeeding activity which is completing first after the achievement of the initial activity. If it is already captured in the original element, the next iteration will begin from the following $2nd$ element.

3.5.10. Kahan Summation Algorithm

IKahan summation algorithm, commonly referred to as the compensated summation, considerably reduces the statistical error in the aggregate obtained by addition of a series of finite-accurate floating-point numbers, in comparison to the obvious method. This is achieved by maintaining a distinct running compensation or (a variable for accumulating minute errors). Specifically, summing, and figures in sequence feature a worst-case fault that develops proportional to *n*, including a root average square error which matures as a code for casual inputs (Figure 3.4).

Kahan summation algorithm

```
T kahanSum(T const * input, size_t n)
T sum = input[0];
T t = 0.0;        // A running compensation for lost low-order bits.
for (size_t i = 1; i!=n; ++i) {
    y = input[i] – t;    // so far, so good: t is zero.
    s = sum + y;         // Alas, sum is big, y small, so low-order digits of y are lost.
    t = (s - sum) – y;   // ( s - sum) recovers the high-order part of y
                         // subtracting y recovers -(low part of y)
    sum = s;             //Algebraically, t should always be zero.
                         // Beware eagerly optimising compilers!
}                        //Next time around, the lost low part will be added to y in a fresh attempt.
return sum;
```

Figure 3.4: Kahan summation is among the most accurate algorithms.

Source: https://www.slideserve.com/maude/ieee-754-standard-expression-opti-mization-approximate-math-vector-algebra-using-simd-instructions (accessed on 6 April 2020).

Moreover, through compensated summation, it means that the worst-case fault bound is functional without *n*; therefore, a large number of values may be summed using an error which only relies on the floating-scale precision. This algorithm is the brainchild of William Kahan. Corresponding, earlier techniques include, for instance, the Bresenham's line code, which keeps track of the gathered error in numerical operations, including the delta-sigma variation (covering, not only summing of the error).

- **Accuracy:** A thorough inquiry of the flaws in compensated summation would be required to realize its accuracy features. While it is more precise than Naïve summation, still it can provide great relative errors for poor-conditioned sums. Presume that one is calculating *n* values x_i, within the $i = 1,\ldots, n$ algorithm. The exact sum would be computed using infinite precision. As for compensated summation, the user instead obtains a code whereby the error is bounded by a unique code.

For the comparative error bound, it means the ratio $\Sigma|xi|/|\Sigma xi|$ is a condition integer of the summation issue. Basically, the condition integer represents the inherent flexibility of the summation issue to errors, no matter how it is calculated. Additionally, the relative flaw bound of each (backwards stable) summation technique by a stationary algorithm in fixed accuracy should also be considered. It is usually relative to the condition number of the algorithm Furthermore, for random inputs having a non-zero mean it means the condition integer asymptotes to a fixed constant. In case the inputs read non-negative, it means that the condition figure will remain to be 1.

Cryptography

CONTENTS

4.1. INTRODUCTION

The communication world has been advancing since the beginning of the world and the creation of creatures. Different creatures have always had ways of communication with each other. Since communication is a component of much importance to God's creations, it should be continuously advanced. The information shared through communication channels might be of different categories and standards. It is obvious to us that the information of higher standards needs to be kept confidential between only the sending and the receiving parties. This is where cryptography comes in (Figure 4.1).

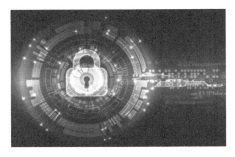

Figure 4.1: Cryptography is an area that deals with protecting transmitted information through various transmission media

Source: https://www.bbc.com/news/business-39341663 (accessed on 6 April 2020).

Cryptography ensures that information is sealed by us of special codes which can only be encrypted by sending party and decrypted by receiving party. This configuration limits access to information by unauthorized users. Most unauthorized access is done during information transmission and might lead to alteration or complete distortion of the information being communicated.

Encryption refers to sealing information when they are being sent such that it cannot be accessed without the acquisition of the decrypting key. The decrypting is always placed at the receiving end such that only the recipient can decrypt the information being communicated to them.

4.2. QUANTUM CRYPTOGRAPHY

Cryptography has really grown over the ages. It refers to the encryption of data with a given motive. Quantum cryptography seems to be the best thing that has come around in the world of cryptography. It is a recent technique that can serve as a confidential channel between two communicating parties.

This type of cryptography is governed by the laws of quantum mechanism that were discovered in the early the centuries. It basically changes the way we must see things. It is well known that the elementary particles do not have a precise speed or location for their traveling and existence as expected by many.

The principle of inconvenience has been the rule in coming up with a cryptography formula which has been well taken care of by quantum cryptography. There is need to have quantum cryptography in the future. It offers a wide range of benefit as Charles and Gilles have laid out in their journal Experimental quantum cryptography that "...*Because the system depends on the uncertainty principle of quantum physics, instead of the usual mathematical assumptions such as the difficulty of factoring.....*" Basically, quantum cryptography allows the exchange of random quantum transmission which consists of very faint flashes of polarized light. It also offers a subsequent public discussion of sent data which makes it possible to encrypt. Basing it on the estimates, it offers high-end secrecy to data transmitted by it.There is a wide range of difference between traditional and quantum cryptography. The following table lays out the differences which serves as a prove that the future with quantum cryptography is bright (Table 4.1).

Table 4.1: Difference Between Traditional and Quantum Cryptography

Traditional Cryptography	Quantum Cryptography
It uses public keys and secret keys for their efficiency.	It uses proton transmission to ensure functionality.
It uses integers and characters as the public and secret keys.	It uses protons emission in encrypting the data transmitted.
It is a two-way traffic in the usage of the encryption keys.	It uses software to encrypt the data transmitted.
It is not a very secure method because secret keys may fall to the wrong hands.	It is highly secure due to a high-end security mechanism which can be decoded only by a receiver.
It uses traditional methods in creating and sharing encryption keys	It uses digital signatures to encode the data and a digital signature reader to decode data.
It is insecure and encourages data copyright.	It is very secure due to the digital signatures.

Source: https://medium.com/@prasathbhuvana89/10-difference-between-classical-computing-and-quantum-computing-5e1777aa590d (accessed on 6 April 2020).

Quantum cryptography is very promising and will offer digitized encryption with the use of digital signatures. This makes it hard for information to fall into wrong hands. It is a well-known fact that cryptographic algorithms should be very reliable and rigorous. Quantum cryptography reduces the risk of copyright as the owner of the signature is the sole responsible on who access the data and who doesn't.

4.3. TRANSMISSION MEDIA

There are various ways used in transmission of information. As the technological age is advancing with each passing millisecond, more transmission techniques are being invented. The invention has catered for both the physical transmission techniques and wireless transmission techniques for most companies do prefer use either of them depending on their current needs (Aumasson, 2017).

Physical transmission mediums deal with the transmission of data signals from source to destination through a restricted physical pathway such as a cable. The cables are based on the speeds required to transmit data, the amount of data signals to be transmitted all at once from source to destination, the type of data to be transmitted among other factors.

Two wire open line cables (TWOLC) is a type of the physical transmission mediums. It is outdated but was used to transmit voice information from source to destination. It grappled with the problem of inter-line interference which caused crosstalk despite their insulation with plastic casing. The crosstalk lead to distortion of transmitted data signals.

Twisted pair cables are part of the physical transmission mediums. They are divided into two categories.

The unshielded twisted pair (UTP) cable is used to transmit data signal in less electronically noisy environments for they are prone to suffering from electromagnetic interference from environments. The Shielded Twisted Pair (STP) cable is the second category which transmits data signal in most environments for it not prone to electrical noise. Twisted pair cable has the advantage of being used massively since they are cheap to purchase and install and are always readily available in the market. However, they do suffer from high attenuation rates where the magnitude and energy of data signals being transmitted decreases progressively from source to destination along the transmission medium. Their advantage includes transmitting data signals at low rates (Aumasson, 2017).

Coaxial cable is used to create network backbones in interconnected computers. They have a central copper core surrounded by a dielectric material that aids in reducing both electromagnetic interference and radio frequency interference. The thinner the central copper core, the higher the loss of energy and magnitude of data signals being transmitted from source to destination and the thicker the central core the low the loss rates of energy. Coaxial cables are divided into two categories based on the dielectric material. The thin coaxial cable, commonly referred to as the thinnet, has one dielectric insulator with thin central core. The thick coaxial cable, commonly referred to as the thicket, has two dielectric insulators with thick central copper core. Coaxial cables are suitable for transmission of high loads of signals. The signals transmitted by coaxial cables are voice signals, data signals and video signals. Coaxial cables transmit audio, video or data information. The main disadvantage of coaxial cables is that they are relatively expensive to buy and install (Aumasson, 2017).

Fiber optic cables use light technology to transmit data signals from source to destination. They convert electrical signals to light using light emitting diodes (LED) at the transmitting end and use refraction principle to navigate the light at the receiving end. At the receiving end, the light signals are converted back to electrical signals which can be processed by the computer by a photosensitive device. Fiber optic cables consist of the core, cladding, buffer, and jacket. The core is the central part of the cable made up of a hollow transparent glass that aids in refraction of light signals for the purposes of their transmission. The cladding is a single protective layer surrounding the core. It bends light and redirects it back into the core during transmission. The buffer surrounds the cladding and strengthens the cable material. Lastly, the jacket acts as the outer cover for fiber optic cable. Fiber optic cables are further divided into two categories: single mode fiber optic cable and multimode fiber optic cable. The single mode fiber optic cable has a very narrow central core. It is mostly utilized for long distance transmissions because it suffers from data loss. The main disadvantage is that it can be very expensive to purchase and requires careful handling during installation. The multimode fiber optic cable has a thick central core and also suffers from the magnitude of signals being transmitted because of modal dispersion. The main advantage of fiber optic cables is that they are suitable for use in hazardous environments, such as areas prone to high flammability rates because they do not generate electrical signals. The general disadvantage is that they are expensive to purchase and require careful handling during installation (Aumasson, 2017).

The Ethernet is the latest make of the physical transmission medium in the market. It one of the fastest cables which transmit data signals within the shortest time possible. The sending end listens to the Ethernet cable to confirm if it transmitting data. If it is not transmitting any data signals, it sends its data signals from source to destination. The carrier sense multi access collision detect (CSMA/CD) is used to avoid collisions occurring in situations where multiple nodes might have been listening to the cable to confirm if its sending data signals and once it is done with its transmission, they all send their signals at once causing collision. Collision detect mechanism simply helps in controlling the sending devices to send data signals one at a time avoiding collisions.

Non-physical transmission mediums also referred to as wireless transmission mediums or unguided or unbounded transmission medium are used to transmit data signals from one point to another without the use of any physical connection in between the two points. They use the transmitting antennae component which is used to detect the signals being transmitted and transmit them from source to destination. At the receiving end, the receiver aerial component is put into place to help in detecting signals around its surrounding and confirming if they are to be received by the node in which they have been installed in, and then after confirmation, the data signals are received (Aumasson, 2017).

Microwave transmission an example of non-physical transmission media makes use of the microwave frequencies of different ranges, which in most cases range from three gigahertzes to forty gigahertzes on the electromagnetic spectrum, to send data signals from source to destination. The signals being transmitted are basically of a short wavelength. They make use of the point to point transmission technique in which data signals to be transmitted are directed through a focused beam from sending node to the receiving node station. They are mostly used in making microwave ovens because of their short wavelength.

The satellite communication is more like the microwave transmission technique only that it has an added component, the satellite. It has three components. The transmitter earth station which is basically the device that sets up an uplink (signal sent to the satellite by the transmitter earth station) which has a unique frequency in order to transmit data. The second component is the satellite. It receives uplink signal, boost the signals by cleaning any distortion, and then retransmits it to the receiving earth station. The retransmitted signal from the satellite to the receiving earth station is referred to as the downlink and it has a different frequency from the uplink for it has been amplified from the original uplink. The third component is the receiving earth station which receives the send signal on the other side of the globe. Satellite transmission is not limited by the distance between both the sending device and the receiving device for the send signal is at some point boosted and cleaned of any distortion. A geostationary satellite is a type of satellite which is seen to be stationary in space by an observer. Satellite footprint is basically the area in which the line of sight can be located. The main advantage of the satellite communication technique is that it is used to send data signals to different recipient earth stations all at once forming a point to multipoint means of data signal transmission. This type of transmission is being used to make very small aperture terminal (VSAT) technology to enable homes, offices, and other locations to access satellite services directly using small dishes. The satellite services include viewing of different television programs with the help of dishes such as the digital satellite television (DSTV) dish, the Go television dish (GO TV) among other types of dishes (Aumasson, 2017).

Radio communication transmits data signals in form of radio waves which are omnidirectional in nature. They basically start from a central point and spread outwards in all directions as they are being radiated into the atmosphere by the radio frequency antenna at the sending end. Radio communication is used in radio station, television stations and data broadcasts stations.

The radio waves used to transmit these signals can be of three different types. The high frequency (HF) radio waves which are transmitted by directing them into the ionosphere of the earth, the last layer of the atmosphere, which in turn reflects them back to the earth's surface and the receiving node picks up the signals over the earth's horizon with the help of the receiver aerial. Very high frequency (VHF) radio waves are transmitted along the earth's surface from the sending end to the receiving end. A repeater station is placed in between the two communicating ends, more at the horizon, so as maintain the line of sight and to clean and boost the signals due to the curvature of the earth's surface at its horizon which leads to reduction of the magnitude and energy of the signal being transmitted. The last types of radio waves are the ultra-high frequency (UHF) radio waves. They transmit data signals through a line of sight hence there should not be any barrier between the sending and receiving end. They require small antennas and aerials at the both the sending node and the receiving node respectively (Dooley, 2018).

Bluetooth technology is a wireless transmission technology which is basically a worldwide and short rage type of radio technology that allows people to use hand held communication devices such as cellphones and personal digital assistant computers to access the internet and share information. It can also be used to share information without allowing connection to the internet so long as the two communicating devices are not far apart. The minimum distance is approximately hundred meters apart. Bluetooth technology is also being used to develop wireless earphones which are connected to mobile phones or laptops so to listen to audios or even make calls.

Infrared transmission technology transmits data signals successively by having infrared transmitters and receivers, all referred to as transceivers. The transceivers must be within a line of sight and in the same room for they cannot penetrate obstacles like walls though they can be reflected off surfaces which are shiny like walls and ceilings until they reach their destination. Their main advantage is that they can be used to connect devices within the same room without the need of having to use cables (Dooley, 2018).

4.4. HISTORY OF CRYPTOGRAPHY

The history of cryptography is usually dates back in the ages before the coming of our Lord Jesus Christ. It was invented back then by the Egyptians since the government officials did not completely trust the messengers to deliver their messages safely without having the temptation of looking at the message and some going to an extend of altering the information contained in the messages. The Egyptians officials come up with a system that replaced the usual characters of the Egyptians language with special characters that only the sender of the message and the recipient of the message could understand what they really represented.

Since the ages before the coming of Christ, this method of encoding information has evolved and many governments have invested huge amounts of money simply for the perfection of cryptography. The governments are interested in cryptography for they do not wish their foes or allies to have any access to their top-unit information for it may put their organization at risk (Dooley, 2018).The cryptography inventions have simply turned into a fight between the best mathematicians in the globe and the best computer scientists. They all are trying to come up with the best coding techniques which cannot be accessed easily by unauthorized personnel. The war has been able to bear some fruits since some of the best encryption and decryption techniques have been availed in the market (Dooley, 2018).

4.5. CRYPTOGRAPHY NOTIONS OF SECURITY

In the modern cryptography techniques, plaintext is being converted into a cipher text, through the process of encryption at the sending end and later decrypted at the receiving end with the help of experts commonly referred to as cryptographers (Figure 4.2).

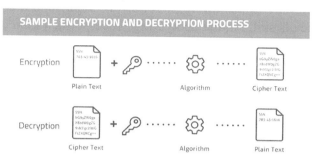

Figure 4.2: The encryption and decryption processes of the modern technology are based on established principles.

Source: https://pediaa.com/difference-between-encryption-and-decryption/ (accessed on 6 April 2020).

The confidentiality principles basically ensure that the information being transmitted will not be accessed by any unauthorized personnel. It basically fights against any tapping attempts of acquiring information by listening through a communication channel and cracking the decryption key to be able to understand the transmitted message (Aumasson, 2017).

Integrity ensures that neither the sender nor the receiver has the right of altering the information being transmitted without it being detected by the cryptography system. An unauthorized third party cannot alter the information being transmitted for the system will be able to detect the security breach and report it to the appropriate personnel or simply stop the transmission process till all the irregularities have been repaired.

Non-repudiation is a technique used to ensure that the source of information and its destination is clearly identified. It simply avoids issues to do with lack of knowledge of the source of a certain kind of information in future in situations where, maybe the government or any other institution has come across some information which might be sensitive. In such situations, the sending end or the intended receiving end cannot deny about their knowledge of such kind of information since the cryptography system will be able to provide the required evidence identifying them as the sender and the recipient (Buchmann, 2004).

Last but not least, the authentication principle ensures that the sending end the receiving end is able to confirm both their identity in the cryptographic system. It basically ensures that, the sending end as it encrypts the information it is transmitting, it is able to understand the recipient end and their specials skills in the decrypting process. Such kind of knowledge avoids overestimated encryption of the message being communicated across giving the receiving end some hard time in the decryption process.

The above principles help us in understanding the fact that the cryptography systems not only major their attention in the mathematical procedures and computer programs for the protection of transmitted information, they are also concerned with the behavior of humans during the entire transmission process from the point of creation of the message, to its encryption, transmission, decryption, and its access by the recipient.

4.5.1. Network Security and Why It Is Important

There has been a recent upsurge in computer security breaches and some even occur around the world daily. Although some of them may be considered minor, causing a little loss of data or monetary resources, there is other whose extent of damage may be considered catastrophic. These adverse effects of security breaches have caused many companies to down play reports about the breaches and deny any claim related to loopholes in their networks. Hackers are continuously coming up with new and improved ways of exploiting vulnerabilities in networks which calls for the same to prevent such vulnerabilities by security experts (Aumasson, 2017).

Network security can be defined as the process of protecting or taking preventive measures so as to protect the primary networking infrastructure from unauthorized access, abuse, adjustment, and disclosure. The implementation of the named measures enables users and applications to work in a secure environment. Network security can be improved and maintained in various ways but one of the most important aspects is the use of multiple layers of security.

4.5.2. Importance of CIA Triad on Organization Objectives

Confidentiality, integrity, and availability (CIA triad) is a model structured to provide guidelines and policies in an organization. Information security is a broad field involving different methods of designing and testing data but the CIA triad is considered as the most crucial components of information security since it is widely accepted due to its simplicity. The implementation of the CIA triad is a step towards achieving organization objectives. First, understanding the underlying meaning of this concept is key before implementing them. The CIA triad which in some instances may be referred to as the AIC triad starts with confidentiality which is the ability to hide content such as files and information from unauthorized access. Information is a priceless asset for any organization especially those that rely on such information to conduct their operations. These organizations may include financial organizations, such as banks containing credit card details for their clients, government agencies such as the immigration department or the election agencies containing voters' details. Confidentiality is implemented through the use of encryption which allows parties that have the encryption key to access the information. Encryption is a widely used system of securing information. An organization whose objective is to transmit information securely must therefore implement this first component (Aumasson, 2017).

Integrity on the other hand is the protection of any information from any modification by unauthorized parties. The value of information lies on its correctness. Altered information may be costly since it may lead to incorrect decision making. The methods used in ensuring this component are cryptography such as hashing of data. The last component is availability meaning that all authorized personnel can access information whenever needed. Information is considered important and of value if the right people access it when necessary. Common attacks such as denial of service (DoS) are used to deny access to information. This has been seen by the common reports of these attacks on high profile websites which in turn turns out costly to the affected companies in terms of revenue. Furthermore, the lack of availability or downtime may also be caused by power outages or other natural causes. Implementing availability is done through introduction of backups which are important in controlling the impact of such incidents. Having an off-site backup in an off-site location meaning there is readiness in restoring services in case there is any issue with the primary data and therefore there is reduction in downtime. Application of the CIA triad is therefore vital in meeting objectives (Aumasson, 2017).

4.5.3. Authentication on Windows

Authentication can be defined as the process of verifying identity of an object, a service, or a person. The goal of authentication is confirming that the item being authenticated is genuine. When authentication is applied in a networking context, it is the act of proving identity to a network resource or application by use of cryptographic operations which uses keys only known to the users or a shared key. There is then comparison with signed data with a known cryptographic key in an attempt to validate the authentication by the server. To improve the authentication's scalability and maintenance, the cryptographic keys are stored in a secure central location (Microsoft 1). The storage of identity information such as cryptographic keys is done using the Active Directory Domain Services which is the default and recommended technology which is a requirement for NTLM and Kerberos implementations (Aumasson, 2017).

Windows implements a variety of authentication protocols such as Kerberos, Transport Layer Security/Secure Sockets Layer (TLS/SSL), NTLM, and WDigest/Digest. Other packages can be combined into authentication packages. The process of basic authentication which is a widely used method of collecting user names and passwords which are normally encoded starts when a user is prompted to enter their names and password. The HTTP request that has the user's credentials is then received by the forefront TMG for validation against a specified authentication server. When the web proxy requests are outbound, the credentials are first validated and then evaluated by the forefront TMG which then authenticate the credentials against a web server configured by a specific method. This is only possible if the web server uses the same authentication scheme as the one used by the Forefront TMG. The relevance of this type of authentication is that it supports a wide range of HTTP clients. However, the web browsers using basic authentication transmits their credentials in an unencrypted form hence may be vulnerable to attacks (Aumasson, 2017).

Digest authentication also starts when users make a request after which the Forefront denies the request and ask the user to enter their Windows credentials. The use of Digest or WDigest is case sensitive and also requires the users to use the names and domains exactly as they appear. There follows a hashing process where an encrypted hash or message digest is produced. There is also addition of values for identification and a time stamp which prevents reuse of passwords after being revoked. This is a more secure way of transmitting credentials when compared to basic authentication.

Windows server 2003 has Kerberos authentication which is based on symmetric cryptography as its default authentication protocol. The process of authenticating clients and resource servers by use of Kerberos starts when clients first authenticate their names and the present timestamp by use of a symmetric key. Encrypted message by the client is then sent to be decrypted by the resource server. The resource server then verifies the client's name and timestamp after decryption and in a successful event, the client is authenticated to the server and the converse is true (Aumasson, 2017).

4.6. CRYPTOGRAPHY BUILDING BLOCKS

Cryptographic blocks are basically the step-by-step procedures used in the production of a certain code to be used in the encryption process of a message being transmitted (Figure 4.3).

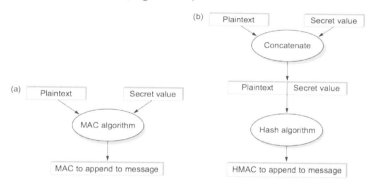

Figure 4.3: Cryptographic blocks ensure that the fundamental notions of cryptography perform well.

Source: https://book.systemsapproach.org/security/crypto.html (accessed on 6 April 2020).

4.6.1. Symmetric Cipher

The symmetric cipher building block is used to encrypt message from source to destination. Uses the technique of encrypting the message being send by use of a special key so as to come up with cipher text. The recipient of the message must have a decrypting key for them to gain access to the message delivered to them. Only the sender of the message and the receiver has access to the decryption and encryption key (Buchmann, 2004).

The encryption and decryption keys keep on changing with each transmission session hence given the name session key. The key space basically increases with increase of characters combined so as to come up with a final key. Longer keys are better than short keys though they do not really guarantee of maximum security of the message being transmitted.

- **Advantages of Symmetric Cipher:** The main advantage of symmetric cipher block is that the key is shared only between the sending end and the recipient hence enhancing the confidentiality of the information being communicated across.

- **Disadvantages of Symmetric Cipher:** Longer encryption and decryption key are quite vulnerable to attacks since most hackers might build a dictionary that generates keys which might be closer or exactly the same as the actual key and then launch the dictionary attack. Once the attacker gains access to the session key, he or she is able to decrypt all the messages being communicated throughout that certain session.

Symmetric cipher cannot support secure communication among several communicating devices. Such a process will require the use of more than one key which will require frequent updating with each session. The updating process will be a tedious one and kind of impossible to achieve.

The symmetric cipher building block does not achieve the cryptography notion of non-repudiation. During transmission process, neither the sender of the message nor the recipient of the message can actually identify themselves in the entire communication process.

4.6.2. Hash and HMAC Building Block

Hashing block is used to ensure integrity of the message being transmitted. The message is usually associated with a hash identification letter or number that assures the recipient that the received message is still intact and the same as the one sent by the sender. The hash identification number is irreversible and two different messages cannot be marked with the same hash identifier for it might cause message collisions (Buchmann, 2004).

Message collision due to use of the same hash identifier for two different messages can be prevented by use of a longer hash identifier component.

The hash can be used as an authentication technique. Once the recipient receives the transmitted message, he or she is able to calculate the added hash identifier to the message and confirm if it's the same message transmitted from the sender.

The problem with hashing is that there may be the presence of a man in the middle who can gain access to the message being transmitted and change the hash identifier. Such breaches lead to transmission of distorted information.

The HMAC technique was introduced to cater for the problem caused by the man in the middle. HMAC deals with having a key for the hash message. It is more like the symmetric cipher technique. Only the sender and the recipient of the message have access to the key of the hash message. Once a message with an appended hash identifier on it has been transmitted, the recipient is able to calculate the hash message since they do have the key (Buchmann, 2004).

Message integrity and authentication is achieved since the man in the middle does not have access to the hash message key minimizing message alteration.

4.6.3. Asymmetric Cipher

The Asymmetric cipher building block was invented as an improvement of the symmetric cipher. It does make use of keys for the encryption of a message.

One of the keys is a public key which is made known to everyone and the other key is the private key, only known by the owner of the message. The send message is encrypted using a public key but it can only be decrypted using only one private key owned by the recipient of the message.

Asymmetric cipher deals with the issue of secure key distribution for there is no need of acquisition of multiple keys as in symmetric cipher. Only one key is owned to encrypt the messages being communicated and the recipient required to have a personal private key for the decryption purpose (Buchmann, 2004).

It is quite scalable, for everyone will need to have the acquisition of only one public key and one private key for protection of information being communicated. Both the public key and the private key do not have to keep on changing with each passing day.

The main disadvantage of asymmetric cipher is that it is slow in transmission of data. It is thus used in secure distribution of keys only and session keys of symmetric cipher are used to ensure the message being communicated is kept confidential (Buchmann, 2004).

4.6.4. Digital Signatures

Digital signatures are part of the hash family. They are used to cater for non-repudiation for by using only the hash identifier, identification of the one who send or received the message via the internet might be tricky.

The sender of the message encrypts their private key using HMAC technique and appends the hash identifier on the message being transmitted. On arrival to the recipient's location, the hash message is calculated with the help of the private key. If the hash messages do match, then the recipient is assured of the true origin of the message, being transmitted (Rubinstein-Salzedo, 2018).

Digital signatures do suffer from attacks from the man in the middle who tries to decrypt the message being transmitted and may alter or distort the entire message rendering it useless to the recipient.

4.6.5. Digital Certificates

Digital certificates are being used to clearly prove that a certain message is from this sender. The sender's private key and name is included in the digital certificate. The certificates have been signed by certified authority and they are further encrypted using the sender's private key (Rubinstein-Salzedo, 2018).

The recipient machine should have a list of the well-known certified authorities to render the attempts of fraud of digital certificates by hackers useless. The availability of certification revocation list will also help identify if a certain digital signature has been revoked by attackers.

Viruses and worms among others can also be used to gain unauthorized access to the well-protected private key used for decryption purposes. In such a situation, the message transmitted using that key are at risk of being accessed by unauthorized users and maybe altered or distorted. To curb such problems, a digital smart card should be used to store the information of a private key. The card usually has a strip that contains the private key details and it enclosed using electronic techniques and can only be accessed by use of digital card reader (Rubinstein-Salzedo, 2018).

4.6.6. Cryptography Primitives

Cryptography primitives are the perfectly made step-by-step procedures used to come up with rules that govern communication in cryptography platforms and further enhance the protection of data being transmitted from source to destination. They follow a certain day to day procedure which most of the time makes use of the one-way hash function and some other encryption functions although they are not really limited to these styles only that they happen to be one of the best styles (Rubinstein-Salzedo, 2018).

Primitives act as the main components required for the establishment of a perfectly working cryptographic system. The primitives are similar to a programming language and do not have to be changed every now and then during the creation of a new cryptographic system because of various reasons.

They must be very reliable in that they precisely meet the expected requirements as stated either in their manuals or any other platform. If it happens to function below its stated expectations, it simply means that all the rules that govern such a system are vulnerable to outside attacks from hackers to name but a few (Rubinstein-Salzedo, 2018).

Developed cryptographic primitives take too long to be tested and declared error-free. Designers who might want to develop a new type of a primitive might not be competent with the mathematical and scientific skills required since they are quite complex.

The process of designing a new cryptographic primitive is a very time-consuming practice. It does not guarantee that the end results will be free of any errors although the process may be designed by experts.

The ability to prove that a certain cryptographic primitive is perfectly working and free of any errors is an impossible practice in most cases (Rubinstein-Salzedo, 2018).

To develop a new and perfectly working cryptographic primitive that meets all the cryptographic standards will require the best and carefully outlined procedures to be put into place.

- **One-Way Hash Function:** It is a step-by-step procedure used to ensure that the message being communicated across communication platforms is well secured. It is basically used to compute the value of the unique identifier added to a message so as to assure the recipient of the message that this message was send by a certain person and it has not been interfered with so far, it is still authentic and of the same integral standards as it was from its source.

- **Symmetric Key Cryptography:** The symmetric key cryptographic primitive is a procedural process of computing for the encryption and the decryption key used to code a message being transmitted from source to destination. Both the encryption and decryption key tend to be the same in most situation. They have to be calculated for the end message received by the recipient to be decrypted from a cipher text format to a normal message format.

- **Public Key Cryptography:** It is the process of computing for the value of the general public key known to everyone that is used to encrypt a message at the sender's end. The computational must somehow match with the unique private key, which is known only to the end user. It affirms that it is the right key to be used for such a message being transmitted from one point to another.

- **Digital Signatures:** These are cryptographic step-by-step procedures used to basically confirm the author of the message. They were designed to ensure that the non-repudiation notion of cryptographic systems is met for both the sender and the recipient of the message are able to be identified with ease by use of the special key attached to the message being transmitted from one point to another.

- **Mix Network:** It is a cryptographic primitive that collects several communications from all transmission channels in a cryptographic system for analysis purposes. It basically analyzes all the communication so as to confirm the source, destination, both authors and recipients of the message being transmitted among other communications information categories.

- **Private Information Retrieval:** The private information retrieval procedure uses kind of a secret and well protected door so as to gain access to a database pool which contains all the communications information for the transmission processes that occur in that system.

- **Commitment Scheme:** It is a cryptographic technique that allows either the sender or the recipient of the message to commit to only one chosen value, may be of an encryption key and ensures they keep it secure from others so as to later expose when the appropriate time comes.

- **Conclusion on Cryptographic Primitives:** These perform at their level best in a combined format. They need to be combined for a stronger, perfectly performing cryptographic environment to be established. Combination overcomes their limitation as individual components of a cryptographic system.

The combination process requires specialization for it quite a cumbersome process. The specialization process is like an art that requires very deep knowledge of what is really required to be done. The experts need to be well skilled and done so many practice activities before the actual combination. Such restrictions must be followed for if any errors occur in the protocol made, the entire cryptographic system is rendered useless and not of any use to anyone.

4.6.7. Private Key Encryption

Private key encryption is a technique used to send information which has been decrypted from the sender to the recipient. It is basically made up of secret keys for they are only accessible to two people. The key used to encrypt and decrypt the message being communicated across a transmission medium is basically the same. It is only made known to only both the recipient and the sender of the message (Rubinstein-Salzedo, 2018).

The encryption technique done using the private key differs. We have the block encryption which ensures that every bit in the message has been encrypted using a private key. The stream cipher encryption technique is used to ensure that only a set of data in a message have been encrypted before transmission process commences. Block encryption tends to be more secure than the stream cipher technique. The main disadvantage of block encryption is that it cannot be used to encrypt large sets of data for the entire process will be time consuming and quite cumbersome. The stream cipher encryptions are mostly used to encrypt large sets of data for they encrypt bytes of information per message and not bits of information. They simplify the encryption process and make it quite easy and less time consuming.

Private key encryption faces the challenge of attacks by the man in the middle who tries to tap into the communication channel and use some tactics to gain access to both the encryption and encryption key. The attacker is now able to decrypt all the messages being exchanged between the sender and the recipient. The message is at the risk of distortion or alteration, for who knows what the attacker's true intentions are. It cannot be trusted to be the true message send by the sender to the recipient (Rubinstein-Salzedo, 2018).

The private key encryption technique does the face the challenge of secure key distribution. Such challenges occur when the cryptographic society for in which it is part of is made up of different communication societies which apparently need to pass across messages using the same private key technique. It means that each communication must design its own set of secret keys a process which is tiresome.

Due to the threat by the man in the middle, the private key set needs to be updates with every transmission session. Such a process is really time consuming and requires lots of hard work for it to be completed.

In case of loss of the private key during transmission process, it is really hard to retrieve it. The transmitted messages have to remain encrypted till the key has been recovered. If the recovery process of the key is not completed within the shortest time possible, the entire cryptographic system is rendered useless and declared to have failed in its operations.

It is quite expensive to set up a complete structure with well-equipped instruments for private key encryption. The entire set up of private key techniques requires really complex and expensive resources for it to function at its level best (Rubinstein-Salzedo, 2018).

4.6.8. Message Authentication

Authentication is the process of verifying that a certain object is real. The message authentication process basically identifies that the message being communicated across is the one and only true message and that it has not been altered whatsoever (Figure 4.4).

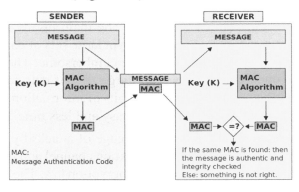

Figure 4.4: Message authentication codes are used to encrypt and decrypt messages with the help of a secret key.

Source: https://en.wikipedia.org/wiki/Message_authentication_code (accessed on 6 April 2020).

The key is only made known to two users. The procedural designing of the code ensures than only a maximum of two users can gain access to the entire message. Once more than two users try to use the message authentication code key, the entire encryption or decryption process is aborted or rendered insecure for use.

At the recipients' end, the client decrypts the message authenticated code to confirm if the message has come across any challenges whatsoever.

Message authentication tries to up-hold the notion of message integrity in the cryptographic society.

Some users might opt to not code the entire message, which means the message contents are not really hidden from access by unauthorized personnel. The trick here is that, everybody, and anyone are able to view the message contents but they cannot be able to alter the message in anyway. In such situations, the message is encrypted using only the message authentication code whose key is only shared between the sender and the recipient (Rubinstein-Salzedo, 2018).

The message authentication techniques without secrecy can also be used to send secret messages. That is, the contents are available to the public, but only the intended recipients are really able to understand its contents. In such situations, the message is still authenticated meaning it cannot be altered in any way.

4.6.9. Public Key Encryption

Public key encryption is a technique that does make use of two keys for the encryption and decryption of messages being communicated across a transmission medium. One of the keys is the public key which does the encryption job and it is globally know while the other key is the private key which does the decryption services and it is only known by the recipient of the message (Dooley, 2018).

For a sender to encrypt a certain message to be transmitted, he or she should be aware of the recipient's public key for them to encrypt the message. It basically means that people who communicate encrypted information need to have a database identifying their recipient's public keys. On arrival to the recipient's receiving machine, a private key, only know to the recipient is used to encrypt the information.

Public key encryption technique is really important for it is impossible for hackers to determine the private decryption technique with only the knowledge of the public key. Public key and private key differ completely for they do not serve the same purpose, one is used for encryption, and the other is used for decryption purposes (Aumasson, 2017).

Public key can serve as the decryption key or the encryption key, same to the private key which can also serve as the encryption and decryption key.

With this technique, the sharing of information is simplified and still the cryptographic system notions are observed. The messages being send are encrypted using public keys which are known to the public, a process which is less tiresome and the private key are used to decrypt the messages protecting the information from access by unauthorized personnel.

Public key encryption technique is basically made up of several components.

- The plain text which is the actual readable message which has been generated to pass information from one end to the other. It is the one fed to the cryptographic primitives for encryption purposes.

- The cipher text is the message which is produced after the plain text has been encrypted using the public key.

- The encryption algorithm is the step-by-step procedure used to convert the plain text to the encrypted cipher text.

- Decryption algorithm is used by the recipient. It is the step-by-step process used to convert the encrypted cipher text back to its original format, the plain text with the help of a decryption key, the private key.

- Public key faces the risk of access by attackers with the use of brute force attacks or dictionary attacks exposing the recipient's decryption private key. The private key can also be altered by the man in the middle in attack situations.

- In case of the loss of the private key, the public key is rendered vulnerable to attacks because its only component that kept the entire system secure has been lost.

- Its main application is its use in secure transmission of messages from one point to another.

4.6.10. Digital Signature Schemes

Digital signature is a cryptography technique which makes use of mathematical concerts to confirm that the transmitted message is authentic and it has not been altered in any way. It simply identifies the origin of message, author of the message and the current state of the communicated message.

Digital signals are mostly used hand in hand with the public key encryption technique. The one dealing with the creation of the digital signature makes use of their own private key to encrypt the information being communicated across. The public key later used to decrypt the digital signature at the recipient's end and be able to access the information encoded in it. Both the sending and the receiving party need to trust that the private key used to encrypt the digital signal was truly a private key to avoid rendering the entire information useless (Dooley, 2018).

Digital signatures are being used by governments for tax returns authentication, business to government transactions avoiding fraud cases or personification cases among other governmental activities.

Healthcare facilities are using digital signatures to ensure that patients' records are stored securely and kept up to date. They are also used for patient admission and treatment procedures for they are able to authenticate the true patient's information avoiding personification of a patient.

Manufacturing companies make us of digital signatures so as to speed up manufacturing processes by enhancing the product design for they affirm that they are of perfect make, assure of the quality of the end products, and enhance the competitiveness of the company in the market among other activities.

Financial systems are making use of the digital signatures for signing of contracts for this limits fraud cases. Paperless banking is also enabled for with digital signatures, one is able to confirm that they made a certain transaction. Loan processing is being done with the help of digital signatures, for in case of loss of signed documents, the digital signatures remind the bank of the loan issued to so and so. Insurance documentation, mortgages assigning among other activities prefer the use of digital signals so as to authenticate the services being offered (Dooley, 2018).

4.7. BENEFITS OF CRYPTOGRAPHY

Cryptography has and will continue to be of great help more so with the ever-growing technological concepts in our generation and the generations to come.

Cryptography enables sensitive and secretive data to be transmitted without many doubts that is will be accessed by a third party or land in the hands of the wrong personnel. Such assurances have been enabled with the help of the many cryptographic primitives which have been put into place (Rubinstein-Salzedo, 2018).

Information being transmitted from one point to another is protected from any form of alteration or distortion. Techniques such as message authentication by use of codes have made the dream of fighting fraud, piracy of information among other defects come true. It only allows two users to access a certain set of information for the attempts of a third user to access the information alts the whole transmission process.

The source of information and its destination are well identified with the use of the various techniques available in cryptographic system. Such information prevents personification of data for its true source and destination is easily identified.

The data being communicated is rest assured that it will be integral with the help of the many techniques put in place in cryptographic systems (Rubinstein-Salzedo, 2018).

4.8. DRAWBACKS OF CRYPTOGRAPHY

The immediate access of encrypted information in situations of urgency in an organization is impossible. It takes time for sensitive large amounts of data to be accessed. The organization decision is then made out of assumption instead of actual facts.

Once the entire organization's cryptography system has been attacked, the entire information is lost and the system rendered useless for it cannot be of any help at that moment (Rubinstein-Salzedo, 2018).

The entire security of information protected by use of cryptographic techniques is dependent on the complex mathematical and scientific concepts put in place. Any achievement by attackers of analyzing the complex concepts of a certain cryptographic techniques renders the entire system useless for it now vulnerable to multiple attacks.

The use of cryptographic systems in protection of information is costly. The experts required to come up with the system will require labor payments, the equipment which need to be set up too are quite expensive among other expenses (Rubinstein-Salzedo, 2018).

In situations where the rules that govern protection of information in cryptographic systems have been weakly designed, the entire system is unable to guard itself from attack threats by hackers.

Availability of information at all times cannot be assured by use of cryptographic techniques for they are only designed to protect information and not to assure the users of constant availability of data.

Algebraic Algorithms

CONTENTS

5.1. INTRODUCTION

Algebra is a term used to refer to different kinds of numerical computations. It may be in the form of equations or in simple basic numerical values. For instance, calculations can be done in the form of algebraic equations and can be solved in different manners such as simultaneously among others. Algorithms different from algebra refer to the rules and the process followed during the problems solving operations and calculations. Algorithms in this case are mostly used in calculations performed by computers. For this to work, the computer is fitted with a set to instructions that will govern the process of calculations. These set of instructions are collectively known as algorithms. In this case, they are used as specifications for carrying out the computation process, data processing as well as automated reasoning among other kinds of tasks. Therefore, algebraic algorithm entails calculations involving numbers, vectors, polynomials, exponential, and differential polynomials, rational functions, for-mal power series, algebraic sets, curves, and surfaces. Algebraic algorithm is a mathematical discipline that is extensively taught in other disciplines such as computer science, engineering, and physics among others (Figure 5.1).

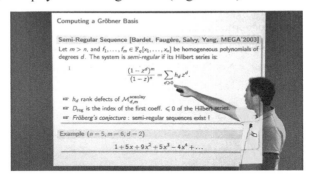

Figure 5.1: Applying algebraic algorithms is a very broad discipline that involves the manipulation of formulas to solve the given problem.

Source: https://www.youtube.com/watch?v=g0GS_Ur7k_w (accessed on 6 April 2020).

As a discipline, it involves the use of matrices and polynomial equations in soling these problems. These two components are essential in carrying out calculations dealing with engineering, signal, and image processing and sciences. They are used to solve a variety of mathematical problems. Some of these problems include polynomial equations, linear systems of equations, polynomial system of equations, univariate, and multivariate polynomial equations, factorizations, and decompositions, interpolation, calculations involving matrix characteristics, minimal polynomials, Newton's polytopes, least, and greatest common divisors, determinants, and ranks among others. These are some of the computational problems that will involve the use of matrices as well as polynomials in solving these equations. To solve them, it may also involve both the matrices and the polynomials being combined with other mathematical formulas for results to be achieved. For high levels of accuracy to be obtained, one must ensure that the formula incorporated during the calculation is certified to provide high levels of accuracy in the results obtained. By convention, there are some formulas that are generally used during calculations globally and are incorporated into various systems of education ensuing the uniformity of the answers obtained by different individuals.

The computational methods therefore ensure infinite precision. There are some systems included during computations to ensure high levels of accuracy. Some of these systems include the maple and mathematical compute solutions. They involve the use of computational techniques such as modular computations, elimination, and resultant methods, Grobner bases computation, Hensel's and Newton's lifting and continuous fraction approximation. These systems are applied when conducting computations by making use of computers. However, to ensure high levels of accuracy there are some requirements needed by the computer to a certain this. The conditions include a high memory space in the computer. The computer should also be set in such a manner that the computer's timing sequence allows the computer to calculate the problems to be done effectively. This means that the processing of the computer will affect how fast and accurate the results will be obtained (Winkler, 2012).

There are various methods of carrying out calculation which may include use of numerical methods in conducting the calculations. The numerical methods make use of operations with binary or decimal numbers that have been rounded up to the nearest fixed precision. It also makes use of the IEEE standard floating point numbers that are represented using double and single precision. These ensures that the computations are quickly done by making use of a smaller memory space though it will require one to make an experimental study on the effects of conducting the round up and how it will affect the accuracy of the results. The experimental study involves one conducting a series of forward and backward error analysis on the rounded numbers. It will also involve linear and nonlinear operations, perturbation, and advanced approximation techniques. There is different computation combinations used in carrying out effective computations. There are various models used in carrying out effective computations (Winkler, 2012).

5.2. COMPUTATIONAL METHODS

5.2.1. Matrix Computation

This is the most common method used in computational processes. It is extensively used in areas involving science and engineering computations. It has proven to ensure high levels of accuracy when the calculations process. The calculations are done with the use of numerical operations. It also uses IEEE standards for double and single precision (Figure 5.2).

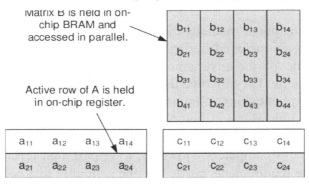

Figure 5.2: Matrix methods simplify computation methods using numerical linear algebra.

Source:https://www.researchgate.net/figure/Matrix-Matrix-Computation-for-Algorithm-1-Load-matrix-A-and-B-to-BRAM-Fori0MAC_fig1_220953365 (accessed on 6 April 2020).

Some of the topics that are covered in matrix computations include the having a background on floating point and cache architecture, linear systems, Gaussian elimination, structured linear systems, least squares problems, unsymmetric eigenvalue problems, symmetric eigenvalue problems, iterative methods for linear systems and eigenvalues. By having knowledge on all these topics an individual will be able to effectively carry out computations with minimal errors in the results obtained. It therefore requires individuals to obtain knowledge on important algorithms and techniques useful in carrying out computation. They focus more on the linear algebra and computation matrix. It involves the use of theoretical as well as practical elements of algorithms. For students that are venturing into mathematics, the skills they gain on matrix computation will enable them to use sophisticated scientific computing and visualization to solve application problems. They will also be able to carry out an analysis on numerical algorithms. They will be able to form relationships between the accuracy of the algorithm and the computational effort. They are able to interpret the results that have been generated by the computer implementations of numerical algorithms. They are able to understand and elaborate on the effects of errors in computations. They are able to give a justification on how such errors affect the solutions in use. They will be able to extensively use the knowledge they have on matrix computation while in conjunction with other disciplines (Winkler, 2012).

Some topics under matrix computation in the matrix manipulation. For one to be able to effectively conduct a matrix computation they the need to have skills in matrix manipulation problems. Matrices can be distinguished through the various properties they contain. A single matrix cannot be used in solving all the problems. There are therefore a variety of matrices available. Take the case of one conducting a computation on the lenses equation. In the lens maker equation, matrices are used in computers to make calculations by lens makers. A single matrix cannot be used to make computation on different lens arrangements. There are therefore a variety of matrices are used depending on the type of lens arrangement that is in use. This applies in the different areas where matrices are used in computations. Depending on the type of computation, the matrix is selected and used. The different properties of the matrices are useful in identifying it appropriate applications. The more special properties a matrix contains the more it is able to be used in a number of computations. Take the case of the matrix-vector when under a product will take up much less time in term of execution. This is attributed to the fact that the matrix contains several zero inputs. In matrix manipulations, the algorithms phrases that are located at the block level are useful when conducting complex calculations. It is then referred to as the block structure. It is known to be recursive meaning that the block entries will exhibit an exploitable resemblance to the general matrix. The matrix vector product is composed of dot products. Matrix computations are built up on a hierarchy of linear algebraic operations matrix can be done either through dot product which may entail the use of scalar operation such as addition and multiplication. The algebraic operations can be expressed in the language of linear algebra. It involves the use of matrix notations, matrix operations, vector notations, vector operations, the matrix-vector multiplication, and Gaxpy. Error-free rational matrix computations involve computations involving finite fields, rings, matrix inverses, determinants, ranks, and characteristic and minimal polynomial. The matrix computations are used in solutions of linear systems of equations. It involves the use of the Gaussian elimination and the banded linear systems with a given band width in solving the equations (Winkler, 2012).

5.2.2. Dense, Sparse, and Structured Matrices

These are applied in storage and multiplication of vectors and require using vector notations. It may be carried out using straight-forward algorithm computations. For the storage of the sparse matrix, they are stored economically by making use of the data structure suitable for it. In the case of singular matrices, when it under goes a product with other vectors, it becomes a null space as the matrix end up vanishing. The spare matrices are created and used in the case of crucial applications. Such applications include solving both partial and ordinary differential equations. The dense structured matrices are commonly defined by use of parameters and they allow one to apply FFT in the multiplication of such matrices. These matrices are extensively used in different applications including image processing, signal processing, ODEs, PDEs, Markova chains, particle simulations, and coding. Extensions can be made on the existing matrices structures in a bid to make general classes of the matrices by associating linear operations on displacements. Such classes include the semi-separable, rank-structured, and the quasi-separable matrices (Cohen, 2013).

5.2.3. Matrix Multiplication, Factorization, and Randomization

Certain formulas and procedures are used during the multiplication or vectors. It involves the process of addition and multiplication. It involves the incorporation of the guidance of the algorithms. It involves the multiplication of the column vectors and then the addition of the given multiplied vectors. Therefore, techniques have been developed and are used. They facilitate the distinct description of the algorithms in matrix multiplications. There are modifications made on the techniques that have led to the increase of the overhead constants that lead to the resultant algorithms being non-competitive. It has been identified that the straight-forward algorithm in matrix manipulations are preferred by most users. This is because it is known to be highly effective on different types of architectures. It is also highly effective when used in computers as it takes a much faster time in solving the problems and also it solves the problem while ensuring high levels of accuracy. It has led to the reduction of various practical problems into matrix manipulations. It has also led to the development of the block matrix algorithms. Matrix factorization is among the common tools in matrix computation. It is a key element contributing to the simplicity and the effectiveness of matrices used in solving problems. It has been made more effective through the use of randomization (Cohen, 2013).

This has brought about the term random matrices. One specific trait of the random matrix is that it is non-singular. It is also well conditioned and quite different for the singular matrices. They are very suitable in carrying out numerical computations as they are non-sensitive to errors. There are various randomization techniques that have been employed. They are implemented in large classes of linear systems and they increase the powers of other of other matrix computations using singular and the ill conditioned matrices.

5.2.4. Solution of Linear Systems of Equations

This involves the use of both the Gaussian equation as well as the banded liner systems. The Gaussian elimination is used the dense structured type of input matrices. An alternative for the Gaussian elimination is the iterative solution which is used in the case of complex problems. It involves as system of convergence of the formulas. The first convergence of the solution should be carefully done to ensure high levels of accuracy of the method used.

5.2.5. Symbolic Matrix Computations

This requires the use of rational matrix computations that includes the solution of a linear system and the computation of matrix of the determinant.

- **Advantages of the Matrix Computation:** One of the advantages of using the matrix computation is that in its structure, it allows the efficient computation of the problems allowing the obtaining of results. It also ensures high levels of accuracy. This is because the matrix system used by convention is proven to maintain high levels of accuracy. In some of the calculations used, it ensures high levels of precision in the values obtained. Another advantage is that it is easy to implement the matrix into the various problems that require o be solved across the various disciplines and hence it is said to be a flexible of algebraic algorithm. In most of the matrix model structures, it is made on a basis of very few assumptions made while developing the matrix used doing the calculations. It is also used in carrying out sensitive analysis of problems therefore the data obtained will be highly accurate and will be able to meet the required variables to be attained by being specific to the issue that is to be solved. As said above, each problem may not be solved using the same matrix therefore different types if matrices may be employed to solve the problem. In the case of a complex problem, then a system of matrices may be used in solving the complex problem. In the case of flexibility, the matrix computation allows the modification of matrices so that it can be incorporated into stochasticity, stage structure and the density dependence. In the case of its use in computer, this method allows a quick process for the results to be obtained. It is also beneficial in that the matrices are very easily keyed in to the computer and they can carry out the computations for extremely complex problems within short periods of time.

- **Disadvantages:** Some of the disadvantages is that a single matrix cannot be used in solving a variety of problems that means several matrices should be in place for them to be selected depending on the type of the problem at hand. The selection process may be quite difficult more so if the matrices almost have the same properties. In some of the problems, computations by use of matrices may be quite difficult therefore; another method may have to be selected in its place. Also, if matrix used is in accurate, it may yield to very inaccurate results. It may some errors that may be produced based on the assumptions made.

5.2.6. Approximation of Polynomial Zeros

An approximation is also referred to as an estimate. It involves making estimates of numerical values. It involves the use of the intermediate value theorem and bound on zeros. The intermediate value theorem is one of the methods used in establishing the roots of a continuous polynomial function. A continuous polynomial function is one that is continuous over given intervals. It contains no breaks; it has holes in the intervals and jumps asymptotes. The polynomial functions are continuous for real functions. Rational functions are different from the polynomial functions are not continuous for real numbers. This is because there are holes in the graphs of the asymptotes. However, at the intervals, the rational functions are continuous. There are various equations and graphs that clearly demonstrate how the intermediate theorem works. When values are fitted in these equations, they are used in plotting graphs that are useful in conduction an interpretation of the equations that have been made. The intermediate value theorem is a corollary to the bounds on zeros theorem. This is because it is not fundamentally different from the general statement of the IVT. It is a special case scenario where the value of n is zero (Cohen, 2013).

The approximation of polynomial function in zeros is used in calculus. There are various methods that are used in the numerical approximation of the roots of the polynomial functions. The finding of zeros in a polynomial function makes use of the intermediate value theorem. In a given continuous function there are various algorithms used though some of them may not be entirely accurate on the results to be produced. Though this is true, it is useful in that it will give off a relatively small interval of the roots. This is because they will produce a relatively good approximation on the roots of the polynomial function. There are some of the applications that will require the method used during approximation should a ensure high levels of accuracy. There are methods that make use of five iterations. The use of such a method may lead to production of roots that are within 0.06 units. This is a good level of accuracy of the method. This is because unlike other methods, this method of algorithm is not used in the calculator. Some of it elements are borrowed and used in the calculator. The calculator makes use of a more efficient algorithm in approximation. It approximates the numerical values to a root of a function to thirteen decimal places. In the corollary of the IVT, there is a unique result of the intermediate value theorem. In an instance where a great circle is drawn round the globe then two points will be brought out which include the antipodal points. These antipodal points are said to have the same temperature. This is also based on an approximation by making use of the formula in the mathematics discipline. It is one of the applications of the numerical method (Cohen, 2013).

The exact zero of a polynomial can be established by use of formula. The formula used is referred to as the quadratic formula. It is the simplest formula that is used in computation compared to others that are more complex. Most polynomials are insolvable and finding their zeros may be kind of difficult. The continuity property of the polynomial function will be useful in determining the zero. This means that the polynomial will not have any jumps or gaps, angles or elbows. The graph will consist of smooth curves in the lines of the curves that are drawn.

5.3. SYSTEMS OF NONLINEAR EQUATIONS AND THEIR APPLICATIONS

This is a system that contains two or more equations that are existent in two or more variables. However, one of the equations is usually nonlinear. It is basic knowledge that an equation that does not take the form of Ax + By + C= 0 is referred to as a nonlinear equation. Normally a linear function is known to be polynomials of a certain exponential. An example of a nonlinear function includes y= X raised to power two. It is referred to as a nonlinear function because the highest exponential is 2 unlike the linear equations that have a highest exponential is usually is 1. n in the solving of the nonlinear the substitution method is applied in solving the equations. It is the same method that is applied in solving linear equations. This involves one equation being solved and the value of a variable being obtained. The obtained value is then substituted in the other equation so that the other value of the nonlinear equation is established. There are also other methods used in establishing values of the variables of the nonlinear equations. There are three well-established types of solutions for the nonlinear equations which involve the use of a parabola and a line. The use of these methods will entail the drawing of graphs that will be useful also in establishing the relationship of the variables plotted in the graph (Mishra, 2013). The possible set of solutions from the graph of such linear equations may involve the outcome being:

- **No Solution:** This is as a result of the line not intersecting with the parabola. This is even though there are extensions made to the line to try and make it intersect with the parabola. This may require one to use other method in order to obtain the values of the variables.

- **One Solution may be Obtained:** This is the cases where the line in question touches the parabola and takes the form of a tangent to the parabola. This is because the line meets the line meets the parabola meets at one point.

- **Obtaining of Two Solutions:** This is the normal case of the equations that are used in solving the equations. The line in these cases crosses the parabola at two points and therefore two values of the variable are obtained.

There is also another method of obtaining solutions for such variables instead of using a parabola, a circle is used it its place. Like in the parabola, there are three possible outcomes as the solutions for the equations. They include:

- No solution which meets that there is no contact between the circle and the line. In basic terms, the line does not intersect the circle.

- One solution for the equation. In this case, the line intersects the circle at one point. It can also be referred to take the form of tangent for the circle.

- Two solutions for the equations. This situation involves the line intersecting the circle at two points. Therefore, two values are obtained for the variables.

When using both cases there is a procedure that is followed for the graphs to be plotted. It involves the solving of the linear equations and obtaining one value for the variables. The value is then substituted and is used in solving the variables for other equations. The solutions that are obtained are then the given values for the nonlinear equations. In solving of the equations there are also other methods used in obtaining values of the nonlinear equations. Another method involves the use of the elimination method (Mishra, 2013).

5.3.1. Elimination Method

This method of solving the computational method is easier compared the use of the substitution method. This method is known to be simple to use when two equations are being solved.

If three equations are to be solved it may be quite difficult to obtain accurate solutions while using the elimination method. In the case of two equations, the steps taken are relatively few. By using the elimination method, it makes use of a circle and an ellipse in getting the possible solutions to the variables. There are quite a number of outcomes resulting from the use of this method. They include:

- **No Solution:** In this case, the ellipse and the circle do not meet. It may involve the circle and the ellipse being at quite a distance from each other. The other scenario may be that the either the circle or the ellipse may be inside each other.

- **One Solution:** This case involves the circle and the ellipse intersecting at specifically one point therefore one value for the equation. They are therefore a tangent to each other.

- **Two Solutions:** which involves both the circle and the ellipse intersecting at two points. Therefore, two variables will be obtained.

- **Three Solutions:** In this case, the circle and the ellipse converge at three points leading to three values being obtained for the equations. For this case the circle is place vertically and the ellipse going through it in a horizontal manner.

- **Four Solutions:** which is a case scenario that involves the circle and the ellipse intersecting at four points. Though this type of solution seems to be absurd, it is actually possible to visualize if one takes the case of the circle and the ellipse being intertwined.

It is therefore determined that by use of this method the values that are obtained in five possible case scenarios. It is important to note that when graph is plotted, the inequality is graphed in the same manner as an equation would be graphed. In this case, a dash line is drawn and there is a shaded region which represents the region that entails the sets of solutions. It is also noted that the inequalities are solved in the same manner as the equalities. The solutions to the systems of inequalities are required to meet and satisfy both the inequalities. The system of the nonlinear inequalities refers to a system of two or more inequalities that contain two or several other variables that are composed of one inequality whose property is that it is not linear.

In the case of solving systems of equations that are composed of three equations, there are methods that are made that perfectly suit it. Such types of equations are commonly referred to as a three-by three systems. In solving this equation, it may involve the solving of each variable present in the equation and each time a variable is obtained it is substituted in the equation. The solution obtained for such a type of equation system, it is referred to as an ordered triple. It involves the obtaining the variables x, y, and z. There is certain operation that is performed. They involve the interchanging of the order of the equations. Then both sides of the equations will be multiplied by non-zero constants. Afterward a non-zero multiple of one equation is added to the other one. This kind of equations may be represented in the 3D format as it makes use of the intersection of three planes. For instance, if one takes the case of a corner, it is composed of three sides: two adjourning walls and the floor. When one takes this case, it is a kind of a representation of the three sides of and intersection of three planes.

In the case where the values of three unknowns are being determined the following process will be followed. First, a pair of the equation is selected and is used in establishing of a variable. Afterwards another pair of the variable is also selected and is used in the solving of the same variable. By doing so, a system composed of two equations will be formed. The equations will then be formed by 2-by-2 systems. After variables have been determined, back-substitution process is carried out using the known variables. Therefore, the variables are keyed into the original equation and afterwards they are used in solving for the missing variable (Mishra, 2013).

Similar to two-system kind of equation, in three system kind of equation the user may interact with inconsistent system of equation. These types of systems are referred to as inconsistent due to the fact that the variables that have been obtained cannot satisfy all the equations. It may involve three planes that may intersect the two other planes. However, the intersection may not be at the same location. If the elimination process is used in computation, it may lead to the production of a false statement.

Additionally, there is a system of dependent equations that may require the solving and determination of three variables. This may lead to the production of infinite number of solutions which are produced as a result of multiple situations. Though the equations used in the system may be different, they may all intersect on a given line that is composed of infinite solutions. The system of three equations is very useful in solving problems that are termed to be real-world. In cases of the three variables equations, if it contains an infinite number of solutions then the resultant after performing the elimination operation is that the resultant value is referred to as an identity (Mishra, 2013).

5.3.2. Applications of the Non-Linear Systems

Applications of the non-linear systems include its use in partial fractions. Fractions are more complex numerical problems and hence they involve the addition of variables in numerator or denominator. By making use of the non-linear systems of equation, solving rational problems will be much easier. The other common application for the non-linear system of equations includes the prey-predator systems. This system is also referred as the Lotka-Volterra systems. This system is applied in the case where two or more species are interacting. One of the species is the prey while the other is the predator. The system is used in the biological equations to draw out a natural periodic variation in the numbers of various species in an ecosystem. The equations are laid out to make a relationship on how the different factors of the ecosystem will affect the number of the species existing in the system and how many of them will die. Matrices can also be applied in solving of these equations to make the solving process to be easier. Graphs are also plotted to assist in drawing the relationships between the factors. By using graphs, it makes it easier to interpret the data and making an evaluation (Winkler, 2012).

The nonlinear equations are also used in systems of the pendulum to establish values such as the angular displacement, length of the pendulum and the gravitational acceleration. This is through the use of the nonlinear pendulum equations. When using such equations is assumed that factors such as friction are kept constant. The equation used is referred to as a conservative equation which can be modified into a two-dimensional system. In these types of equations, there are two types of equations. While solving of these equations, it involves use of values that are either real or imaginary. When the pendulum is pushed within a given space, there is the angular velocity which is determined. Its values are fitted into the equation and are used to determine the other values such as the line of displacement among other things. In an equilibrium solution, there are critical points. It is assumed that the value of the angular displacement is zero (Winkler, 2012).

There are various case scenarios of the pendulum used when solving the equations. If the be obtained value is zero, then angular velocity has to be small. These are some applications of the non-linear system of equations.

5.4. POLYNOMIAL FACTORIZATION

The polynomial factorization is also referred to as the factorization of polynomials. This is the expression of a polynomial with coefficients of a given field. It is also the expression of integers as a product of their irreducible factors containing coefficients in the same domain. It is one of the essential parts of the computer algebra systems. The polynomial factorization is also existence in the form of polynomial factorization algorithms. In current systems, there is the use of the computers in solving the problems. It also entails the solving of polynomials with higher levels of degrees and coefficients with huge digit numbers (Cohen, 2013).

When using polynomial factorization to solve problems, we also use polynomial domains. Depending on the type of the problem at hand, the domains used may be unique according to the problem. This introduces the term polynomial rings. The polynomial rings can identify domains of the given equation. The use of the polynomial rings is also useful in developing the factorization questions. The elements of the rings are each product of a constant and also a product of an irreducible polynomial. There is a deposition that is experienced that is known to be unique to a certain level. For factorization tone conducted, it is required that there is a presence of a base field. The polynomial factorization is sensible when used in a problem involving coefficients in a field that is computable. In this case, the elements are each represented in a computer and a given set of algorithms are provided to conduct the algebraic operation.

In some special cases, there are fields that will not require a factorization algorithm. A great example is Shepherson. The field coefficients used is referred to ad prime fields. They are known to be field generated extensions. The algorithms used are conducted by a succession of the following: the first one is the square-free factorization and factorization in finite fields. It also involves cases of reduction.

Polynomial factorization involves various conversions which may include conversion from a multivariate case to a univariate case, conversion from rational coefficients into integer coefficients, conversion from integer coefficients to coefficients of a prime field of p elements, and conversion from coefficients of purely transcendental extensions to a multivariate case over a ground field (Cohen, 2013).

There is the primitive part-content that involves factorization over the rational numbers and the integers of the same problem. It therefore defines the factorization of the quantity Q as the product of an integer and a primitive polynomial. The factorization is therefore unique with respect to the sign of the content which in most cases is positive. The Gaussian law proves that the product of two primitive polynomials is referred to as primitive. Therefore, implying that a primitive polynomial cannot me reduced over the rational. This is only possible if it is not reducible over the given integers. This goes to show that factorization over rational of polynomials entailing rational coefficients are similar to the factorization over integers in its primitive parts. In the same manner, factorization over integers of a given polynomial entailing integer coefficients is the multiplication result of the factorization of its primitive parts after factorization of its contents.

In order to reduce the factorization of a polynomial over its rational to become the factorization of a primitive polynomial consisting of integer coefficients we make use of the GCD integer computation. It also conducts the factorization over integers to factorization of an integer as well as a primitive polynomial (Cohen, 2013).

5.4.1. The Square-Free Factorization

To understand square-free factorization, we need be aware of the square-free polynomial. This is the case where two or more factors of a polynomial have similar characteristics i.e., they are identical. The polynomial is referred to as a multiple of the square of the factor. If univariate polynomials are used, the results obtained will be the multiple of the roots. The multiple factor is then the polynomial's derivative. In conducting this factorization, the Gun's algorithm is applied. Is carries out a thorough exploitation that contributed to the effective factorization of the polynomial so that the result is the square free factors. It is important to note that the factors are not multiples of squares used on mathematical computation. In conducting a polynomial factorization algorithm, it is essential for one to conduct a Square-free factorization as the first step.

The advantage of using the Gun's algorithm is that it can be used in to cade scenario. One including the polynomial being univariate while the other involves it being multivariate. This will involve the multivariate polynomial being considered as a univariate polynomial and the computation is done over a polynomial ring. Other cases involve computations in a finite field. The Yun's algorithm is applied in the case where the degree used is quite small if not it may result to the value being zero (Cohen, 2013).

5.4.2. Classical Methods

These consist of computerized methods that are used in carrying out integral factorization. These methods are good though when currently used they end up to carry out computations at a much slower speed. It obtaining linear factors through the use of rational root tests. It entails using combinations of integer factors which its validity can be tested. Polynomial pond division is used in ruling out valid factors. In the case where the polynomial is of a degree of two or more then partial factorizations is used in conducting the complete factorization. If the equation consists of both a linear and a nonlinear factor, then the linear factor will be ruled out if complete factorization is conducted.

5.4.3. The Kronecker's Method

This is used in the case where a finite number of the polynomial factors are to be obtained. It involves a variety of the ways being used in conducting the computation. It may involve use of possible combinations in solving the problems. The degrees of the polynomial have to be checked and tested before they are used (Cohen, 2013).

One of the major elements of algebraic algorithm is the symbolic computation. This is a sector that has been implemented in computers being used to conduct such calculations. The symbolic computation before being released to the public was first conducted by a modern computer program. The program used is as differential type and was developed by Kahrimanian.

It was developed for UNIVAC. This program expressed its input in the form of a linearized binary tree and afterwards it produced a derivative of the expression. To first develop this program was a challenge but after other languages such as the Lips language, this obstacle was brought down and made to be quite easy. This allowed easy development of symbolic mathematical systems. After several advancements of the programs being used, it led to the development of the SAINT Lips program which is an integration program. This program was good in that it had great capabilities in conducting calculations in the lowest level such as the case of an ordinary calculus student. The limitations of this program were that it did not have a strong mathematical foundation and it was also referred to as rudimentary (Mishra, 2013).

This led to the great need for the development of a general-purpose system. This was needed for the aim of making computerized mathematical computations to be readily available to laymen. Some of these developments include the ALPAK and the ALTRAN. There were other developments that were made but were not generally used as the contained some limitations. Take the case of the FORMAC. This development had the challenge that it was limited in scope. This is if it is compared to the ALPAK and the ALTRAN. The limitation in scope is attributed to the fact that the program developed majored in polynomial and rational functions. Since most of the system used were dealing with calculations involving polynomials, it was essential that there was a polynomial manipulation system. The polynomial system made use of an efficient canonical recursive representation of polynomials. It also embraced the use of arbitrary precision arithmetic. The system was put in conjunction with as SAC-1 which facilitated the conducting of operations dealing with multivariate polynomials as well as rational functions. The advantage was that it allowed the use of coefficients with infinite precision. The SAC-1 is fitted with several algorithms. The choice of the algorithms was based on a procedure that made use of the elementary theory of a real closed field. The algorithms are beneficial as they have wide spread applications more so in the field of computer science and robotics.

There are various versions of the SAC-1 with the latest one making use of the algebraic language Alde's. Further developments were made so that the manipulations systems were advanced that they allowed a natural interactive usage. Such systems include the Engelmann's MATHLAB-68, CAMAL system, Tony Hearn's REDUCE-2 system, MACSYMA, SCARTCHPAD system and the AXIOM system. The AXIOM system was a development from the SCRATCHPAD system. These systems are almost similar. If placed in comparison to one another, the only difference that would come out would be their design goals. For instance, MATHLAB-68 was developed as a general-purpose system created to conduct a series of functions. The functions include performing differentiation, infinite integration, and polynomial factorization, using symbolic coefficients to solve differential equations and conducting direct and inverse Laplace transformations. The REDUCE system is also a general-purpose software system able to allow the creation of programs that allow the easy solving of very complex problems by making use of the system's in-built algebraic simplification mechanisms (Mishra, 2013).

Some of the outcomes of this system is that it has allowed solving problems in QED, QCD, fluid mechanics, celestial mechanics, plasma physics, general relativity and various engineering disciplines. These problems have been solved with high levels of success through the use of these software systems.

The CAMAL software though small, it is quite fast and powerful. It is also a general purpose software system that has been extensively used. The Motivations 9 system is a system that is made up of three modules that include the E-module used in conducting exponential series, the H-model also known as the HUMP which is a general purpose package and finally the F-module that is a Fourier series. Among the systems, the MACSYMA and the SCRATCHPAD systems are the major one. They both make use of the state-of-the-art techniques and have incorporated them to be used in carrying out operations involving symbolic algebra and software engineering. Research did not end there. The development of algebraic systems has tremendously increased bringing about more systems that will be an improvement of the already existing systems.

The more notable ones among the SMP, MAPLE, PROLOG-based SYCOPHANTE system, SYMBAL system, muMATH system and the SCRATCHPAD/AXIOM system. The MATHEMATICA is the latest system to be developed. It is a product of the Wolfram Research Inc. this system runs in most of the personal computers and has facilitated symbolic computation being done by most users. It is almost similar to the SCRATCHPAD/AXIOM and MAPLE. These systems were developed with the main goal of them facilitating high degrees of computing as well as reasoning and teaching of mathematics. They were also developed in an aim of them being able to conduct efficient algorithmic practices. Some of the issues of concern were the developing languages used that would properly fit symbolic computation, graphical displays of the algebraic objects, compute architecture that facilitates symbolic manipulation and the easy-to-use user interfaces (Mishra, 2013).

5.4.4. Applications Symbolic Computation

Symbolic computation has a wide area of applications. For instance, in biology it is used to conduct calculations dealing with the secondary structure of the RNA. In chemistry it is used in operations dealing with the nature of the equilibrium in chemical processes. In mathematics, it is useful in proving the Macdonald-Morris conjecture. In physics, it is applied in the evaluation of the Feynman diagrams. In computer science, symbolic computation is used in designing the IEEE standard arithmetic while in robotics it deals with inverse kinematic solutions in a multilinked robot. Symbolic computation algebra is applied are areas of computer science such as:

- **Robotics:** In robotics, many computational algebra applications use the robotics stem derived from the algebraic-geometric nature of robot kinematics. Some of the problems involved in kinematic modeling include the modeling of a robot having the inverse kinematic solution for a robot. The computation of the workspace as well as the workspace singularities of a robot and the planning of an obstacle-avoiding motion of a robot while in a cluttered environment among others.

- **Vision:** One of the applications of symbolic computation is the representation of various surfaces or the classification of a variety of algebraic surfaces. There could also be algebraic or geometric in variations involved with a given surface. It is also used on the surface boundaries among others.

5.4.5. Computer-Aided Design

The symbolic computation is used in nearly all computer-aided design (CAD) applications. It entails the description of surfaces, smoothing surfaces, the parameterization of surfaces and curves, a variety of Boolean operations such as the intersection of surfaces and union among others. Other applications, include graphical editors, computational algebraic number theory, coding theory and the automated geometric theorem. Some of the solutions include robot motion planning. In the initial and final configurations of a robot in the rigid subparts in the two or three-dimensional spaces. It is also involved in the description of stationary obstacles in the provided space. In such spaces the assumption is that, they can be represented as the finite union as well as the intersection of algebraic surfaces (Vasconcelos, 2004).

Given this representation, we have to find some variables. In the case there is the continuous motion of the robot in the stage of the initial and final configuration, solution takes place in multiple steps. The major initial step includes the translation of the problem to a parameter spaces referred to as the C-space. This is the space of all points that corresponds to the possible configurations in the robots. The C-space is commonly a low-dimensional with a similar dimension as the number of degrees of liberty of the robot, algebraic manifold within a possibly higher-dimensional Euclidean space. It deals with interesting problems in computation algebra. The second stage entails the classification of the points in the C-space into two classes. They include forbidden and free points. Forbidden points in C-space will result into a collision of two subparts of the robots or a subpart of the robot in an obstacle. Free points correspond to a legal configuration of the robot in the course of the obstacle. Description and computation are composed of the connected components in important in computational algebra. In some cases, the free space is represented by use of stratification or decomposition but will require the one to establish the connectivity properties. As the initial and final configurations correspond to two points in the C-space, there are tests conducted to verify whether they lie in a similar connected component. The tests entail computing the adjacency relations in the variety of strata present in the free space and their representation in a combinatorial structure that is appropriate for fast research in algorithms used in a computer (Vasconcelos, 2004).It is then used in surface construction used in solid modeling. If the polynomial is given in the three present vectors: x, y, z, it will be required that 3D space can be described in an algebraic surface. In the case of computation, the envelope of the family of spheres with radius r and who's their centers lie on the given surface f. The surface is referred to as a two-sided offset of the given surface f. It describes the set of points at a given distance r on both sides of the surface f. It is required that a set of equations be outlined that give a description of the points.

There are sets of equations which describes hyper surface in a six-dimensional space and have coordinates consisting of (x, y, z, u, v, w). These coordinates when projected into a three-dimensional space containing coordinates x, y, and z the result will be that the surface will have an implicit form.

Therefore, the offset will be calculated by carrying out an elimination of the variables u, v, and w from the initial coordinates in the preceding equation. It is important to note that the initial equation states that the point hx, y, zi on the offset of the surface f is at a distance r from the footprint hu, v, wi. The final equations ensure that hu, v, wi is the footprint of hx, y, zi. It entails the use of the envelop method. The disadvantage of this method is that it contains quite a number of problematic features. They include that the method does not deal with self-intersection in a clean manner and may at times generate more points that are not in the offset surface.

In the geometric theorem proving if, a geometric statement that entail finite sets of hypotheses as well as a conclusion. Some of the assumptions made include the geometric being able to predicate in the hypotheses while the conclusion being translated into an analytical setting. It is done by first assigning symbolic coordinates to the points and afterwards using their polynomial identities to give a description of the geometric relations (Vasconcelos, 2004).

Parallel Algorithms

CONTENTS

6.1. INTRODUCTION

In the field of computer science, the parallel algorithm, as opposed to the traditional sequential algorithm, this is an algorithm that can perform multiple procedures in a particular time. This has been the custom of computer science to illustrate a sequential algorithm in the theoretical machine replica, frequently this is the one recognized as the Random-access device. Alike, a number of computer science researchers have implemented the one known as the parallel random-access device as the parallel abstract device or the shared-memory. Most of the parallel algorithms are accomplished at the same time as, although in general, the accomplished algorithms are the dissimilar concept and therefore these ideas are frequently conflated, with which the characteristic of an algorithm is the parallel and that is concurrent and which is not being clearly illustrious. Furthermore, the non-similar, non-synchronized algorithms are frequently known the sequential algorithms which by contrast through the concurrent algorithms.

6.2. PARALLELIZABILITY

The algorithms differ significantly in the way the parallelizable; they vary from the simply parallelizable to absolutely unparallelizable. Furthermore, the specified problem might accommodate the different algorithms, which can be extra or even fewer parallelizable. A number of these problems are simple to divide them up into bits in this manner; these are normally referred to as the embarrassingly parallel crises. Such examples are the numerous algorithms to explain the Rubik's Cubes and discovering the values which the outcome is a specified hash. Most of these problems cannot be divided up into comparable portions, as they all need the outcome from the preceding stride to successfully carry on through the next step, thus these is known as the inherently serial crises. Such examples are the iterative arithmetical methods; this includes the Newton's technique, the iterative result to these three-body crises, and the majority of the accessible algorithms to compute. A number of these sequential algorithms may be transformed into the parallel algorithms by means of the automatic parallelization (Roosta, 2012).

6.2.1. Motivation

The comparable algorithms on the individual tools have become extra common ever since the early years of 2000s, because of the substantial progress in the multiprocessing organization and the increase of the multi-center processors. Until the conclusion of the year 2004, the single-center processor performance swiftly increased through the frequency weighing, and hence it was simply to build a computer which had a single quick core than the one with several slower cores which had the identical throughput, therefore the multicore structures were of more restricted use. However, since 2004 occurrence scaling hit a dead end, and hence the multicore structures have since become more common in development of corresponding algorithms (Roosta, 2012).

6.2.2. Issues

1. **Communication:** The price or the complexity of the sequential algorithms is projected in the terms of the gap in the memory and processing time. The parallel algorithms are required to optimize one more supply. Here are two parallel processors to make the message transient. The shared memory dispensation needs the additional fastening of the data, which entails the visual projection of the additional computer and the bus cycles, and in addition serializing a few fragments of the algorithm. The message passing dispensation implements the channels and the communication boxes but this message increases the transfer visual projection on the bus, the additional recollection required for the queues and the message containers and the latency in messages. The plans of the parallel processors implement the special buses such as the crossbar so as the communication, visual projection will be tiny but the parallel algorithm is the one that decides the capacity of the interchange. Even if the message overhead of the added processors overshadows the advantage of adding an additional processor the one which encounters the parallel slowdown.

2. **Load Matching:** The other problem with the parallel algorithms is to ensure that they all are rightfully load unbiased, by making sure that the loads general work is unbiased, as opposed to the input dimension being reasonable. Such examples include the checking of all figures from one to hundred thousand for mainly it is trouble-free to divide amongst the processors; but on the other hand, if the figures are simply separated out equally, the quantity of the work will be unstable, because the smaller figures are easier to develop by the algorithm which is easier to examination for the primality, and hence some processors will acquire more work to perform than the rest, which will sit inactive until the weighed down processors complete.

6.3. DISPERSED ALGORITHMS

The subtype of the parallel algorithms, the distributed algorithms are the algorithms planned to operate in the cluster computing and the distributed computing surroundings, where the extra concerns past the span of standard parallel algorithms required to be attend to.

6.3.1. The Agent Established Model

The agent-established model is a group of computational models for the simulation of the procedures and relations of the autonomous causes which are either individual or even the combined entities like the association or the groups via a view for evaluating their effects on the structure as a whole. It unites the elements of the game hypothesis, difficult systems, appearance, compute sociology, multi-causes systems, and the evolutionary training. The Monte Carlo procedures are implemented to introduce the randomness. Particularly inside the ecology, the agent established models are also known as the individual-established models and the individuals inside the individual established models can be easier than the fully independent agents within the agent established models. A review of the current literature on the individual-established models, the agent-based replica, and the multi agent structure indicates that the agent established models are implemented on the non-computing connected scientific area such as biology, ecology, and the social science. The Agent-established modeling is connected to, but separate from, the idea of the multi-means systems or the multi-agent imitation in that the objective of the agent established model is to investigate for explanatory approach into the combined behavior of the agents by obeying easy rules, normally in the natural structures, as opposed to the scheming agents or for the solving of precise realistic or the engineering crises (Roosta, 2012).

The agent-centered models are a particular type of micro scale form that is implemented to replicate the concurrent operations and the connections of the multiple agents in an effort to re-generate and to predict the manifestation of the complex phenomena. This procedure is the major of the emergences, which a few stating as the entire is better than the total of its bits. In other terms the higher-rank structure properties that appear from the connections of the lower-rank subsystems. On the other hand, the total-scale state alters the surface from the micro-level agent manners. On the other side, simple behaviors which are the meaning of the rules ensued by the agents that are generating the complex manners the meaning of state modifications at the entire system ranks. The Individual causes are usually characterized as the boundedly balanced, and it are alleged to be the acting in what they distinguish as their individual benefits, such as the duplicate, financial benefit, or the social ranks, by implementing the heuristics or the simple result-making system. The agent-based model causes can experience the knowledge adaptation, and the duplicate. Majority of the agent-established models are collected of the various agents that are specified at a variety of the scales that are typically known as the agent-granularity; the decision-creation heuristics; the knowledge of the rules or the adaptive procedures; the interaction topology; and the surroundings. The agent-based model are usually implemented as the computer simulations, which are either as the tradition software, or through the agent-based model toolkits, and this particular software may be then implemented to test how the modification in the individual behaviors which will influence the system's up-and-coming overall performance. The thought of the agent-established modeling was created as a relatively easy notion in the late years of 1940s. Ever since it needs the computation-concentrated procedures, it did not develop into widespread not until the year 1990s (Roosta, 2012).

The early developments of the agent-established model can be followed back to the Von Neumann mechanism, the theoretical mechanism which is capable of replica.

The tool that the von Neumann planned would trail the accurately detailed information to fashion a duplicate of it. The design was then created upon by von Neumann's companion Stanislaw Ulam, who also was a mathematician; Stanislaw recommended that the device be was built on the paper, as the gathering of all the cells on a framework. The plan intrigued von Neumann, who later sketched it up; generating the primary of the strategy which was later labeled as the cellular automata. One more advance was commenced by the mathematician known as the John Conway. He created the well-recognized Game of Life. Not like the von Neumann's device, John's Game of Life worked by the extremely simple policies in the actual world in the shape of a dimensional of-2 checkerboard.

Majority of the computational modeling study describes the structure in the equilibrium or as the moving connecting the equilibria. The agent-established modeling, on the other hand, implements the simple regulations, that can result in dissimilar sorts of the difficult and the interesting performance. The three thoughts of the central to the agent-established models are the agents as the objects of appearance, and the difficulty (Roosta, 2012).

Agent-established models are made up of more energetically interacting rule-established agents. The structure inside which they relate can build real-world-similar to the complexity. Usually the agents are located in space and the time and be located in the networks or in the lattice-like areas. The position of this agents and their receptive behavior which are encoded in the algorithmic shape in the computer agendas.

In most cases, although not always, the vehicle can be considered as the intellectual and the purposeful. In environmental the agent-based model which are frequently known as the individual-established models which are in the ecosystem, these agents can be such like the trees in woodlands, and should not be consider as intellectual, even though they can be focused in the sense of the optimizing entrance to a particular source, such as water. The modeling procedure is best illustrated as the inductive. The modeler creates those hypotheses thought the majority relevant to the circumstances at hand and later then observes the phenomena materialization from the agents' connections. Occasionally that outcome is equilibrium. Occasionally it is a developing pattern. From time to time, though, it is an incomprehensible mangle. In most ways, the agent-established models complement the traditional logical methods. Where the logical methods are allowing the humans to differentiate the equilibria of a structure, the agent-established models permit the possibility of the creation of those equilibria.

This generative involvement can be the majority of the mainstream of the possibility of the benefits of the agent-established modeling. The association models may explain the appearance of the higher-arrangements of patterns, the network arrangements of the terrorist associations and the web, the power-rule distributions in the dimensions of the traffic mess, the wars, and the stock-market collapsing, and the social separation that persists in spite of populations of open-minded people.

The agent-established models also may be implemented to recognize the lever points, described as the moments in occasion in which the interventions have tremendous consequences, and differentiating among categories of the path dependency. Rather than concentrating on the stable condition, majority of the models consider a structure's toughness, the customs that difficult systems settle in to the interior and the external stress so as towards upholding their functionalities. The chore of controlling that difficulty requires a deliberation of the causes themselves, their variety, and their connectedness, and the level of connections (Roosta, 2012).

6.3.2. Uses

- **In the Area of Environmental Science:** The agent-established modeling has been implemented extensively in the scope of biology, as well as the investigation of the stretch of the epidemics and the dangers of the biowarfare, and the biological implementations which including the inhabitants dynamics, the stochastic genetic material expression, the vegetation ecosystem, the landscape variety, the growth and the decline of the primeval civilizations, the evolution of the ethnocentric performance, the forced dislocation or the relocation, the language variety dynamics, cognitive representation, and biomedical functions such as the 3D reproduction of the breast tissue structure or the morphogenesis, the effects of the ionizing emission on the mammary stem unit the subpopulation applications, irritation, and the human resistant system. The agent-established models have as well been implemented for the rising decision support example of the breast cancer. Agent-established models are more and more being implemented to the modeling of pharmacological structures in the early phases and the pre-clinical study to help in the drug growth and the gaining more and more knowledge into the biological structures that would not survive likely a priori. Military uses have as well assessed. Furthermore, the agent-established models have occurred lately employed to investigate the molecular-stage biological structures (Hoffmann and Meyer, 2007).

- **In the Areas of Business, Knowledge, and the System Hypothesis:** The agent-established representations have been implemented ever since the middle of the year 1990s, to tackle a number of trade and equipment problems. Such examples of these applications are the modeling of the organizational performance and the cognition, team operations, supply sequence optimization and the logistics, representation of the customer behavior; examples are the statement of mouth, the social system effects, dispersed computing, labor force management, and the portfolio administration. They have as well been implemented in the scrutinizing of the traffic jamming.

Lately, the agent established modeling and the imitation has been implemented to a number of domains like the investigating of the blow of publication venues by the scientists in the computer science sphere such as the journals against the seminar. In addition, the agent-based models have been put into practice to simulate content delivery in the ambient supported by the surroundings. An article in November 2016 in arXiv summarized an agent established simulation of the posts dispersed in the Facebook public online network. In the area of the peer-to-peer, ad-hoc, and extra self-managing and the difficult networks, the value of the agent established modeling and the simulation has been revealed. The implementation of a computer science-established formal requirements structure attached with wireless antenna networks and an agent-established simulation have lately been verified. The agent established evolutionary exploration or the algorithm is a latest research theme for tackling the difficult optimization crises (Hoffmann and Meyer, 2007).

- **In Finances and Social Disciplines:** Recently, more attention has been focused on the agent-based models as possible devices for the economic study. The agent-based models cannot take for granted the economy and can attain the equilibrium and the representative mediators are later replaced by the agents with a diverse, dynamic, and the co-dependent behavior such as the herding. The agent-based models take the approach from the base to up and can also produce extremely difficult and volatile replicated economies. The agent-based models can symbolize the unstable structures with crashes and explosions that increase out of the non-linear or uneven, answers to proportionally tiny changes. A 2010 July commentary in the Economist looked at agent-based models as option to the DSGE replica. The journal nature as well encouraged the agent-established modeling with an viewpoint that recommended the agent-based models can perform a better duty of representing the economic markets and other financial complexities than the normal models alongside with an thesis by Doyne Farmer and Duncan Foley who disagreed that the agent-based models could accomplish both the requirements of Keynes to stand for a difficult economy and of Robert Lucas to build models established on the microfoundations. Doyne and Duncan pointed towards the progress that has been created by the implemented by the agent-based models to replicate parts of a financial system, but they disagreed for the formation of a very broad model that integrates the low stages models. By replicating a difficult system of forecasters that were based on three separate behavioral summaries that the copying, the anti-copying and unresponsive financial marketplaces were simulated to far above the ground correctness. Consequences demonstrated a link between the system morphology and the contribution of the market index.

Ever since, the start of the 21st century the agent-based models have been positioned in the architecture and the urban preparation to estimate the design and to suggest the pedestrian flow in the town environment. There is besides a growing area of socio-financial analysis of the infrastructure venture impact implemented by the agent-based ability to distinguish the systemic contact upon socio-financial networks (Hoffmann and Meyer, 2007).

- **Organizational Agent-based Models: Agent Aimed Structure at Simulation:** The agent-aimed at simulation figure of speech distinguishes among two groups, to be precise the structure for agents and agents for structures. The structures of Agents, occasionally known as the agent's structures this are structures that implement the agents for the utilization in manufacturing, human, and the public dynamics, military uses, and many others. Agents for structures are later separated in two subcategories. Agent-sustained systems deal with the utilization of the agents as a maintainer's facility to enable computer aid in the problem tackling or the enhancing cognitive experience. The agent-established systems are the center on the use of agents for the creation of the model manner in a system assessment this is the system learning and the summarization.

6.3.3. Implementation

Majority of the agent-based model frameworks are planned for the serial von-Neumann processor architectures, restricting the pace and the scalability of the used models. Ever since the developing behavior in broad-scale agent established models is reliant of the population dimension, scalability restrictions may delay the model validation. Such restrictions have mostly been addressed by means of the dispersed computing, with frameworks like the spread HPC. In particular, the one dedicated to these kinds of implementations. At the similar occasion the same as such methods map well to the bunch and the supercomputer architectures, matters related to the communication and harmonization, as well as the exploitation complexity, relics potential parallel problem for their extensive adoption. A latest expansion is the implementation of information-similar algorithms on the Graphics dealing Units for the agent-based simulation. The tremendous memory bandwidth joints with the absolute number crunching control of the multi-processor graphics dealings unit has facilitated the simulation of millions of causes at tens of boarder per second.

6.3.4. Parareal

Parareal is a corresponding algorithm from the mathematical analysis and is implemented for the resolution of the initial worth of problems. It was commenced in the year 2001 by Lions, Maday, and Turinici. Ever since then, it has happened to be one of the major widely calculated parallel-in-occasion integration procedures. Parareal can be resulting as equally a multigrid technique in time process or as the multiple shooting beside the occasion axis. Both thoughts, multigrid in occasion as well as accepting the numerous shooting for occasion integration, to go to rear to the year of 1980s and 1990s. Parareal is an extensively studied procedure and has been implanted and customized for a variety of different request. Thoughts to parallelize the resolution of the initial worth of problems going to the rear even further, the initial paper proposing a corresponding-in-occasion incorporation method emerged in the year 1964 (Hoffmann and Meyer, 2007).

6.4. PARALLEL PROGRAMMING MODELS

In the area of computing, a corresponding programming replica is a concept of the parallel processor architecture, that which it is appropriate to express the algorithms and their composition in the programs. The worth of a programming replica can be evaluated on its generalization and how well the variety of the different crises can be articulated for a variety of dissimilar architectures, and its presentation of how they efficiently accumulated programs can perform. The accomplishment of a parallel programming replica can take the shape of a records invoked from a chronological language, as an addition to an accessible language, or as a completely new language. Agreement around a specific programming model is significant because it guides to dissimilar parallel computers that are being created with support for the model, thus facilitating the portability of the software. Hence, the programming models are known as the connection between hardware and the software. Classifications of the parallel programming replicas it can be subdivided largely into two fields; the process communication and the problem disintegration.

6.4.1. The Process Communication

The process communication relates to the instruments by which the parallel procedures which are able to converse with each other. The majority of the common shapes of interaction are common memory and the message transient, but the interaction can as well be understood which is imperceptible to the programmer.

1. **Common Memory:** The common memory is a competent means of transferring data amidst the processes. In a common-memory replica, a parallel procedure can share a global address gap that they can read and inscribe to asynchronously. Asynchronous simultaneous access can lead to race circumstances and the mechanisms like the locks, the semaphores, and the monitors can be implemented to avoid all these. Predictable multi-core processors openly support the shared memory, in which most of the parallel programming speeches and libraries, like the OpenMP, the Cilk and the Threading construction Blocks which are planned to develop.

2. **Message Momentary:** In the message-momentary replica, a parallel procedure exchange of information through momentary of messages between one another. These exchanges can be asynchronous, whereby information can be transmitted even before the recipient is ready, or the synchronous, whereby the recipient must be ready. The corresponding sequential procedure formalization of the information passing employs the synchronous communication routes to connect processes, also to led to vital languages like the Go, Limbo, and Occam. In the dissimilarity, the performer model implements the asynchronous information momentary and also been engaged in the planning of languages like the Scala and the SALSA.

3. **Implicit Interaction:** In an implied replica, no process relations are evident to the programmer and in its place the compiler or the runtime are accountable for performing it. Two such examples of the implied parallelism are by way of area-specific speeches whereby the concurrency inside the high-level operations is agreed, and by way of its useful programming speeches because the absence of the area-effects permits the non-reliant functions to be performed in parallel. On the further side, this type of parallelism is complex to manage and the functional speeches like the simultaneous Haskell and the simultaneous ML providing the features to control the parallelism openly.

6.4.2. Problem Disintegration

The parallel plan is collected of the simultaneously performing processes. The problem decomposition relates to the method in whereby the constituent procedures are formulated.

1. **Task Parallelism:** A duty-parallel model concentrates on the procedures, or the threads of implementation. These procedures will frequently be behaviorally separate, that highlights the requirement for communication. The duty parallelism is the ordinary way to articulate the message-momentary communication. In the Flynn's classification, the duty parallelism is normally classified as the MISD, MIMD, or the MPMD.

2. **Data Parallelism:** The information-parallel replica is centered on the performing procedures on a content set, typically a frequently structured collection. The set of duties will act on this content, but separately on displaced partitions. In the Flynn's classification, the content parallelism is normally divided into MIMD, SIMD, or the SPMD.

3. **Implied Parallelism:** As by way of implicit procedures the interaction, an implied model of parallelism discloses nil to the programmer the same as the compiler, the operating time, or the hardware that is accountable. Such example includes, in the compilers, routine parallelization is the procedure of converting the sequential system into parallel systems, and in processor architecture, superscalar implementation is a device whereby teaching-level parallelism are subjugated to perform procedures in the parallel.

6.4.3. Technology

Similar programming replicas are directly related to the replicas of computation. A replica of similar computation is a concept implemented to study the value of computational procedures, but it doesn't essentially requirement to be sensible, with the aim of it to be used efficiently in the hardware or the software. The programming replica, in dissimilarity, does in particular imply the sensible deliberation of the hardware and the software realization. The similar programming verbal communication can be established on an individual or a mixture of programming models. Such examples include the High presentation FORTRAN which is established on common-memory connections and the information-parallel dilemma decomposition, and the Go provides devices for the common-memory and the message-momentary interaction (Hoffmann and Meyer, 2007).

6.5. PARALLEL ALGORITHM TECHNIQUES

The major progress in the parallel algorithms has been the recognition of the fundamental algorithmic procedures. Majority of these procedures are as well been implemented by the sequential algorithms, but hole a more important role in the parallel algorithms, at the same time as others which are exceptional to parallelism. Below is a list some of these methods with a brief explanation of them:

1. **Divide-and-Overcome:** Divide-and-overcome are a normal paradigm for the parallel algorithms. Subsequent to dividing a dilemma into two or several others the sub-dilemma, the sub-dilemma maybe tackled in the parallel. Normally the sub-dilemmas are tackled recursively and hence the next separate step yields still more sub-dilemmas to be tackled in parallel. Such examples, assuming we want to calculate the curved-hull of a group of the points in the plane for example to calculate the smallest curved polygon that surrounding all of the positions. This may be executed by splitting the positions into the leftmost and the rightmost, recursively discovery the curved hull of each group in the parallel, and later merging the both resulting hulls. Divide-and-overcome has then proven to be the individual one of the most influential methods for tackling problems in the parallel with applications varying from the linear structure to the processor graphics and from the factoring big figures to n-body imitations.

2. **Randomization:** This is the implementation of the random figures in ubiquitous in the parallel algorithms. Spontaneously, the randomness is useful because it permits the processors to create local choices which, with the top probability, included up to better global conclusion. Such example includes, presume we need to sort a set of the integer keys. This may be accomplished by the dividing the keys into containers then sorting inside each one of the buckets. For this to perform well, the containers must have symbolized by the non-overlie intervals of the integer principles, and the box approximately the similar number of inputs. The randomization is implemented to decide the particular boundaries

of the intermission. Then initially each processor chooses a random example of its keys. Subsequently all of the chosen keys are arranged together. Lastly, these solutions are implemented as the boundaries. This random example is furthermore used in the several parallel computational geometries, diagram, and the string corresponding algorithms. Other implementations of the randomization comprise of the symmetry breaching, the load harmonizing, and the routing algorithms.

3.   **Parallel Indicator Manipulations:** Majority of the long-established sequential methods for manipulating records, the trees, and the diagrams do not interpret easily into the parallel methods. Such example of this methods such as the traversing of the basics of a connected record, paying a visit to the nodes of a tree in post order, or by performing an intensity-diagram traversal of the graph appearing to be intrinsically sequential. Luckily, all of these procedures may be replaced by the well-organized parallel methods. These particular parallel methods such as the pointer skipping, the Euler-visit technique, the ear disintegration, and the diagram contraction. Such examples include the, one method to label each particular node of an n-node record or the tree with the brand of the final node or the root is to implement the pointer skipping. In each particular pointer-skipping step each specific node in parallel restores its pointer with that of its descendant or the parent. Subsequent to the majority steps, each particular node indicates to the similar node, the last part of the list or even the root of the tree.

Other helpful methods comprise of finding the tiny diagram separators for the dividing of the information among its processors to decrease communication, mixing up for the harmonizing load diagonal processors and the mapping direct to memory, and the iterative methods as a substitute for the shortest methods for the tackling of the linear structures.

These particular procedures have led to the well-organized parallel algorithms in the most dilemma regions for which competent sequential algorithms are recognized.

However, most of these procedures at first developed for the parallel algorithm have led to enhancements in the chronological algorithms.

6.6. GRAPHS

Graphs can be referred to as:

- Graphs: This is class of verticals and the edges. Graph theory is the investigation of this particular graphs and their features.

- Graph topology: This is a topological gap resembling the graph in the common sense of the disconnected mathematics. It can also be the graph of function f is the group of prearranged pairs like x, y, whereby f (x) = y. In the ordinary case where x and f(x) are the actual figures, these duos are the Cartesian coordinates of the positions in the Euclidean flat surface and hence shapes the separation of this particular flat surface. The graph of a function is an extraordinary case of a relation. In the scope of science, manufacturing, knowledge, finance, and other fields, graphs are devices implemented for a lot of functions. In the easiest case, one patchy is plotted as the purpose of another, usually by implementing the rectangular alliance. In the present foundations of arithmetic, as well as, the usually, in place theory, a function is the in fact equivalent to its graph. On the further side, it is frequently useful to observe functions as the mappings, which comprise not merely of the relation among the input and the output, however as well as the set is the field, moreover which is the set codomain. For instance, to utter that a purpose is onto the subjective or even not the codomain ought to be considered. The diagram doesn't decide the codomain. This is ordinary to implement both conditions purposes and the graph of a purpose because even if measured the similar thing, they point out the viewing it from an unusual perspective.

6.6.1. Relation of Graphs

- Paper graphs the graph piece, the synchronize paper, the network paper, or the four-sided figure paper is writing paper that is printed with well lines manufacturing up the usual grid. The outlines are frequently used as channels for the plotting of functions of graphs or the experimental information and the drawing of arcs. This is usually found in arithmetic and the engineering learning settings and in the laboratory pads. Paper graphs are accessible either as the loose-leaf article or the jump in notebooks.

Charts are a graphical illustration of the information, within which the information is characterized by the symbols, for example the bars in a chart appearance in a chart line, or segments in a tart diagram. A chart can represent numeric tabular information, purpose or a number of categories of the qualitative arrangement and provides different information. The word diagram as a graphical illustration of information has several meanings:

- The content chart is a kind of illustration or the graph that arranges and corresponds a set of arithmetical or the qualitative information.

- Diagram decorated with added information in the map environment for a precise purpose is referred to as charts, for example a marine chart or an aeronautical illustration.

- Other constructs are known as charts, for example the chord diagram in the music data or in the evidence chart for the album recognition.

6.7. SORTING

This is a procedure to organize items methodically and has several meanings:

- The ordering: these are items in a particular series ordered by a number of criterions.

- Classifications: this is the assemblage of particular items which have related properties.

In processor disciplines the assembling is a planned sequence which is known as the sorting. Categorization is ordinary processes which happen in several applications and are well competent algorithms to execute it has been created.

The roles that sorted series do include:

- Creating the lookup or making investigation efficient;

- Creating the integration of the series efficient; and

- Facilitating the dispensation of information in a distinct order.

Random rescheduling of items is known as the shuffling. For the categorization both a weak arrangement ought not appear after, this can be particular or a firm weak arrangement which should appear before, indicating one describes also the further, both are the balance of the opposite of each other. To ensure an excellent organization, the balance should be limited to a whole order and several other orders. Sorting n-tuples consists of areas which can be performed based on one or several of its components. These objects can be classified based on the property known as the sort key.

To illustrate the above theory with a practical example, suppose that the items are books, the classification key is the heading, and the order is the alphabetical.

The latest sort input can be fashioned from two or extra sort inputs by the lexicographical arrangement. The initial is then known as the initial sort input, the subsequent one is known as the secondary sort input, and so forth.

For instance, the addresses would be sorted by the implementing the city as the initial sort input, and the boulevard as the secondary classing input.

If the classifying of the key principles is completely ordered, then the sort input describes a feeble order of the items these items with the similar sort input are equal with respect to the sorting. If the dissimilar items have, diverse sort inputs the values, then later defines an exceptional order of the substance.

6.7.1. Ordinary Sorting Algorithms

- The bubble or the case sort this is the replacing the two adjoining elements if they are not within the order, replicating until the array is classified.

- The inclusion sorting the examination of the successive basics for an absent order item, which is later then inclusion the item within the proper position.

- Assortment sort the searching of the least or the even biggest factor in the collection and the put it in the appropriate place. Substitute it with the worth in the first situation, again replicate until the array classified.

- The rapid sort which dividers the arrangement into the two sections. In the initial section, all the elements are not as much of as or equal to the spin around value. In the subsequent section, all the elements are either superior than or the equivalent to the turn value. In conclusion, arranging the two sections recursively.

- The combining of the arrangement by dividing the record of elements into two pieces, arrange the two sections individually and then later combine them.

6.7.2. Physical Categorization Processes

An assortment of sorting the tasks is necessary in the industrial procedures. For instance, during the withdrawal of the gold bars from ore this is a tool known as the shaker board which implements the severity, the tremor, and the current to detach the gold from the lighter equipment in the ore which happens by the sorting by dimension and the weight. The categorization is as well as the naturally happening process that its consequences in the absorption of the ore or the residue. The categorization outcome from the request of some criterion or the discrepancy stressor to an accumulation to divide it into its mechanism based on a number of the variable quality. The resources that are dissimilar, but only somewhat so as well as the isotopes of the uranium they are very hard to disconnect.

The visual sorting is a mechanical process which involves the sorting of concrete products by implementing the cameras or the lasers and it has an extensive implementation in the food manufacturing. The antenna-based arrangement which is implemented in the mineral dispensation (Gebali, 2011).

6.8. COMPUTATIONAL GEOMETRY

The computational geometry this is a branch of the computer discipline that is dedicated to the investigation of the algorithms which may be affirmed in words of the geometry. Some merely geometrical dilemmas happen due to the learning of computational arithmetical algorithms, and these particular problems are besides considered to be a fraction of the computational geometry. Whereas the current computational geometry is the latest development, it is among the oldest areas of computing with a narration stretching all the way to the rear to the distant past. Computational convolution is an essential component to the computational geometry, by means of great practical significance if algorithms are implemented on very huge datasets that consists of tens or hundreds of millions of places. For the particular sets, the distinction between $O(n2)$ and the $O(n \log n)$ can be the disparity between the days and the seconds of the computation. The major impetus for the growth of computational geometry as a regulation was the progress in the processor graphics and the computer-support design and the developing of the CAD or the CAM, but majority of the dilemmas in computational geometry which are typical in nature, and can come from the mathematical revelation. Other significant applications of the computational geometry comprise of robotics the motion preparation and the visibility dilemmas, the geographic content systems the geometrical place and investigation, the route arrangement, integrated route design the IC geometry plans and the confirmation, computer-supported engineering the mesh creation, computer visualization the 3D renovation. The major branches of this computational geometry are the:

- Combinatorial computational geometry, known as the algorithmic geometry, which operates with the geometric objects as the separate entities. A ground placed book in the topic by Shamos and Preparata provides the initial use of the word computational geometry in this logic by the year 1975.

- Mathematical computational geometry, also known as the device geometry, computer-supported geometric design or the geometric representation, which deals initially with the on behalf of the actual-world objects in shapes suitable for the computer computations in the CAM or CAD structures. This branch can be seen as a additional growth of the expressive geometry and is often measured as a branch of the graphics computer or the CAD. The word computational geometry in this particular meaning has been implemented ever since the year 1971.

6.8.1. Combinatorial Computational Geometry

The initial objective of the investigation in the combinatorial computational geometry, used to expand the efficient algorithms and the information structures for the tackling of crises stated in terms the vital geometrical objects like the points, column segments, the polygons and the polyhedral and many others. Majority of these crises seem so easy that they were not considered as problems at all in anticipation of the advent of the computers. Think about, for instance, the closest duo of problem: Given that the points in the flat surface, discover the two with the minimum distance from one another. One would compute the space among all the match up of the points, of which there are $n(n-1)/2$, later on pick the match up with the minimum distance. This brute-energy of the algorithm obtains the O ($n2$) occasion, for example, its implementation time is the relative to the quadrangle of the quantity of points. The classic outcome in the computational geometry is the formulation of the algorithm that obtains the O ($n \log n$). The randomized algorithms which obtain the O(n) predictable time, also the deterministic algorithm which is obtained as O($n \log n$) occasion, they have as well been revealed (Gebali, 2011).

6.8.2. Geometric Query Crises

In the geometric query crises, usually referred to as geometric investigation of problems, the input comprises of two sections, the investigation space section and the query section, they differ over the crises illustrations. The look for space usually wants to be preprocessed, in a method that numerous queries can be replied efficiently. Some of these basic geometric query crises are:

- The choice of searching the preprocess of a group of points, in organizing the competent count the figures of points within the query area;

- The tip location which is given a detachment of the gap into the cells, to create a information structure that is competently telling in which the cell is a inquiry point is situated;

- Nearby neighbor the preprocess is a group of points which are arranged to efficiently notice which point is the nearby to a query position;

- Beam tracing which is achieved by giving a group of objects in the gap to create a content structure that professionally tells which particular object is a query beam intersects initially.

If the exploration space is set, then the computational difficulty for this group of crises which is frequently estimated by the:

- The occasion and the space required to build the information structure to be investigated in; and

- The occasion and at times the additional space to reply to queries.

6.8.3. Dynamic Crises

However, another main class is the dynamic crises, whereby the aim is to discover a competent algorithm for discovering the solution continuously after each and every incremental adjustment of the key data the addition or the deletion contribution of the geometric essentials. The algorithms for crises of this kind usually consist of the dynamic information structures. Several of the computational arithmetical crises can be transformed into a dynamic individual, at the value of the increased dispensation time. For instance, the variety searching crises may be transformed into the dynamic variety searching crises by providing for the addition or the removal of the positions. The dynamic curved hull dilemma is to maintain the track of the curved hull for example the dynamically altering set of positions that is at the same occasion as the input positions are inserted or erased.

The computational difficulty for this group of dilemmas is anticipated by:

- The occasion and the space needed to build the information structure to be looked for in;
- The occasion and the space to adjust the searched content structure following an incremental modification in the search gap; and
- The occasion and at times an additional space to respond to a query.

6.8.4. Variations

Some dilemmas can be treated as the belonging to both of the groups, depending on the circumstance. For instance, regarded as the following crises. The position in polygon to dictates whether a position is within or external a particular given polygon. In a lot of applications these crises are treated as a particular-shot one for example belonging to the initial class. For instance, in majority of the functions of the computer graphics this is a familiar problem which is implemented to discover which field on the screen is ticked by a pointer. However, in majority of these functions, the polygon in query is the invariant; at the same time as the point correspond to a query. For instance, the contribution polygon can represent a frame of a state and the point is a place of an airplane, and the crises to settle on whether the airplane violated the edge. Lastly, in the beforehand mentioned for instance of the computer graphics, inside the CAD applications the altering input information which are usually stored in the dynamic information arrangement, which can be investigated to increase the speed in the point-in-polygon question (Gebali, 2011).

In a number of contexts of the query crises which are reasonable prospects on the series of the questions, which can be exploited also for well-organized data arrangements or for tighter computational difficulty estimates. For instance, in various cases it is vital to know the most horrible cases for the whole time for the entire sequence of the N questions, to a certain extent than for a particular query.

6.8.5. Numerical Computational Geometric

This particular branch is as well referred to as geometric representation and the computer-support geometric plans. The center problems are arced and the surface representations and the demonstration. The majority important devices here are the parametric arc and the parametric exterior, like the Bézier arcs, the spline arcs, and the exterior. A significant non-parametric advance is the rank-set technique. Application fields of the computational geometry comprise the shipbuilding, airplane, and the automotive manufacturing.

6.9. NUMERICAL ALGORITHMS

Numerical investigation is the learning of the algorithms that implement the numerical rough calculation, as contrasting to the representative manipulations by the problems of the mathematical investigation this is as it's distinguished as of the discrete arithmetic. The numerical position of view trails back to the most basic mathematical writings. The arithmetical linear algebra this is a investigation about the arithmetical algorithms for the linear algebra dilemmas.

The basic theory includes:

- **The Thin Matrix:** In the numerical investigation and the technical computing, the sparse matrix or even the sparse array this is a matrix in which majority of the essentials is zero. By difference, if the greater part of the essentials is nonzero, then the matrix is well thought-out to be dense. The figure of the zero-valued essentials divided by the entirety number of essentials for example m × n on behalf of an m × n matrix is known as the sparsity of the medium, which is normally equivalent to 1 minus the depth of the intermediate. By implementing this, descriptions a medium will be thin when its sparsity is superior to the 0.5.

- **The Band Medium:** In the field of arithmetic, predominantly the matrix hypothesis, the band medium is a sparse medium whose non-zero access are restricted to a slanting band, consist of the major diagonal and the zero or extra diagonals on both sides.

- **Bidiagonal Matrix:** In the field of mathematics, the bidiagonal medium this is a lined matrix with non-zero accesses alongside the major diagonal and both the slanting above or the slanting below. This states that there are precisely two-some none zero diagonals within the matrix. While the diagonal over the main diagonal have the non-zero accesses, the matrix is the higher bidiagonal. While the diagonal underneath the main diagonal have the non-zero accesses, the matrix is the lesser bidiagonal.

- **Tridiagonal Medium:** In the linear algebra, the tridiagonal prevailing conditions is the group matrix that have nonzero rudiments on the foremost diagonal, the initial diagonal underneath this, and the initial diagonal higher than the foremost diagonal merely.

- **Block Medium:** This is matrix that is made up of smaller matrices.

- **Hilbert Medium:** This is illustrations of a medium which are tremendously ill-accustomed and hence complex to handle.

- **Stieltjes medium:** A symmetric optimistic specific by way of non-positive off-diagonal way in.

- **Wilkinson Medium:** This is a paradigm of the symmetric tridiagonal medium with two of a kind of almost, but not precisely, equal to the Eigen values.

- **Convergent Medium:** This is the four-sided figure matrix whose consecutive powers move toward the zero medium.

- **The Diagonally Foremost Medium:** In the scope of mathematics, the quadrangle matrix is thought to be a diagonally foremost if, for all the rows of the medium, the degree of the diagonal access in a line is bigger than or even equivalent to the amount of the magnitudes of all the added non-diagonal access points in that line.

6.9.1. Interpolation and Approximation

Interpolation is the building the purpose of going via several given information points.

- **Polynomial Interruption:** Polynomial interruption this is the interruption by the polynomials.

- Linear interruption in fields of mathematics the linear interpolation is a procedure of the bend fitting by implementing the linear polynomials to build the latest data positions within the variety of a discrete group of known content points.

- Runge's occurrence in the scope of the mathematical area of the numerical study. The Runge's occurrence is an oscillation at the limits of a period that happens when implementing polynomial interruption with polynomials of an elevated degree in excess of a group of equ-distanced interruption points. It was revealed by David Runge in the year 1901, when investigating the behavior of mistakes when implementing the polynomial interruption to approximate the certain purpose. The finding was significant because it demonstrates that going to elevated degrees does not constantly improve the accuracy. The occurrence is comparable to the Gibbs occurrence in Fourier sequence approximations.

- Lebesgue constant interruption in the field of mathematics, the Lebesgue constants which depends on a group of nodes and of its dimension providing a thought of how better the interruption of a function at any particular given nodes is in the contrast with the most excellent polynomial rough calculation of the function in which the amount of the polynomials are obviously set. The Lebesgue invariable for polynomials of the amount at the majority n and in favor of the set of the n + 1 nodes the T is more often than not denoted. These variables are identified following Henri Lebesgue.

6.9.2. Approximation Theory

- Modulus of stability this is implemented to calculate the efficiency of a function;
- Unisolvent point location this is the role from a particular function gap which is resoluted by uniquely by principles on a particular set of positions; and
- Rock-Weierstrass theorem this is an uninterrupted functions and may be approximated evenly by the polynomials, or the convinced other function gaps.

Numerical techniques refer to procedures resembling the algorithms that may be implemented to tackle certain mathematical troubles such as the ODE's or even the PDE's in the numerical manner. While the numerical study refers to the implementing the developed procedures to scrutinize a specific physical dilemma of importance. The numerical scrutiny is implemented in the field of arithmetic and computer knowledge that generates, investigates, and later puts it in action these algorithms for achieving the numerical explanations to crises involving incessant variables. Such rises take place throughout the ordinary sciences, the common sciences, manufacturing, medication, and the commerce. Error in the area of numerical algorithms happen when how distant a respond is as of the actual value and this may be calculated in two dissimilar ways as the absolute worth, or even as a virtual value. The complete error is the divergence connecting the computed or the estimated respond and the actual answer. While the virtual error is the complete error divided by the actual answer (Gebali, 2011).

The root cause of numerical analysis within mathematics and computing fields is that it's a root-discovery algorithm and is an algorithm for discovering the zeroes, also known as the roots, of the continuous tasks. The zero of a purpose if, as of the actual numbers to the actual numbers or even from the difficult figures to the complex statistics, is a figure x such that the f (x) = 0.

6.9.3. Parallel Difficulty Theory

The parallel difficulty Theory researchers in this field have created a theory of the equivalent complexity of the computational crises comparable to the theory of the NP-wholeness. The concept of Nick's group in the parallel difficult theory holds the position of P in the chronological complexity for instance the crises in the NC are considered to be tractable in the corresponding.

CHAPTER

7

Randomized Algorithms

CONTENTS

7.1. INTRODUCTION

In addition to the input data, an algorithm that is able to receive a stream of random bits that it utilizes to make random choices is referred to as a randomized algorithm. It is possible to receive different results from different trends of a randomized algorithm even when the input is fixed. This means that it is inevitable to have the involvement of probabilistic statements in the description of the properties that are found in randomized algorithms. For example, the time that a randomized algorithm takes to be execuet, is a random variable.

When you look back into the very early days of computer science, it is possible to trace isolated examples of randomized algoriths. Hhowever, the centrally important concees,was developed abonty50 years years ago. Solovay and Strassen were able to develop the randomized primality test which was considered as one of the key early influences in the recognition of randomized algorithms. In addition, the paper that was written by Rabingdrew attentionthe main aspects of a randomized algorith to computational geometry, and number theory. There was also a paper that was written by Gill that helped in laying the foundations for extending the abstract computational complexity theory for the inclusion of randomized algorithms (Hromkovic, 20tat Cconstruction of algorithms in a wide range of applications requires randomization as one of the most important tools. Randomized algorithms are able to provide two main advantages. Firstly, randomized algorithms normally provide a space requirement and execution time that is much smarisoncompared to the deterministic algorow easySecondly, randomized algomsthey are to understanso to implement. Most of the time, introducing randomization is used for the conversion of worst-case behavior deterministic algorithms that are naïve and simple into a randomized algorithm that can perform much better in providing probabrite up,Here we will be able to cover the many different ways in which randomized algorithms can be utiled. Welt will cover the manner in which randomized algorithms are used in algebra and number theory, randomized techniques in combinatorial and enumeration, and distributed computing, data structure and graph theory maintenance, randomized algorithms in computational geometry, sorting, and searching, and randomized algorithms for pattern matching. The main aspect that will be discussed is the fact that there are a few major principles that are used for the construction of randomized algorithms, no matter how wide their application is.

Some of the aspects that will be discussed include:

1. **Abundance of Witnesses:** Making the decision of whether there is possession of certain properties by the input data is a principal covered in randomized algorithms, such as whether it is possible to factor an integer. Most of the time, the establishment of the property is made possible by the ability to find a specific object referred to as a witness. Despite the fact that it may be difficult to deterministically find a witness, there is still the possibility of showing that witnesses are available in abundance in a specific probability space, and therefore it is possible for one to efficiently search for a witness through repetitive sampling from the probability space. It is much more likely to find a witness within less trials if the property holds, and therefore, when the algorithm is not able to find a witness after many different trials, it provides evidence that is strongly circumstantial, however not absolute proof, that there is no available property within the input.

2. **Foiling the Adversary:** The ability understands the advantages of a randomized algorithm are made possible by a game-theoretic view. The computational complexity of a problem can be thought of as the value of a specific zero sum two-person game, whereby, the algorithm is being chosen by one of the players, while the other player (mostly referred to as the adversary) is able to foil the algorithm by choosing the input data. The algorithm's running time on the chosen input data is the adversary's payoff. It is possible for one to view a randomized algorithm as a probability distribution over deterministic algorithms, and this means it can be seen as a mixed strategy for the player that is able to choose the algorithm. One is able to create uncertainty on the actions of the algorithm on a specific input by playing a strategy that is mixed, therefore making it much more difficult for the adversary to choose a complicated algorithm that may end up leading to the creation of difficulties for the algorithm.

3. **Fingerprinting:** This technique is used for the representation of objects that have large data by short "fingerprints" that have been computed for that specific manner. There are many situations in which the availability of two objects that have fingerprints that are the same helps in providing strong evidence that these two objects are very identical. This technique is used for pattern matching problems.

4. **Checking Identities:** The ability to plug in random values for specific variables, in addition to the ability for one to check whether the expression provided evaluates to zero, helps in making it possible to check whether algebraic expressions are identically equal to zero. If there is occurrence of a nonzero value, this means that the expression is not an identity. If there is repetitive occurrence of the value zero, this helps in providing strong evidence that the expression is identically zero.

5. **Random Sampling, Ordering, and Partitioning:** Information about the distribution of input data is gathered by randomized algorithms for tasks such as selection and sorting, through drawing of random samples. The order in which the input data is considered can be randomized so as to solve certain problems. In such situations, it is possible to prove that almost all orderings of the data, for every fixed array of input data, normally lead to a performance that is acceptable, despite the fact that some of the orderings may lead to the failure of some algorithms. In the same fashion, divide, and conquer algorithms that are randomized are mostly based on partitioning the input randomly.

6. **Rapid Mixing of Markov Chains:** It is possible to find approximate solutions to combinatorial enumeration problems through several randoized algorithms, based on the fact that it is possible to make random samples from a set of combinatorial objects that are large and well structured. This process if sampling is based on a Markov chain where there is correspondence of its states to the combinatorial objects. One of the major aspects when it comes to the Markov chain is to show that it converges in a rapid manner to its stationary distribution.

7. **Load Balancing:** When it comes to distributed computation, the use of randomization helps in evening out the process of computational tasks assignment to the different processing units.

8. **Symmetry Breaking:** When it comes to distributed computation, most of the times, it is important for the computational processes' collection to make choices that are consistent, while still arbitrary, from a set of possibilities that are essentially indistinguishable. In such a situation, for breaking symmetry, randomization is very

useful.

In addition to being able to describe and illustrate the manner in which the stated ideas are normally utilized in constructing randomized algorithms, there are some other concepts that will also be discussed in relation to randomized algorithms. These include:

9. **Randomized Complexity Classes:** There are some studies that have been done within the computational complexity theory on the solvable class of problems by randomized algorithms in polynomial time. Due to the fact that the performance guarantees for randomized algorithms are of a problematic nature, there have been several proposals of a number of different reasonable definitions.

10. **Interactive Proofs:** In this situation, a demonstration is made by a prover that a certain theory is true, through the performance of certain tasks that cannot be performed if the theory was false. In general, these tasks normally consist of providing answers that are correct to a set of question that have been picked at random from a certain group.

11. **Randomness as a Computational Resource:** In actual practice, it is not possible for randomized algorithms to access unbiased and independent random bits at a supply that is unlimited. There is a tendency for the production of bits that have a correlated sequence by physical sources of randomness. As of now, there are many computer scientists that are dealing with research when it comes to the use of sources of randomness that are imperfect, as well as with the ability to stretch random bit strings that are short into strings that are much longer which, despite the fact that they are not random, it is not easy to distinguish them from strings that are truly random with the use of computational tests.

12. **Elimination of Randomization:** Obtaining a deterministic algorithm can be done by ensuring the construction of a randomized algorithm and thereafter eliminating the randomization.

7.2. THE BASIC PRINCIPLES UNDERLYING THE CONSTRUCTION OF RANDOMIZED ALGORITHMS

7.2.1. The Abundance of Witness Technique

There are two main reasons why the abundance of witnesses technique is very important between the techniques of the design of randomized algorithms:

- One needs to use deep results from mathematics so as to be able to apply this technique efficiently.

- When using this technique, the main question is if it is possible or not, for a certain provided problem, to be much more efficiently solved using the randomize mode of computation in comparison to the deterministic mode.

If a certain blem (P) and an in (x)*(x)* had a witness (y)*(y)*, that is information that is additional, it helps in solving the plem (P) for the input (x)*(x)* in a manner that is much more efficient than there was no witness (y)*(y)*. This is why it is important to understand why this technique is very useful for the design of randomized algorithms. There are some studies that have shown that the fingerprinting technique can be considered as an abundance of witnesses technique that has been simplified, in a situation where it is much easier to find witnesses (Hromkovic, 2006).

So as to be able to utilize the abundance of witnesses technique, it is important for one to have a set of candidates for witnesses for every input instance, whereby the witnesses are in abundance (around more than half). If the situation is as so, if one randomly chooses a certain element from these candidates for witnesses, then one is able to get a witness that has sufficient probability.

In accordance to the previously discussed question, of whether randomized algorithms for a provided algorithmic problem (P), can be much more efficient in comparison to the deterministic algorithms, we can see there it is highly related to the question of whether there is random distribution or deterministic order of the witnesses for the problem (P). In a situation where the witnesses are ordered, it is possible for one to make a discovery of this order for a specific input instance, which means that the witness can be found in a deterministic way, and in this situation, it is correct to say that for a given problem, deterministic algorithms can be efficient. When it comes to randomized algorithms, they can only be considered more efficient in a situation where there is random distribution of the witnesses in the set of potential witnesses, and only if the witnesses are of a high number (Bubley, 2012).

It is also possible to have a situation in which there is an order in the set of witnesses, however it is very hard to find this order. This can be found in the primality testing problem. The algorithm that is used for making determinations on whether an input number is prime is referred to as a primality test. This test among the different various fields of mathematics, it is mainly utilized for cryptography. In comparison to integer factorization, these tests are not used for providing prime factors, but are used to state whether the input number is prime or not. In comparison to factorization which is considered to be a problem that is computationally difficult, primality testing is considered to be much easier, due to the fact that the time in which it takes to run is polynomial in the input size. Some of these tests that are used help in proving that the given number is prime, and there are also others such as the Miller-Rabin that help in proving that the given number is composite. This means that the Miller-Rabin tests can then be referred to as a compositeness test.

When it comes to the characterization of witnesses, there are some things that need to be considered. For a witness to be considered a good witness that is able to prove a fact, such as "n is prime," it needs to have these specific conditions:

- A fact witness is required to provide the possibility of verifying the fact in an easy manner.

- A witness should also be able to make verification of whether the next witness to-be is actually a good witness.

- A good witness should also be able to make specifications of a group of candidates for witnesses while still providing an abundance of witnesses.

7.22. Foiling the Adversary

The process of foiling an adversary comprises most randomized algorithms. The goal ofis section is to presenting its appgorithm developmentrecisely for problems where:

- Every deterministic algorithm (policy) has certain worst-case instances by which the algorithm isn't able to effectively compute the accurate output.

- However, there exists a group of deterministic algorithms which can efficiently caion for ealculate the co outcome.

If (ii) holds, thus,then for any specified input case, one may choose an algorithm from this class at random, and then expect to derive the accurate result proficiently with reasonable possibility. Because of the perspective preseabove, this technique is also known as the process of avoiding worst-case inputs. We talk preferably about foiling an adversary since one can watch the whole process of algorithm development as a game pitting the algorithm developer and their adversary. The objective of the developer is designing an effective algorithm for a particular problem (Hromkovič, 2013).The work of an adversary is investigating any algorithm provided by the developer in order to discover cases at which algorithm behaves poorly. It'sIt is a standard game for examining algorithms oered bounds on the quantity offor computs needed to solve a particularthproblem. In conditions whereby the adversary is fruitful in building tough inputs for any particular deterministic algorithm, this developer can seek to tire the adversary by developing a random algorithm. Therefore, the work of the adversary gets harder than for the deterministic case. Even though the adversary may learn the developed randomized algorithm, they don't know which of these possible shall be picked at random. PlusAnd, finding an input which is tough for all or barely for many, moves is a highly complex task than discovering a hard problem case for the particular run.

The task of applying the technique of foiling an adversary is based on finding a proper sequence of deterministic algorithms (stratagems) so that, for any given problem case, most algorithms effectively compute the accurate result.

Basically, a randomized algorithm employs an amount of randomness within its logic. This algorithm normally uses evenly random bits being the auxiliary input for guiding its behavior, hoping for attaining decent performance for the "average situation" over all probable choices of chance bits. Officially, the algorithm's output shall be an unsystematic variable decidm bits;therefore, the eithor output or both (or altogether) are randomzed variables (Hromkovič, 2013).

One must differentiate between algorithms which use the randomized input such that they aoning a failure or not terminating. For some instances, probabilistic algorithms constitute the only practical way of solving the problem. Commonly, randomized algorithms are estimated using a pseudorandom digit generator instead of a real surce of randomized bits. However,; this implementation may diverge from the anticipated theoretical behavior.

7.2.3. Motivation

As a motivating illustration, consider the matter of finding ' within in an array consisting of n n elements. For Input: A range of $n \geq \geq 2$ components, where half are considered 'a's while the other half is made of 'b's. For Output: Detect 'a' in the sequence where two algorithm versions are presented, one for Las Vegas (LV) algorithm while the other for Monte Carlo algorithm. The amount of iterations is normally less than or equivalent to k. Assuming k is the constant underlining the d co{\display style \Theta$\Theta(1)$}\ Theta(1).

Random algorithms are mainly useful when facing malicious "adversary" programs, or attackers who intentionally try to feed a poor input into the althm, like in Prisoner's dilemma. It'sIt is for this particular reason that randomness is pervasive in cryptography. For cryptographic applications, the pseudo-random digits can't be used, as the adversary can easily predict them, thus making the algorithm successfully deterministic.

Hence, either a resource of truly randomized numbers or cryptographically safe pseudo-random digit generator is needed. Another part where randomness is integral is quantum computing. Here, the LV algorithm constantly outputs the accurate answer; however, its run time is more of a random variable. Also, Monte Carlo algorithm is assured to complete in the volume of time which can be bounded through a function that the input scope and its stricture k, but permits a small possibility of error (Hromkovič, 2013).

Note that LV algorithm may be transformed into the Monte Carlo algorithm (through Markov's inequality), through having it output the arbitrary, probably incorrect answer in case it fails to finish within a given time period. Alternatively, if an effective verification process exists to determine if an answer is accurate, it means that a Monte Carlo algorithm may be turned into LV algorithm via running the first algorithm continually until an accurate answer is found (Hromkovič, 2013).

7.2.4. Computational Complexity

Computational complexity concept models randomized algorithms in form of probabilistic Turing xamples include LV algorithmsare considered to be part ofe complexity classes.are also examined.

The most fundamental randomized complexity group is RP, whi of decision problems whereby there's anwith effective (polynomial interval) randomized process (or the prlistic Turing engine). This processwhich distinguishes NO-instances with complete certainty and identifies YES-instances with the probability of almost 1/2. The complementary group for RP is the co-RP.

Moreover, problem classes with (probably nonterminating) algorithms having polynomial time average instance run time with correct output are often believed to be at ZPP. The group of problems where both NO and YES-instances are permitted to be recognized with some fault is called BPP. The class serves as a randomized equal of P, that is, BPP represents the group of effectual randomized algorithms.

7.2.5. Randomized QuickSort

Quicksort is a popular, commonly used algorithm where randomness might be beneficial. Any determintic edition of this gorithm needs O $(n2n2)$ interval to sortn n figures for some distinct class of de-generate inputs (like a presorted array), with the particular class of inputs which produce this behavior described by the pivot choice protocol. Nevertheless, if the algorithm chooses pivot components uniformly at random, then it hs a certainly high chance of ending in $\Theta O(n \log n)$ duration irrespective of the input characteristics (Hromkovič, 2013).

Randomized Quick Sort largely is a Quick Sort extension where the pivot component is chosen randomly. The worst case interval complexity for tialg, according to scholars is $\Theta O(n2n2)O(n2n)$, since the worst case occurs when randomly selected pivot is chosen in organized or reverse sorted in order. Though in some texts, the worst-ase intlexity is scripted as $\Theta O(n\log n)$ O (nlog[70]n).

Quicksort normally has a copte ase interval requisite of $\Theta O(n2n2)O$ $(n2n)$. While the worst case happens when, at each stp, the partition process subdivides an nn-len sequence into arrays of length 11 or $n-1n-1$. The "u"choice of pivot components needs O (n) crve calls, which lead to the O $(n2n)$ $\Theta O(n2n2)$ worst-case (Hromkovič, 2013).

Selecting the pivot randomly, even randomly scuffling the array before sorting produces the outcome of interpreting the worst-case rather unlikely, especially for large arrays. In other terms, "the possibility that quicksort shall use a quadratic integer of comparison when organizing a massive array on the computer is lesser than the possibility that your computer shall be hit by lightning."

You can still abolish the worst-case pivot choice sequence by continually choosing the median component as the piBeause finding the median requn) $\Theta O()$ duration, this provides $\Theta(n\log n)\Theta(n\log n)$ as the worst-case performance. Nevertheless, since randomized quicksort is quite unlikely to step upon the worst-case, the determinant median-identification variation of quicksort is seldom applied (Bubley, 2012ally, uicksort may require only $\Theta(n\log n)\Theta(n\log n)$ duration in worst case for instances where one applies a linear-time algorithm for finding the median point as the pivot. Definitely, randomized quicksort provides a better applied performance index. For Quicksort implementation involving a random component, normally you get a deterministic algorithm, which is an algorithm that for a particular input shall always dliver the exact same phaes. To find the "worst case running time must assess all possible inputs and, plus choose the one which generates the worst runtime.

In some inputs, the algorithm may not always perform these same steps since some randomness is entailed. Rather thana run-time for every fixed input, tere's there is an "anticipated runtime," -where we check every poial value of the randomized decisions plusand their probability, while the "anticipated runtime" is counted as the weighted runtime average for every combination of randomized decisions, though still for a permanent input.

When calculating the "anticipated runtime" for every possible input, you will finally arrive at the "worst-case estimated runtime." The goal is finding one possible input iich the anticiparuntime is worst. PlusAnd, apparently it'sit is revealed that the worst situation foimated runtime" is only $\Theta(n\log n)$ O(n log n) (Bubley, 2012).

Remember that there are just two things for taking expectation/average over: first is the input variation and the pivots (a single unit per partitioning). For a few inputs and applications of Quicksort all the pivots are bad meaning (nn times a similar amount sometimes works) thus randomization won't help. In these cases, the anticipatede (which averages over pivot choices) plusand may be quadratic or the worst circumstance (a bad input).

Nevertheless, the "overall" anticipated time which (averages over these inputs andlections) would still be $\Theta(n\log n)\Theta(n\log n)$ for practical implementations. Various other implementations have realistic ting runtime in the code $\Theta(n\log n)\Theta(n\log n)$, namely the ones that pick the precise median as the pivot and dealing with duplicate content in a decent manner. The bottom line is, remember to review your source(s) for the implementation they apply and which amount they consider to be randomized and fixed in their data analysis (Bubley, 2012).

7.3. RANDOMIZED INCREASING CONSTRUCTIONS IN GEOMETRY

For computational geometry, the normal technique to create a structure such as a convex casing or Delaunay triangulation would be to permute randomly the input spots and then include them individually into the existing configuration. This randomization ensures that anticipated number of variations to the arrangement caused by the insertion is negligible; therefore, the expected runtime of the algorithm may be bounded from the top. The method is called randomized incremental development.

The Karger's algorithm is a classic case, where the input is basically a graph G (V, E) Output. An incision partitioning the indices into bits L and R, where the minimum amount of edges amid L and R are considered. Rememr thathe narrowing of two nodes, which areu u andv, v within a (multi-)graph produces a fresh node $u,$ wre the edges have a union incidentnu $u$rv, $v,$ apart from any edge(s) joiningu u tov. $v.$

Following contraction, the subsequent graph might have parallel edges, though has no self-loops. The average cut has magnitude 3 and is specified through the vertex colors. In every implementation of the external loop, the algorithm reiterates the inward loop until just 2 nodes endure, the equivalent cut is attainf one implentation is {\dityle O (n)} $O(n)$, wheren n dotes the amountnumber of vertices. Following times applications of the external loop, it'sit is possible to output the lowest cut among every outcome (Bubley, 2012).

Following execution, we obtain a cut size of 3. For Lemma 1: lowbe the mium cut size, then allowC c equals= $\{e1, e2., ,\ldots, ek\}$o beimum cut. When, ringterationi, $i,$ there's there is no edgee $e \in Cc$ designated for contraction, it means Ci= =C. $c.$ In Proof: If G isn't connected, then G may be subdivided into L and R sections without any definite edge between them. Therefore, the minimum cut in a disjointed graphis 0.

Assume that G is connted. Allow for V= =L∪R t the divider ofVv prompted by C: C= = $\{\{u, vu, v\} \in E: u \in L, v$ $v \in R\}$ (properly-ded becau G is connected Ta an edge {u, vu, v} ofC. $c.$ Originally,u, $u,$v v areong alay ste f\nee}$f \neq e$\{\displaystyle f\neq e\}, thenu u andv v don't get merged. Therefore, at the termination of the algorithm, there are two compound nodes which cover the whole graph, one containing the L vertices and the alternative comprising of R vertices.he e size of a minimum cut is 1, whileC c equals= $\{(A, B)\}$. If not selecting (A, B) for the contraction, then we can have the minimum cut (Hromkovič, 2013).

In Lemma 2, if G is a multi-graph having p vertices and where min cut has scope k, then G contains at least pk/2 edges. Pof: Since the min cut here is k each vertexv v should satisfy quotient $(v) \geq\geq k$. Thus, theunt of the quotient is roughly pk. Though it'sit is winown that the amount of vertex qutient equals= 2|E|.

7.4. ALGORITHM ANALYSIS

Te possibility that the algorithm ths is $1;-$ the likelihood that every attempt failfails. Following independence

$$i\}\neq C) =\prod _{\{i=1\}} ^{m}(1-\Pr$$

$(C\_)$. th lemma 1, the possibility at Ci equals= CC is the possibily that no C C edge is chosen during iterationi. i. Take the inner loop,hen allow Gj to represent theraph followingj$j$ edge contractions, wherebyj $j \in \{0, 1,...,n$ $n-3\}$. Gj contains $n-j$ vertices. The algorithm detects the min cut having probability ratio of $1-\dfrac{1}{n}$, with time $O(mn) = O(n^2 \log n)$.

7.5. DE-RANDOMIZATION

Randomness may be seen as a resource, such as space and time. to minimizin applying as minimal of it as conceivable). It'sIt is not presently known if every algorithm can be de-randomized wthout considerably aggregating their run .

For example, in ctional complexty, it'sit is unknown if P equals= BPP, that is., we don't know if we can have an arbitrary randomized algorithm which moves in polynnomial durthout applying any randomness. There are diverse different techniques that can be applied to de-randomize specific randomized algorithms. The means of conditional possibilities, including its generalization, and pessimistic estimators also form a big part of this process (Hromkoič, 2013).

7.6. EXAMPLE WHERE RANDOMNESS HELPS

When a computti is limited to Turing machines, it i's presently an open question if the capacity tmake random selections permits somelved in polynomial interval wtis capacyHenc, this translates to tnof ifertheless, in some contexts, there are particularcan be examples of problems in which randomization produces strict improvements.Depending on the original motivating example and: assuming an exponentially extensive string of $2k$ typescripts, half (a's) and half (b's), a random access engine needs 2k−1 lookups for thest-case to discover the catalog of a; whether it'sit is allowed to make random selections, it may solve this issue in an anticipated polynomial amount of lookups. The usual way of performing a numerical calculation in embedded structures or cyber-physical units is providing a result which approximates the accurate one with great possibility (or Perhaps Approximately Correct Calculation (PACC)). The hard part related to the assessment of the divergence loss between the estimated and the accurate computation may be effectively addressed through reverting to randomization.

For communication complexity, the equivalence of dual stris may be confirmed to some reliability through logn n parts of contact with randomiztocol. Whichever deterministic protocol needs \Theta$\Theta(n)$ components when defending against a tough opponent.

The capacity of a convex form may moreover be projected by a randomized system to arbitrary in polynomial time. Researchers showed that there's there is no deterministic algorithm which can perform the same. This is accurate unconditionally, that is, without depending on any complexity-theory assumptions, supposing the convex body may be queried just as a black case.

A complexity-theory example of the place where randomness looks to assist is in the IP class. An IP comprises of all languages which are acceptable (having high probability) with a polynomially extensive interaction between the all-powerful prover, together with a verifierwhich implements the BPP alghm. Abbreviated as IP = = PSPACE.

Nevertheless, if it'sit is necessarythat the verifier is to be deterministic, it means IP = = NP. For a chemical interction netork (the finite group of ons such as A+ + B → 2C+ + D working on a finite amountnumber of particles), the capacity to ever achieve a particular target state from the original state is decidable, whereas even approximating the possibility of ever getting to a particular target state is considered undecidable.

CHAPTER

8

Pattern Matching and Text Compression Algorithms

CONTENTS

8.1. INTRODUCTION

Pattern matching can be described as the activity of finding a particular pattern within raw data. This pattern is typically a pool of strings defined in formal style. Applications need two types of solutions based on which string is being used, the pattern, and text provided. Some solutions reliant on the usage of automata and combinatorial elements of strings are typically implemented for pre-processing the pattern (Figure 8.1).

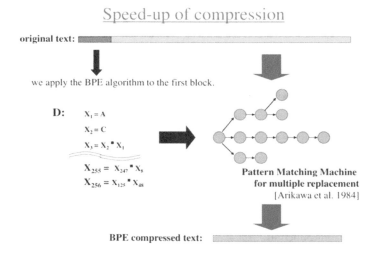

Figure 8.1: Text compression condenses otherwise large files into manageable bits.

Source: https://www.slideserve.com/adolfo/speeding-up-pattern-matching-by-text-compression (accessed on 6 April 2020).

The concept of indices covered by virtual trees or automata can be applied in the second form of solutions. The goal of data condensing is providing data representation in a condensed form so as to save storage space and transmission ere's There is no loss of data, the compression procedures are reversible.

Generally, pattern-matching, and text-condensing algorithms are some of the essential aspects of broader text processing domain. This applies to text manipulation (word editing), storage of textual information (text compres), plusand data retrieval structures (whole text search). These are fundamental modules used in applications of practical software existing under many operating systems. Furthermore, they highlight programming methods which act as paradigms in different aspects of computer science (software designing and system).

Ultimately, they also play a significant role in theoretic computer science by offering challenging problems. Even though data are documented in different ways, text still remains to be the key way of exchange data. This is especially obvious for literature and linguistics where information is comprised of large corpora and vocabularies, though applies also to computer science whereby a large volume of data is recorded in linear files.

This is also the situation, for example, in molecular biology since biological molecules may often be estimated as structures of amino acids or nucleotides. Additionally, the amount of accessible data in these aspects seems to double after every 18 months. Probably, this is the goal behind algorithms being efficient even when the rate and storage volume of computers surge continuously (Wayner, 2000).

There are two types of textual patterns available which are: approximating and single strings. In many applications, texts should to be organized before being reviewed. When no additional information is identified regarding the syntactic sture, it'sit is feasible and indeed very efficient at building a data structure which supports searches.

Out of different data structures that are equal for representing indexes, t searchux tree is among the most common. The assessment of strings is inherent in the estimated pattern-search prot. As it'sit is sometimes needed to compare only two ngs, it'sit is possible to present the basic technique based on longest shared subsequences. This publication features examples of classical text condensing algorithms. Some variations of these algorithms may be implemented in applied compression software, where they are also quite common (Wayner, 2000).

The publication also provides a raft of methods for pattern correspondence in condensed text and images. Typically, compressed data must be expanded before it is processed, though if the condensing has been performedhtly, it'sit is commonly possible to review the data without needing to decompress it, or even partially decompress it. This problem may be subdivided into lossless or lossy compression tiques, plusand for each case the pattern matching technique may be closely related. A lot of work has been stated in the publication concerning these cases, covering algorithms which are ideal for pattern-matching for different compressiothods, plusand compression methods developed particularly for pattern matching.

8.2. PROCESSING TEXTS EFFICIENTLY

There are a few regular algorithms which can be applied to process texts efficiently. This applies for cases of text manipulation (word editing), storage of text information (text cossion), plusand to data retrieval structures. The algorithms presented are fascinating in different aspects. First, they're basic modules used in the applications of practical apps. Secondly, they introduce programming techniques that act as models in other aspects of computer science (structures and software design).Thirdly, they play a central role in theoretic computer science by presenting challenging problems. Even though data is memorized in different ways, the text remains similar as the primary form of exchangingormation. It'sIt is especially evident in linguistics and literature, whereby data consists of massive corpus and dictionaries (Wmputer scienceThis is also applicable to them wherewhereby a large quantity of data is kept in biology sinceAs an example, consider biological molecules which may typically be estimated as structures of amino acids or nucleotides. Additionally, the amount of available data available in these fields seems to double after every few ms.

This isIt's the reason behind algorithms being efficient even when the rate of computers rises regularly. Generally, pattern matching refers to the activity of locating a particular pattern within raw data. The sequence is typically a gathering of strings defined in a formal language. There are two forms of textual patterns available, which are single and approximated strings. There are various algorithms for corresponding patterns in photos that are additions of string-sequencing algorithms (Wayner, 2000).

For different applications, texts must be designed before searched. In cases where no further data is identified on their syntactic nization, it'sit is possible and really extremely efficient to develop a data structure which supports searches. Out of the many existing data structures representative of indexes, the suffix tree is part of its construction.

The contrast of strings is contained in the estimated pattern-searching problem. Coering that it'sit is sometimes needed simply to compare a pair of strings (documents, or molecusequences) it'sit is possible to introduce the general method depending on some of the extensive subsequences. Ultimately, the report comprises of a pair of classical text condensation algorithms. Variations of these algorithms may be applied in realistic compression software, whereby they are typically combined alongside other elementary techniques. The proficiency of algorithms is assessed based on r run time, plusand sometimes also through the volume of memory space that they need at run-time (Wayner, 2000).

8.2.1. Text Processing in Machine Learning

Text Processing is among the most significant aspects of ML systems. A few examples of these applications include: (i) Language Translation: Meaning translation of the sentence from a particular language to another; (ii) Sennt Analysis: It'sIt is simply to decide, from the text corpus, if the sentiment towards whichever topic or item etc. is constructive, negative, or impartial; and (iii) Spam Filtering: Detecting unwanted and unsolicited messaging.

The software addresses a large amount of text for performing classification or even translation tasks, including lots of backend work. Converting text into something that an algorithm may easily digest is a complex process. But, generally, it comprises topics like data pre-processing, tokenization, stemming, and lemmatization among other measures. Additionally, stemming, and lemmatization allows for reduction of words such as 'studies' or 'studying,' in order to achieve a shared base structure or root term 'study.'

The python code can be used to perform various text pre-processing procedures. For instance, NLTK or The Natural Linguistic ToolKit comprises one of the most-renowned and commonly utilized NLP libraries, practical in all kis of chores fromt t tokenization, parsing, stemming, and tagging among others (Sayood, 2006).

8.2.2. Feature Extraction

Feature eaction refers toFor text processing, where words represent distinct, categoriunctions. The goal question is how to encode this daeady for use by the algorithms can use. Generally, mapping from textual information to tangible valued vectors is known as featutically symbolize, text chun is knon as the bBag-of-wWorf-wordsBag-of-Words, users employ a list of unique texting words within the text corpus known as vocabulary. Next, every sentence is presented in context or document in form of a vector whereby every word is represented as 1 meaning present, and 0 meaning lacking from the vocabulary. A different representation may also count the amount of times every word shows in a document (Sayood, 2006).

Among the most common techniques is employing the Term Frequency-Reverse Document Frequency or (TF-IDF) method. Term Frequency or (TF), refers to the aunt of times thatt t shows up in a file, or ratio of terms foun document. There's There is also Inverse Document Frequency or (IDF), symbolized $\log (N/n)$, here,efers to the amountmber of files andn n means the quantity of docunts that a phraset t has shown in.

Generally, the IDF from rare words is high, while the IDF available in a frequent word most likely is low. Therefore, having the capacity of highlighting terms which are unique. The TF-IDF rate of a term can be symbolized as TF * IDF also.

This protocol has special features, for instance, the TF-IDF technique heavily reprimands the term 'beautiful,' but assigns more weight tods like 'day.' It'sIt is because of the IDF portion, which provides greater weightage to words which are distinct.

For instance, 'day' is a significant word from the pretext of the whole corpus. The Python scikit-learn catalog provides sufficient tools for text information mining and offers functions for calculating the TF/IDF of text vocabulary taking into consideration a text corpus (Sayood, 2006).

Among the main drawbacks of using the BOW system is that it eliminates word order, therefore ignoring the framework and consequently the meaning of words present in a document. As for the natural language processing procedure or (NLP), preserving the word context is of great importance. In order to resolve solve this matter, another approach can be applied known as Word Embedding.

Word embedding refers to a text representation procedure, where words which have similar meaning possess a unique representation. Generally, it showcases words in a synchronized system where connected words, depending on a variety of relationships, may be grouped together (Sayood, 2006).

8.2.3 Word2Vec

Word2Vvec considers as its contribution a massipus of text and, plus develops a vector space frctor across the space. Typically, word vectors are locatedin the vector system, so that words which share mutual contexts within the corpus are found in near proximity to each other in the system (Akhgar, 2009).

Furthermore, Word2Vec is quite popular at ualculation of analogysolving similarity qucoming in the form of "if a islent to b thenwhilec c is equivalent to d". By using such a basic vector offset technique based osine distancing, it'sit is much easier to process the algorithm.

Similarly, this type of vector composition allows users to answer the basic questioing (minus) an (plusplus) Woman $= = ?$" which arrives at the outcome "Queen"! These are truly remarkable if you think that the knowledge basically comes from observing various words in context, with no other data availed about their semantics (Akhgar, 2009).

8.2.4. Glove

Global Vectors (GloVe) are commonly used fo   lso known as GloVe, Tthis algorithm is basll an epan Wword2Vvec technique for competently learning word vectors. The GloVe system creates an open word-context or terminology co-occurrence matrix through statistics across the entire text corpus. Ultimately, the outcome is a learning system that could result in a characteristically improved word embedding (Wayner, 2000).

Allow P (k|w) to be the possibility that the term k shows in the framework of word w. Take, for instance, a word that's associated to ice, though not to steam, like solid. Moreover, the P (solid | ice) shall be considerably high, while P (solid | steam) would be comparatively low.

Therefore, the rate of P (solid | ice) and P(solid | steam) shall be massive. By taking a word like gas which is linked to steam though not to ice, though the rate of P (gas | ice) or P (gas | steam) shall rather be negligible. As for terminologies similar to icesteam, like water it'sit is expected that the ratio must be near to one.

Moreover, word embeddings have been designed encode every word into a unique vector which captures some kind of association and resemblance between words inside the text corpus. It means even the variants of words such as case, spelling, and punctuation, among others shall be spontaneously learned. Consequently, this means that to some extent the basic text cleaning procedures highlighted above may not actually be necessary (Wayner, 2000).

8.3. CHOOSING ML ALGORITHMS

Some of the different approaches of building ML systems for different text-based applications are based on what the lus the data accessible. Variou classicl thods,, such as, 'NaiveNaïve Bayes' and 'Support Vector Machines' used for spam filtering, have further been widely adopted (Figure 8.2).

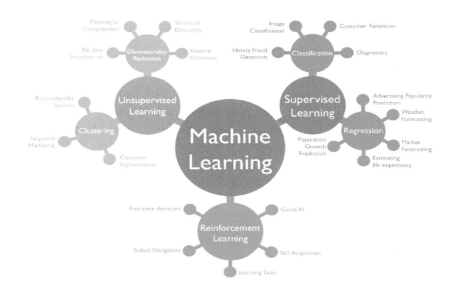

Figure 8.2: Machine learning uses complex algorithms to do clustering, classification, and *einforcement learning.*

Source: https://towardsdatascience.com/machine-learning-algorithms-in-laymans-termspart-1-d0368d769a7b?gi==f970a0d70cf4 (accessed on 6 April 2020).

Deep learning (DL) methodologies are providing much advanced resultsfor NLP issues, such as, sentiment inquiry anage translation. BesidesHowever, Dlatively ratherslow to train, plus it'sand it assification issues the ML techniques equally provide similar results with faster training time (Wayner, 2000).

8.3.1. Pre-Processing

A dataset is programmed in form of a test set, having a training set consisting of roy 25000 files each. It'sIt is important to first go through the files and translate them int a standard python data-frame, which is essential for additional processing and visualization. Besides, the testing and training sets have further been subdividedinto a total of 12500 '++VE' and '–VE' reviews each. Every file and label has –VE review represented as '0,' whereas the positive review is '1'

In order to attain the frequency rate of certaords within a text, it'sit is important to use the nltk.FreqDist() feature, listing the main words applied in the text, offering a rough notion of the key topic present in the text inforon, as presented in the this code: import *nltk*. Ultimately, this provides the top 50 phrn in the English dialect (Sayood, 2006).

Check closely and you will find various redundant punctuation and tags. Through excluding single and double letter words, it means the stop words such as the, this or that assumes the greatest spot in the word rate distribution plot. It appears like a cleaned sentence corpus now and texts like went, movie, and saw etc. assuming the best slots like expected.

Yet another useful visualization tool which is the word cloud package, allows for development of word clouds through putting words on the canvas randomly, through sizes which are proportionate to their frequency within the text: from word-cloud import word-cloud.

8.3.2. sifier

Following cleanupng the data, it's time towe develop the classifier to detect sentiment of every record review. Borrowing from the IMDb system, division test, and preparation sets of 25,000 per unit: The scikit-learn tool offeome cool appliances, plusand the text corpus can be subdivided iuntio vectors., besides Iit i's possible to limit the maximum functions to 10,000.

In total, there are multiple algorithms to pick frou can use the basic Naivve Bayes Classifier, plusand fine-tune the model straight on the training system (Sayood, 2006).

8.4. STRING-MATCHING ALGORITHMS

In computer studies, string-matching algorithms, also known as string-search algorithms, are an essential component of string algorithms which tries to detect a place whereby one or multiple strings (commonly called patterns) can be found within a bigger string or text. One common example of string matching is when a pattern and searched text become arrays of components found in an alphabet or (finite group) Σ.

The symbol Σ might be a human dialect alphabet, for ince, the texts A to Z plusand other similar applications may employ a bnary alphabet such as ($\Sigma = = \{0,1\}$), or te DNA phabet known as ($\Sigma= = \{A,C, C, G, T\}$) for bio-informatics. Practically, the technique of practical string-search algorithm might be affected through the string encoding method (Sayood, 2006).

Particularly, if the variable-width programming is in use, it means that the system might be slower to detect the N-th character, possibly needing me that's proportionate toN. *n*. It might considerably slow certain search algorithms. Among the many feasible solutions is searching for the code sequence units rather, though doing so might produce wrong matches unless the programming is particularly developed to avoid it.

8.4.1. Types of Searching

Among the most fundamental examples of string, searching comprises of one (typically very long) string, oftent known as the haystack, plusand one (frequently very short) string, occasionally known as the needle. One objective is to detect one or multiple incidences of a needle the haystackse in pointFor example, it'sit is possible to 'search for' a text within a sentence.

One may search for the original occurrence of "to," that is the 4th word; or just about evert occurrence, whereby there are 3, or the final part, referring to the 5th word coming from the last section. More commonly, nevertheless, different constraints are included. For instance, one may want to correspond the "needle" simply where it comprises of one (or multiple) full words—possibly described as not getting other letters directly adjacent on whichever side (Sayood, 2006).

For that case, the search for terms like "low" or "hew" can fail for the illustration sentence mentioned above, while those literal strings may not even occur. Yet another common example features "normalization." In many purposes, the search for a term like "to be" must even in areas where there's there is another topic existing between the terms "be" and "to."

Moreover, other "whitespace" characters like tabs, non-breaking portions and line-breaks are commonly used in organized texts, tags, and even arbitrarily big but "parenthetical" items like footnotes, list-numbers, and other markers, implanted images, and much more. Symbol systems, on the contrary, comprise of characters which are identical (but for some few purposes). For Latin-based alphabets, typically they differentiate lower-case texts from upper case, however, for other reasons string search may be required to disregard the distinction.

A lot of languages comprise of ligatures, whereby a single composite character may be characterized as equal to two or several other characters. A lot of writing systems comprise of diacritical marks like vowel points or accents, which might vary in terms of usage, or be of divergent significance in matching.

Moreover, DNA sequences may consist of non-coding components which can be ignored for certain reasons, or polymorphisms leading to no variation in the programmed proteins, that may not pass the actual difference for certain other reasons. There are languages with rules whereby a unique character or character form should be applied at the start, midpoint, or conclusion of words (Akhgar, 2009).

Ultimately, for strings representing natural language, elements of the dialect itself become included. For instance, one may want to find multiple "word" occurrences in spite of it carrying alternative spellings, prefixes, and suffixes.

Yet another more complicated form of search is typical expression searching, whereby the user develops a sequence of characters that are unique to the text or some symbols. Besides, certain matches to the pattern must accomplish the search.

For instance,n order to capture both theU. u. S. English term "color" or the UK equivalent "color," rather than looking for multiple different literal strings, a person may employ a typical expression like: color whereby the "?" typically makes the previous character ("u") elective.

- **Naïve String Search:** A basic method of seeing where a particular string arises inside another is checking every place that it might be, vidually, to determine if it'sit is existing. Therefore, firstl is to check whether there's there is a replica of the needle present in the haystack's first character; ot check to see whether there's there is a replica of the needle beginning from the haystack's second character.

Otherwise, check from the third character. For a typical case, there's there is need to check one or multiple characters for every wrong posi in order to determine if it'sit is an erroneous position, such that in the typical case, ths will take the form oO ($n ++ m$) procedures, wheren n the haystack length whereasm m refers to the needle length; though in some scenarios, looking for one string such as "aaaab" within a string such as "aaaaaaaaab," ultimatly this reuires O(nm Finite- condition- automaton- oriented searching.

- **DFA Searching Mommy. svg:** For this technique, the goal is to Prevent backtracking by developing a determinant finite automaton (DFA), which identifies stored search string. They are costly to build—however they're commonly formed through a powerset construction—despite being rather fast to use. For instance, DFA has been shown to distinguish the term "MOMMY."

The methodology is typically generalized in practice for purposes of searching for arbitrary standard expressions. Besides, StubsKnuth-Morris-Pratt calculates a DFA which identifies additions with the string towards searching for a particular suffix. The Boyer-Moore protocol begins searching from one side of the needle, such that it can typically jump past an entire needle-length for every step (Akhgar, 2009).

Alternatively, Baeza-Yates chks on whether other precedingj j characters constitute a prefix that's similar to the search sequence, and is thus adjustable to fuzzy string seas. As for bitap algorithm, it'sit is a Baeza-Yates' application technique that carries rather the same format. Quicker search algorithms pre-process the text. Following the creation of a sub-string index, for instance, the suffix tree or array, pattern sequences can be determined much faster.

For instance, a sufplay-style \Theta(n)} od, and every {\displaystyle z} z happenings of a ed in the {\display-style O(m)}$O(m)$ period under the pretext that the alphabet contains a constant size while all inner nodes within the suffix tree determine wbranches are beneath them. PlusAnd, the latter may be realized by operating a DFS algorithm coming from the suffix tree's root (Akhgar, 2009).

- **Knuth-Morris-Pratt Algorithm:** It covers t search for pattern occurrencex x within a primary text string by using the basic observation: following any mismatch, a word by itself shall allow people to decide where to start the subsequent match in order to surpass the re-examination of formerly matched characters. In the pre-processing stage, time complexity and $O(m)$ space are of utmost importance, wheras in searching phase the $O(n ++ m)$ period complexity is the one that's considered (independently from the alphabetic size).

Moreover, the single greatest amount of comparisons within a typical text chacter can be dfine as: $\leq \log \eta m$ m whereby $\eta == 1 + + \sqrt{52}$ constitutes the golden ratio. This algorithm was developed in 1977 as a result ofearch from Pratt and Knuth, plusand autonomously by Morris, though the three officially published their findings together later on (Zelkowitz, 2005).

8.5. TWO-DIMENSIONAL PATTERN MATCHING AL-GORITHMS

A 2D pattern matcng algorithm attempts detectm m occurrences throughm m pattern sequence PAT (containingymbol presented in a specificn n byn *n* script array TEXT, referring to mdn. Every algorithm can be effortlessly protracted to the example of rectangular non-square patterns or texts. Meanwhile, a position within the text array means a set of integers found within a given scope [1,…, n] (Figure 8.3).

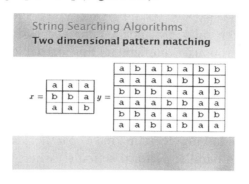

Figure 8.3: 2D pattern matching is a simple algorithm that can be represented in square boxes.

Source: https://slideplayer.com/slide/4697098/ (accessed on 6 April 2020).

With the occurrence of a 2D pattern PAT within a TEXT, it means that the left higher cornepoition will be represented a x (i, , wereby 1~ I andj j <<n n –m m ++ 1 represent the pattern alignment present in the text nc TE

It thatheT [i+ + kI ki minus – 1,j j plus+ $k2$–l] is equal to PAT [k, $k2$] where ery integer including 1~k, dm m capd. By denotingN n = = n2n2, it'sit is possible to determine the overall scope of the matter (Zelkowitz, 2005).

Through investigating the equivalent complexity of a 'D'-matching issues. The computation model can be defined as CRCW PRAM, meaning parallel random access mechanism (PRAM), a parallel variant of the random open machine, can be applied as a standardized model for representing parallel algorithms.

The program comprises of a series of processors that function synchronously while communicating via a shared random access memory (RAM). Every processor carries a random access mechanism with special functions. The novel 2D matching algorithm is showcased which is more openly designed for 2D objects. It doesn't employ the multitext or multi-pattern approach like in KLP algorithms.

There are various methods available for building parallel photo identification algorithms, reducing images into smaller factors, and condensing images through a parallel lessening of a huge number of these independent elements into smaller items. The significance of fiveighlighted. A fresh useful factors is eventually presented: thin factors.

These processors generally are indexed thr successive natural integers, plusand they synchronously implement this particular central program. Nevertheless, the activity of a particular processor relies equally on its integer (which is recognizable through the processor). With just a single step, this processor is capable of accessing a memory position. Besides, parallel algorithms are offered in a similar manner like [S]. The parallelism can be expressed through following a certain kind of parallel statement: such as, for every 'I' in X and in parallel perform action (i) where the implementation of this statement comprises of various processes. Such as ~ transmitting a processor to every aspect of X._ and implementing in parallel by allotted processors the techniques mentioned by action(i) (Zelkowitz, 2005).

Typically t potion "i in X" resembles "l< <i $i < < n$" where X is an intermission of integers. In this example, users are typically faated in the parallel interlude T(n)$T(n)$ and in the amount of processors P(n) needed for executing parallel algorithms.

The overall work performed by parallelorithms cos the object T(n)$T(n)$ P(n). There's There is an overall fact which pins the amount of processors to general work and the parallel time. Allow A to be the parallel algorhm having a computation period oft. t. Considering that A for instancincludes an overall amount of allm m computational operations, it means then that A can be executed using pcessors present in the O (m/p (plus+) t) schedule.

Moreover, Brent's lemma covers an implementation issue pertainingthe consignment of processors. PlusAnd, there are no complications for submissions of the theory within the algorithms provided. Processors relate to positions that certain texts have. Effective parallel algorithms refer to those which function through the polylogarithmic (polynomial of a log's iize) period with a polynomial amountnumber of processors (Zelkowitz, 2005).

The 2D pattern matching through optimal equivalent algorithms represent a class of problems which are sble through algorithms like NC, plusand this is associated with NC-algorithms. This algorithm can only be optimal when it works in a linear format. The goal is to develop an optimal NC-algorithm that's 2D and a solid pattern matching problem. There are multiple quick parallel algorithms applicable for 2D-pattern matching which have been presented autonomously in the [lo], and [S].

The above systems are known as KLP and dictionary algorithms. Besides, the first program is optimal while the second is optimum within a factor log (m). The KLP algorithm utilizes log (n) processors much less, however the dictionary algorithm has a much simpler format and is associated to a sequence of algorithms for different other problems having similar complexity.

Additionally, the dictionary approach of matching problems has been identified as an old notion. It fundamentally shows subliminally in some situations. In cases of fixed-dimension alphabets n/log (n) processors that are matching with the algorithm, the proof was basically omitted. The critical aspect of KLP algorithm is usually the suffix-prefix corresponding subprocess. For some of the contemporary algorithms, a rather direct solution may be applied which makes the sub-process redundant.

An original algorithm for 2D-structural matching is presented, most probably developed for two-dimensional items. This program nevertheless doesn't use the multi-text or multi-pattern technique like the KLP algorithm or other algorithms do. There are 4 kinds of factors (typical pieces) which are commonly used, and these are: basic, regular-basic, smalegular-small elements. Besides, there's there is another 5th useful form of 2D factors known as thin factors (Zelkowitz, 2005).

The applicability of this is layed in 2D-pattern corspondee. It'sIt is assumed that bothm m andn n constitute powers of both. It nevertheless doesn't affect the generalization of the matter, considering that every patan be de-composed into one regular amountnumber of patterns where the edges are factors of two.

For the case of 1-D patterns, in case thetern-size isn't a factor of two then it'sit is possible to search a pair of sub-patterns which comprise of the prefix as well as suffix of a particular configuration with size being thggest possible factor of two. In 2D, it't is impossible to disintegrate the (m)x x (m) square into a total of 4 sub-squares (not actually disjoint) whose sidonsist of factors of two. Therefore, it'sit is assumed henceforth that the dimensions of sides of every considered pattern comprises of factors of two.

8.5.1. Types of Factors

Some of gorithm , plus the dictionary algorithm, are directly from dictionary constructions which allow for check-in at constant periods whether some elements of text and pattern are equal or otherwise. There are factors of 1-dimensional strings and substrings comprising of consecutive positions (Wayner, 2000).

For the 2D case, factors are categorized as rectangular components of 2-dimensional images, in which factors where the length consists of an elemactors. 1D The one dimensional fundamental aspect of the pattern generally is known as the regular basic factor, in case it begins in the configuration at (i) position.

Analogously, for the case of 2D, it can be saidhat e two-dimensional factor of figures s xs s is regular in case it begins (its leftmost corner). At the position so that both horizontal and vertic vertces are respective inthe order,i. i. s+ + 1 as ll as j.s s + + 1 for a few integers ofi, i, j.

The modified algorithm moreover is optimal with regards to the task spent on patterns. This is fundamentally the same algorithm as the standard version. But the main difference is that for the pattern only systematic basic factors are recognized. Therefore, the overall work expended on patterns can be said te to their overall size (being optimal), whereas for the text every fundamental factor is considered.

The algorithm can identify every basic factor available in the text. Consequently, there are names available for every pattern and text factors which are aspiants for matching these patterns. The i's a manifestation of patterns at site x in case the factor beginning at pointx x and of similar format as the pattern contains the same symbol as the pattern. This modified algorithm is known as partly optimum sequencing (Wayner, 2000).

The optimality of an algorithm is in regard to the overall size of patterns. Basically, the lemma is fundamentally provedn representations. Assume that there aret t patterns, every one of scope M. It means, the partially optimal matching algorithm detects every pattern in a sgle-dimensional or 2D image of magnitudeN n in period O (M) ving an overall task O(N. log(M) plusandt. t.

Proof is also essential. Basically, the algorithm identifies every basic factor in the transcript and all standard basic dynamics within the pattern for the same case point. The overall work of the algorithm is proportionate to the amount of considered aspects. The vital point is that for the pattern only standard factors must be processed. On average, there are just O (M) regular standard factors in the sequence. Thus, the work done on one pattern is defined as O (M). Likewise, fort patterns of dimension M would be O (t M).

It completes the etire proof which is represented by 0Let k= = log (m). The matt al assumes w.1.o.g. is standard wheren, n,m m are separable by k. Some factors of dimension k of the sequence are known as sml factors These factors begin apointsi. $i.$ or $k++1$, which is integeri, $i,$ and is known as systematic small factor.

2D pattern matchinby optimum parallel algorithms 40lowsx x to be a sequence of length it plusand alws for small(x, i) as te minor factor ofx x beginning at point i< < m. Consider, for technical purposes, that the transcript has k–1 unue final markers at the finish. For everyi i defineXi (is equal to) name (smull(x, i)), in which the name (f) reflects the identy of the orall factor similar tof f (in there's there is no such feature then it'sit is some unique symbol).

These names must be consistent: in case. SWIU~/X, i) is equal to small(x, j) it means xi = = xj, besides the labels are integers ranging from the points [l. M]. The equivalence of dual names may be paterned with regular work. The structure (x= = x1 x2 x3 xq.g) is known here as the vocabulary of smullfactors. One basic way of computing this dictionary is using a parallel edition of the Kap-Miller Rosenberg algorithm. It providesn n log(log(n)) the total work, which is adjacent to optimal.

Additionally, the optimality is attained using the (modified) multi-pattern equivalent automata.

The vocabularof small factors may be calculated in logn n time using linear work. Besides, the f provided scholars iather complex. It'sIt is compatible withthe albets of random size. Nevertheless, if antht features a constant scope, then it is possible and , plus the inction of steady-small factorsn't beisn't (Wayner, 2000).

InFor this case,, it means the lemma follows a rather basic presentation of the "4 Russian" trick of programming tiny sections by numbers for string factors. Every small factor receives regular names (including non-regular ones) which categorize all non-equal minor factors, whereas in the KLP-algorithm non-regular m factors receive a standard single name plusand are indiscernible.

Consider for simplicity purposes that the alphabetic sysem is binary, then allow for the equation s= = log (m)/4. Possibly there are only a few "m" double sts of size 2.s. On each of these systems, it'sit is possible to pre-compute the names of different small elements of length s; the names may be integers consistent to binary system of factors.

The averagmount of processors is represented as is $n$isn/log(m), meaning there are roughly m112 processors for every small section of logarithmic scope. Subsequently, users take independently and equallsegment every one of the second size, wheres s begins at a point divisible by s. A processor may encode the (in binary representationbinaryrepresentation) through log (m) time.

For the fifth kind of factors known as thin factors, this is a natural overview of basic factors representing th2D case. The thin factors are represented asm m by log (m) text sub-arrays or pattern structures. These arise when users cut the 2D sequence through m/log (m) slice-lines, or the 408 M (Wayner, 2000).

The establishment of the dictionary structure for these factors is mentioned in the segment on two-dimensional pattern matching. This is begun with the segment on single dimension string-matching. Additionally, the algorithm for double dimensions is theoretically a natural extension of single-dimensional case algorithm.

- **1-D String Matching:** The fundamental aspects of 1- and 2-dimensional pattern-matching processes presented in ID string matching appear similar. There aro auxiliary functions required: which are sfshift and compression (cm, in brie. Allowx x to be the sequence osize m, andy y becomeh transcrof sizen, $n,$ then permifor $k =$) log m. It'sIt is assumed here thatn n andm m are derivatives of k. The configuration and text are provided as vectors of specific symbols where the original point is 1.

For a sequencez z whose overall ls a co h, it s repreented asdenoe:$cm(z)$ is equal=, $k+ + lZZk+ + 1.Z(k-l)k+ + 1$, whereby $h ==$j jz z I/k. Remember that zj works the name of a minimum element (of length k) beginning from j. Moreover, the string $cm(z)$ comprises of the same data as z, but is briefer through a logarithmic factor.

Generally, every letter captured in the fresh string a logarithmic-scale block of z. instinctively Instinctively speaking $cm(z)$ consists of a configuration of names of sequential small factorsġ-i, comprising of a particular string.

The solidity ratio refers to the limitation of inormation; where Ishift(x, r)II and IpatternxlXm--kw are the main programs. Forration shift, in order to detect the match, i'sit isropriate to detect the sub phrases $h\$(x, r)$ plusand he st and final full small elemes. x, and xr, _, k, which form part of patternx x or (the trishadowed factors).

Moreover, the identity of *sh$(x, r)* typically is done through searching for the compressed form in an efficient manner because of the fact it begins at a systematic position. 2D pattern matching through optimal parallel algorithms for this case a minor factor (sequence of length log(*m*) would be replaced by a single symbol. Largely, the compression rate is log(*m*) (Waer, 2000).

Single-dimensional items of scope logm   *m* are limited to 0-dimensional. This idea may be generalized by extendg the sequence for dual dimensions. The positionj *j* found in the text my be referred to as regular status iff *j* (mod) $k == 1$. This entire idea is for limiting the search to beginng points '*j*' which are regular.

Conr that ifj *j* covers aandposition then it'sit is basically the (*j*div/*k* plus+ 1)th structured position (by enumerating standard positions by consecutive digits). The proof of different obvious oervations is also presented. Theccurrence ofx *x* begins at pointi *i* in the copyy *y* in case certions are met first.

8.6. SUFFIX TREES

It's amongSuffix trees are one of the most complex data structures available today. The journey of suffix trees begins in 1970, when a researcher called Knuth highted that the topic "Considering strings S1 plusand S2, detect the largest standard substring" is tougher tan simplading in a pair of strings which are (>>O(plus+ |S2|)). To symbolize all sublines of S, it'sit is ideal to create a keyword tree covering all S suffixes, since all suffixes are prefixes of a suffix at some point. An example of this application is in biology. Checking for a nucleotide series in the human gene is synonymous to finding the amount of times sub-string shows in a 3 to 109-character series, 2009).

For purposes of reading the tree, there's there is a path stretching from the root up to the leaf which is often suffix. A new branch moreover can be formed if it'sit is topologicallptivating. It causes a lessening of the nodes, plusand ultimately it ends up with the |S| leaves including lower than (S) non-leaves, based on some theories. Every node can act as a subng, and not simply a character.

To save space, it'sit is needed to represent every node through a set (index, len) within the string, rather than the whole substring. O (|S|) space/O (1) per component. The single failure links reserved are between internal nodes but not the actual leaves. For keword trees, t failure link is represented as $(n)= = m$, wherebym m acts as the node equivalent to the biest prefix within theSM, a suffix of the stringn. n. For suffix trees,m m works as the no matching with the original appropriate suffix ofn. n.

Failure links typically point towards branching internal nodes since w must be an outward suffix. Inconsistencies in suffix trees usually are a bit complex, but there are certain steps that can be followed to ensure the process is a success. For instance, follow the parent's link then rematch to position at the center of the Failures, equaling to the node's substring. Alternatively, trail the node's link so that STFSM achieves a scan duration of O ($|A\|T|$) whethe tree has finally been built. In this example,T t constitutes the whole text (Akhgar, 2009).

8.7. ALIGNMENT

Sequence alignment algorithms optimally align a pair of short sequences using advanced systems, then look for matching proteins through using a computer system to align multiple, much longer, chains. The DP algorithms usually are recursive algorithms tailored to store intermediate outcomes, which enhance efficiency for various systems. Smith-Waterman is an example of an alignment algorithm which applies a DP system for finding the otimmlocal(niversal) alignment of dual sequences- – b and a.

Additionally, the alignment lorithm relies on discovrg t matrix elements H whereby the component H_{ij}i nptia ark for aligning h tutu ($\_ \$a\_2$.,…,$a_i$) together with ($b\_1$,$b\_2$,$….$, b_j). Two similar sequences get a high score, while two dissimilar strings get a low score. Basically, the greater the score of the path along a matrix, the moeimproved the alignment (Zelkowitz, 2005).

Matrix H can be detected by graday intifying the matrix elements, beginning at $H_{1,1}$ thnadvanig in the directions towards increment of i and j. Evrelent is set depending on a unique code where $S_{i,j}$ serves as the iiaritysoe used frcomparing the amino acids a_i and b_j, while d is considered the drawback for any giveng. Mover the matrix is primed using the code $H_{0,0} = = 0$. he oaining local Smith-Waterman sequences, the $H_{i,j}$ code is modified to achieve the necessary results.

Th ap penalty, meanwhil, ca bemodified lk d may be swapped for $(d \times k)$ hereby d acts as the penalty for one gap while k is an integer of successive gaps. When the optimalaignment mark is identified, the "traceback" from H across the optimal route is found, that matches with the optimal structural configuration for the score.

For the next group of exercises, users will manually execute the Needleman-Wunsch alignment protocol for a set of short sequences, and then conduct global sequence alignments using a computer program established by Anurag Sethi, that's based on edlan-Wuschcode with a ffine space penalty, $d+ +$e $e(k-1)$, in which e is the extended gap penalty. The production file shall be in a GCG format, which is one of the dual standard layouts in bioinformatics used for storing sequence data (the alternative standard setup is FASTA) (Zelkowitz, 2005).

To manually implement the Needleman-Wunsch alignment, the first activity you will examine is the Smith-Waterman code on a s series aspect of hemoglobin or (PDB code 1AOW) plusand myoglobin 1 (PDB program 1AZI). For this, you will arrange theis HGSAQVKGHG to a sequence KTEAEMKASEDLKKHhe Ssequences begin at the top right corner and: the original gap penalties are mentioned at every offset starting point. With every move from the beginning point, the original penalty increase frohe single gap penalty goes up by 8. Meane empty matrix has initial gap penalties on its own as well.Aligned pairs form the boxes through which the route exits from the upper-left side. When there are vertical and horizontal movements across yath, it means there shall be a space (or dash, "-") "–") within the sequence. For al gnmt boxes, it means the similarity score is $S_{\{i,j\}}$ from a BLOSUM40 matrix checkup that is provided as(small text, base of square). There are a total of four alignment scores which are offered as examples (big text, uppermost of square) (Zelkowitz, 2005).

8.8. APPROXIMATE STRINNG

Approximatring matching technology iscommory string appears similar to , though not similar to desired matches and patterns, which can be figuratively encoded as strings. This process involves searching for optimum alignment of double finite-length strng, whereby equivalent patterns might not be clear.; Eextended so typical variations or random sound , for instance, may share delicate, characteristic, fundamental patterns of symbols (Figure 8.4).

Figure 8.4: Approximate pattern matching relies on character matching and gaps to form letter sequences.

Source: https://www.slideshare.net/mailund/approximate-matching-string-algorithms-2007 (accessApril 2020).

The use of approximate pattern macthingmatching here simply highlights the fact that the perfect match might not be attainable and that imperfections like missing and extraneous signs must be considered. For a number of applications, a few of the strings are a prototype sequence that represents a sequence class while the other option is a testing string which must be analyzed and/or classified (Zelkowitz, 2005).

Moreover, the edit space between sequences $a1$, ..., am or $b1$ ... bn constitutes the basic costs of the series of editing steps namely (insertions, deletions, and variations) which translate one string to another. A renowned tabulating technique computess s and the mching editing sequence in duratand space O (mn)., Beginning from this technique, it'sit is important to develop an enhanced algorithm which works in duration and in interval O(s · min (m, n)). Yet another enhancement with time labelled O(s · min (m, n)), or space O(s · min(s, m, n)) can be provided for special cases where every editing step has the same rate independently of the typescripts iolved.

In case the editing series that provides costs s isn't needed, it means algorithms cabe pplied in span O(min(s, m, n)). Considering thats s = = O(max (m, n)), then the new procedures are often asymptotically as functional as the unique tabulating method (Zelkowitz, 2005).

Being duct, the algorithms are hievable, provided there's ther a threshold ratet, t, time test t ·mim, n)) plusand in span O(min(t, m, n)) wheres s ▢ ▢t. t. Ultimately, diverse generalized edit spaces are analyzed and situations are provided under which these algorithms may be used together with comprehensive edit operation groups, including, for instance, swapping of adjacent characters.

8.9. TEXT COMPRESSION

Text compression is commonly used in Huffman coding processes. During texting, there is a unique alphabet that, for any given class, has comparatively stationary possibilities. For instance, the probability structure for a given novel won't differ considerably from the probability system for another vel.

Likewise, the probability structure for a group ofC c programs won't be a lot diffent from the probability system for a different group ofC c programs. In an example, the odds of 26 letters (both upper- and low-case) are acquired for the American Constitution which is illustrative of English texting.

Additionally, probabilities were attained by calculating the frequency of incidents of letters present in the earlier edition. Whereas these two documents may look substantively different, their sets of probabilities look very much similar.

By encoding the previous versions of the texts using Huffman codes which were developed using the occurrence probabilities obtained, the file size can be reduced in size from roughly 70,000 bytes to around 43,000 bytes using Huffman coding.n though this limitation in file scope is beneficial, it'sit is still possible to obtain enhanced compression standards by first removing the structure present in formelation between the codes in the file.

Noticeably, there's there is a considerable sum of correlation within the text. For instance, Huf is commonly followed by fman! Regrettably, this correlation isn't amenable to basic numerical models, like was the situation for the image documents. Nevertheless, there are other rather more complex methods that can be applied to remove the connection in text files (Zelkowitz, 2005).

8.9.1. Markov's Text Compression Model

Markov's text structure is particularly valuable in text compression, whereby the possibility of the following letter is highly influenced by the previous letters. As a matter of fact, use of Markov systems for written English shows up in the unique works by Shannon.

In present text compression writings, the kth-sequence Markov models are broadly referred to as finite context systems, with the term context being applied for what has earlier been described as state. Take the word preceding for instance. What if the word preceding has already been processed, or about to encode the subsequent letter? If no account is given concerning the framework of the system, and treats every letter like a surprise, it means the possibility of letter g appearing is comparatively low.

By using the first-order Markov structure or one-letter cot (which is, checking the probability structure given *n*), it'sit is possible to determine that the possibility of g will increase significantly. Through increasing the context scope (moving from n-to in or din for instance), the possibilities of the alphabet turn to be skewed, thereby resulting in reduced entropy (Zelkowitz, 2005).The author Shannon applied a second-order system for English text involving 26 letters, and one space for obtaining the entropy of 3.1 bits per letter. Applying a model whereby the output signs were words instead of letters, leveled down the entropy model to 2.4 bits per letter.

Furthermore, Shannon applied predictions produced by people (instead of statistical models) for estimating the top and bottom bounds present on the second sequence entropy model. As for situations where the topics were cognizant of the 100 preceding letters, users can estimate these bounds as 1.3 or 0.6 bits per letter, correspondingly (Zelkowitz, 2005).

8.10. RESEARCH ISSUES AND SUMMARY

Pattern matching and text compression have paved the way for other topics like Prediction via Partial Match (PPM). Largely, text prediction is based on a procedure that's similar to text compression, apart from the fact that encryptiext condensation are binary, instead of human application. There's There is a close relation between text-compression and effective entry: code structures that compress properly are usually applicable in text entry.

Different studies have been carried out on dynamic methods of compressing text, where one of the techniques that offer the most ideal compression rate has been identified as PPM. By and large, PPM was proposed to utilize high order context forecast in mathematical coding. Moreover, PPM interposes the *n*-gram figures in the user corpus using initial statistics, symbolized as Pinit(w) (Sayood, 2006).

In addition, the adaptation effect explained through these algorithms as well. Research shows that there's there is a relation een the amount of learning data (parallel axis, in amount of words), plusand the amount of keystrokes a word known as (vertical axis).

Besides, the entry technique of single-key through disambiguation with completion can be used. For such, the horizontal line is slightly over 5.5 keystrokes a word which specifies the baseline, and constitutes the average amount of keystrokes requirprocess one word using a whole keyboard (covering spaces).

The numberamount of keystr refers to the quantity of the keystrokes a word needed for the inpu plusand selection operations. The selection keystrokes are calculated asn n when picking the nth candidate. For predicting texts, there are several points through which the target text can be selected (Sayood, 2006).

8.11. SEARCHING COMPRESSED DAT

With text data amounts increasing by the day, the question of storing theis massive data and detecting a sequence in these t is getting more apparent. The answer lies in compressing the text data plusand the answer to the latter rests on using an effective string-corresponding algorit A few compressed texts may be searched instantly without decompression, plusand this procedure is generally known as compressed pattern sequencing or compact string matching.

Recently, there have been many algorithms which have been established to resolve the compressed pattern sequencing problem. The compressed desiatching algorithm is normally specific to just one compression algorithm, plusand can't be applied with another. The word compressed string matching originally was seen in the works by Amir and Benson (Sayood, 2006).

While any string sequencing algorithm may be applieth this scheme, the compression rate and string matching tempo are moderate. It'sIt is been proved that searching basic patterns in texts which are compressed using a byte-based word-style Huffman coding algorithm can be twice faster than looking for them in standard texts.

Moreover, dense codes are represented as statistical codes which apply a word-based technique, besides they are effective when looking for one word within a compressed text. There are two unique semi-static dense codes, and they were first established in 2003 known as the End-TCode (ETDC), includis, c)-Density Code (SCDC). Consequently, thesedeveloped dynamilents of them,are known as Dyna, which are ideal for compression speed, though not effective in decompression speed (Sayood, 2006).

8.11.1. Compression Algorithm for Quick Text Search

The CAFTS decids which sub-dictionary shall be applied by checking the final encrypted diagram (LED), and integrates the subsequent three characters following this LED to develop the searched trigram. Afterwards, the sub-dictionary scope of the LED can be derived froimension hash table.'

In case the sub-dictionary dimension is 0, then it s there's there is no sub-dictionary for the LED present in the 'dictionary.' But if it'sit is not 0, then the address of ttart of that sub-dictionary can be achieved from the program's 'address hash table,' plusand the trigram is equally explored in that sub-dictionary having a dual search mechanism.

When the trigram is established, the ofset protocol of trigram (or index integer of the trigram for that sub-dictionary) $++\sigma$ is encrypted, plusand the final two typescripts in the trigram have been allotted to the LED. In case the trigram is not established in the parallel sub-dictionary then a shifting procedure is performed: It means the second element of the previous LED becomes the original character of the fresh LED, the primary element of the previous trigram becomes the succeeding character of the novel LED, and the final two typescripts of the old tri-gram become the original two typescripts of the fresh trigram, while a new character can be read directly from the resource for the previous character of the frtrigram (Sayood, 2006).

Assume that the text document to be condensed is 'dickens.txt' plusand we are now condensing the text "Oxford Univey" using an identified alphabet. Then the algorithm reads double characters (O and x), plusand cs their presence in Σ. Since they are present in Σ, it means they're allotted to the LED plusand their Σ codes which are (28 and 58) become encoded. Besides, the algorithm is capable of reading the subsequent three characters namely (f,o, and r), that are also present in Σ.

Typically, the trigram is developed where these three3 characters are present and this trigram examined in the 'Ox' sub-dictionary. Considering that 'for' is the single trigram available in the 'Ox' sub-dicionay, it forms part of the original index. Following the encoding of σ value or index (60 ++ 1 == 61), the subsequent and third fonts of the trigram from (o a r) become allotted to the LED (Sayood, 2006).

To develop a new trigram, eans the next 3 three elements would be derived from the resource, where (d, is 'space,' plusand U). While the first versions of these are present in Σ, the final one is nohus, the Σ codes found in 'd' plusand 'space' are encrypted, and in order to encode 'U,' it'sit is a must to first ensure the escape element (0) is encoded, then later ASCII encryption of this character would be encoded.

A total of two characters would be derived from the (n and i) source to develop the new LED, besides a total of three characters shall be borrowed from the source consisting of (v, e, and r) to create the fresh trigram (these are all present in Σ). Moreover, the Σ codes which are 'n' and 'i' or (48 and 43) become encoded while the trigram 'ver' becomes searched through the diagram 'ni' sub-dictionary.In thihe trigram can be detected in the 188th catalog of the sub-dictionary while 60 ++ 188 (equals) = 248 is encrypted. Besithe2nd and 3rd typescripts of the trigram which are (e and r) will be altted to the LED, plusand, to develop the new trigram, and the subsequent three typescripts (s,i, nd t) shall be taken directly from the source. These typescripts are all available in the Σ plusand allotted to the trigram, though this trigram isn't presented in the 'er' sub-dictionary (Sayood, 2006).

Genetic Algorithms

CONTENTS

9.1. INTRODUCTION

Genetic algorithms are typically used in biology to quantitatively describe the resemblance of various organisms and their traits (Figure 9.1).

Genetic Algorithms

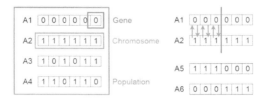

Figure 9.1: Genetic algorithms illuminate relationships amongst different organisms.

Source: https://towardsdatascience.com/introduction-to-genetic-algorithms-including-example-code-e396e98d8bf3 (accessed on 6 April 2020).

The word genetics is derived from the term gene. Although it is a biological term, it can be used in other disciplines to describe various relationships, be it when showing relationships in mathematical formulas among others. It is also used in physical formula as well as other disciplines. Algorithms, on the other hand, refer to the processes and set of rules that govern the process of calculation as well as other problems solving operations. The algorithms are used by computers to solve the problems input in the system. It can therefore be referred to as an instruction that is to be followed when a mathematical operation is being conducted. They are fitted to solve the problems keyed into the computer. Some of the algorithms used are automatic and may run well in the computer as they solve the current problems in the computer. Some of the algorithms are made in such a manner that they can solve the most complex of problems. They are made to suit various complex problems in the various physical, chemical, mathematical, and biological problems.

Genetic algorithms have different definitions depending on the area of applications. For instance, in the world of computer science and research refers to a metaheuristic that is part of a large group of evolutionary algorithms. In the genetic algorithms, we focus more on the biological uses. The term metaheuristic refers to a high-level procedure that is based on a heuristic design that is extensively used in generation of partial algorithms with an aim of coming up with high levels of efficiency and accuracy when solving optimized problems. They are also used in solving problems that may have complete or incomplete information. It also solves those with a limited computational capacity. This algorithm involves the use of stochastic optimization. The use of such optimization ensures that the generated solutions are dependent on the random set of generated variables. It incorporates the use of other optimization tools as well as iterative methods in solving of such problems (Jacobson and Kanber, 2015).

The metaheuristics in the genetic algorithms have various properties that define them. They include their characteristics of containing strategies that control the search process. They also have techniques that entail the use of a wide range of algorithm that vary from simple local search procedure to very complex learning and searching engines. Another characteristic is the fact that they are non-deterministic and approximates. They are also made in a way that they are not specific to a given problem. This is also one of its advantages. The genetic algorithms make use of biologically inspired operator in conducting optimization as well as conducting search problems. Such operations include mutations, selection, as well as crossovers.

The operations were generated on the basis of Darwin's theory of evolution. There are various methodologies that are used in genetic algorithms. They include optimization problems, initialization, selection, genetic operators, heuristics, and termination methodologies. The optimization problems are a methodology that seeks out to come up with better solutions. There are a variety of solutions and are therefore referred to as a population of candidate solutions. An individual candidate solution has its own characteristics. The candidates can undergo alteration and mutation. The solutions are represented by use of 0 and 1 in the binary formats. In some cases, the encodings are used in the representation of the candidates. The evolution process involves the use of generated individuals referred to as an iterative process. The population in the iterative process is called a generation. There is an evaluation that is carried out for each candidate on its fitness. The optimization process involves the establishing of an objective function. Candidates that have a similar characteristic are classified under the same population and hence the stochastically selection. The genomes then undergo modification resulting to the formation of new generation. The newly generated population is used in the following iteration of the algorithm. In a basic genetic algorithm, there are various requirements. It is required that there be a genetic representation in the given solution domain. Also, there should be a fitness function that will be used in evaluation of the solution domain. A typical representation of each candidate solution is known as an array of bits. The main characteristic of the genetic representation of the genetic representation that brings about the efficiency is the fixed size attribute of the candidates that allows for simple crossover operations. In cases that involve computations with longer representations of variables, the crossover operations may end up being more complex. The representations vary according to the type of programming. For instance, in genetic programming the tree-like representations are used while in the evolutionary programming the graph form representation is used. In a special case, the genetic programming the representation used is a mixture of both the linear chromosomes and the tree is used. Once the representation of the candidates is done, the initialization process follows (Jacobson and Kanber, 2015).

9.2. INITIALIZATION

The nature of the problem is a major determinant in identification of the population size. It may therefore contain several solutions. After the random generation of the initial population thereby creating a large rage of possible solutions which are applicable in a large area. After the initialization, the selection is done.

9.3. SELECTION

In a generation that has occurred, there is a part that is selected to be bred into a new generation of candidates. Through a fitness-based process the selection occurs which involves the filtration of the solutions to identify the most likely to be selected. It employed the use of given methods to conduct the filtration whereby they rate the fitness of each solution and by far this is the most effective method to be used. The methods that conduct random sampling of the solution of the candidates. This process is disadvantageous in that it is time consuming. Therefore, the fitness function is defined as the genetic representation as well as the measure of the quality of the given solution. The fitness function is always dependent on the problem. Some of the solutions involve the use of the knapsack problem that involves the use of a fixed capacity of the knapsack. It involves the definition of a fitness expression. In complex situations, the definition of fitness expression may be difficult and therefore there is use of simulation in determining the function value of the phenotype. It involves the use of interactive genetic algorithm are incorporated into the operations (Jacobson and Kanber, 2015).

9.4. GENETIC OPERATIONS

This is the following step is the generation of a second-generation population. The second generation is carried out through combination of generic operations such as the case of mutation and crossover.

A pair of parent solutions to be used in production of new solutions are selected from a pool of solution with the consideration that they meet the set standards. The selected parents are combined through the use of mutations and crossover and therefore the resultant solution referred to as the 'child' is composed of the characteristics of both the parent genes. The combination process continues further until a population of the solutions is produced. The process continues and results in the production of solutions that are of high quality.

The chromosomes present in the end solution are different from the initial solutions. Therefore, solutions that initially had poor characteristics in the end result of the combination may end up having a better quality of the properties of the chromosomes.

Therefore, genetic diversity is allowed and it facilitates the improvement of the chromosomes. The resultant chromosomes are therefore genetically diverse. In most cases, mutation is carried out as most researchers have their second thought about the crossover method in the process of combination. The argument being that crossover may not produce the required size of the chromosomes. The parameters may be turned to produce different results. This therefore entails the use of the elitist selection. There are also the heuristics methods (Jacobson and Kanber, 2015).

9.5. HEURISTICS METHOD

This method is also incorporated into other methods used in conducting the operations. Though they play a role in the operations, they are also used in conducting their operations in a faster manner. The operations are therefore done in a more robust manner.

It therefore conducts a modification of the system making it able to conduct the operations quickly. In the case where the specialization heuristic is used, it conducts a penalization of the crossover conducted between the solutions that tend to have similar characteristics.

The advantage of this being that is allows for population diversity and thereby assists in prevention of convergence in a minimal optimal solution.

9.6. TERMINATION

This method involves the generation process is done continuously unit a terminal point is attained. Some of the terminating conditions include the solution satisfying the least criteria required. It also involves a certain number of generations being attained. The terminating condition being that the allocated budget has been attained. It may also be that the highest level in ranking the fitness of the solution may have been attained. For instance, if plotted in a graph, a plateau state is obtained signifying that the highest level has been attained. The terminating condition may be established as a result of the manual inspection of the solution on the point established. In some cases, all the above descriptions may lead to the solution being referred to as they have attained termination.

Genetic algorithms are not as complex as thought to be. They are in fact quite simple to implement and incorporate. The challenge may be that to some extent they are quite difficult to understand. The complexity may be in the aspect that the frequency of the algorithms may succeed the generating solutions of high fitness. It may therefore be quite difficult to implementing the algorithms in practice problem. It therefore requires the hypothesis which consists of the description of the algorithm and its adaptability by obtaining it identity and recombining the building blocks of the chromosomes. Some of the identities involve the order of the chromosomes as well as the defining length. The hypothesis may entail the genetic algorithm performs an adaptation by involving the use of implementation of the heuristic (Chambers, 2019).

The heuristic is constantly evaluation as there has been no consistency in the hypothesis used. It therefore requires the making of various estimations in the distributions of the algorithms. This has brought about the production of good results. The challenge has been that it limitations in the case of the classes. There have also been some sceptics concerning the generality of the algorithms used in operations.

There are various features of the genetic algorithm though there are five important features. They consist of encoding, selection, mutation, crossover, and fitness function. Encoding involves the problems to be solved being considered as individuals in a given population. It involves the solutions being divided into small building blocks also called steps. The steps represent the genes. A collection of the genes will end up in an encoding of the entire situation. The problem will be represented in the form of GA chromosomes (Chambers, 2019).

Fitness function is the representation of the requirements of the solution expected of the problem. The function in this case performs the calculation and afterwards gives the result of the fitness of individual solutions. Selection involves the operator defining how individuals in the given population are selected and used in reproduction. It entails the use of various strategies in identifying the most suitable solutions to be used during the selection. The genes with the suitable characteristics are selected. Crossover different from selection involves the operator defining the parents of the chromosomes to be generated. They therefore identify the chromosomes to be mixed. Once mixed there are genetic codes of the offspring that is obtained. The operator therefore makes use of inheritance properties. Mutation involves the operator making changes in the genetic coding in the offspring. Therefore, there is production of random diversity in the genetic coding (Chambers, 2019) (Figure 9.2).

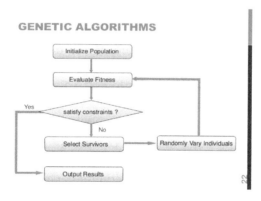

Figure 9.2: The figure illustrates how genetic algorithms work.

Source: https://www.ozassignments.com/solution/genetics-algorithm-research-proof-reading-and-editing-services (accessed on 6 April 2020).

9.7. EXAMPLES OF GENETIC ALGORITHMS

The examples of genetic algorithms are the various representations of the genetic algorithms. In this case, we discuss them step-by-step using the following examples. The step-by-step allowing the solving of simple optimization problems. There are various expressions that are used in the solving of problems in genetic algorithms. The solving involves identification of optimal values that may satisfy the various variables in the equation. Take the case of an equation such as $4a^2+b= 64$. The solving of the problem involves identifying an objective function. The function may be in the form of a and b. Hence solving the equation may involve establishing the values of a and b. To solve the equation, we go through the four major steps that are coded as R for a given iteration. The first step involves guessing of the initial sets of a and b. The values may be inclusive or not inclusive of optimal values. The values in this case are referred to as chromosomes while the steps taken are referred to as the initialized population.

The term population in this case are the sets of values of b and a. There are uniform functions that are used in the generation of initial values. There are possible six sets of values that are generated. The values vary between 1 and 10. The R code mentioned earlier is used in the generation of the initial chromosomes. The second step involves a process known as selection. As mentioned earlier selection involves the operator identifying and choosing chromosomes that can be considered to be the parents to the chromosomes to be generated. The selection involves computation of the function of the individual chromosomes. The fitness function also referred to as the objective function is obtained. By so doing, selection allows the fittest chromosomes being used in subsequent operations. According to the fitness value, chromosomes with the lowest values of the fitness function are selected. Chromosomes that have an objective function of 0 are the most preferred to be used in operations (Jacobson and Kanber, 2015).

In the selection process, the most commonly used method used is the roulette wheel method. This method involves the use of a pie plot that use values of fitness probability are the common way of expression. In the optimization problem, there are different ways in which the problems are expressed. In one way, the chromosomes that produce low fitness values tend to have high fitness probabilities. Therefore, the fitness probability is computed through use of fitness values. There is a formula used in the computations to obtain the values of the fitness probability. The roulette wheel is usually in the form of a pie chart with the sum of all the values of the fitness probabilities should add up to 1. Afterwards a scale is selected. A scale of cumulative fitness probabilities. The obtained segments are then used in the following step. It is important to note that the given segments signify the chromosomes. In some cases, there are some chromosomes that will be discarded as they are deemed to be unfit. There are pieces of R-codes used to represent the fittest chromosomes.

The next step is the crossover. This involves the expression of the genes. It involves the conversion of the values of a and b. They are converted into binary strings therefore the values are expressed in terms of 0 or 1 as the case of the binary language in computers. Crossover involves the changing of a group of genes. It involves the mating of the parent chromosomes resulting to the production of a new chromosome known as the offspring. During crossover, there is a parameter that is followed. The parameter is called the crossover parameter.

The values in this parameter commonly range between 0 and 1. In the case where the value obtained is 0.5 then this implies that three chromosomes will be allowed to be involved in the crossover and therefore results in the production of three off springs. The crossover will occur at selected points or positions in the chromosomes. The positions used during mating may be several depending on the type of mating. The next step will be mutation. Mutation involves the altering of values in the gene. It involves replacing of certain values in the binary format using values such as 0 and 1 (Jacobson and Kanber, 2015).

Take the case of a chromosome with a gene sequence of (0, 0, 0, 1) after mutation will end up being (1, 0, 0, 1) in this case the first value has undergone mutation so that it value changed from 0 to 1. In other cases, more than one position of the gene sequence may be altered. It is therefore the mutation parameter that will govern the process of mutation by deciding the number of genes that may undergo mutation. In the case where the parameter is 0.1 then the mutation will occur 0.1 times and it will be the number of genes that will be allowed to undergo mutation. Random values are selected in the given rows and columns to be used during the mutation process. After the mutation process is done, the binary chromosomes are converted into the integer form.

Afterwards the fitness values are then calculated. In the case where after the computation the chromosome value produces a value resultant to zero then the mutation process will end there. If the value is not zero, then it will be required that the process be repeated from the second step (selection) and the fourth step (mutation) will be repeated by having the mutated chromosomes being equated with a new population. The R-block code may be used to represent the process.

The resultant of the optimization problem may involve the fitness values computed for 10 values. The values of the yielded chromosomes a and b is therefore the optimal solution. In this case their fitness value yields to 0 (Jacobson and Kanber, 2015).

9.8. UNDERLYING PRINCIPLES IN GENETIC ALGO-RITHM

Genetic algorithm is based on principles of natural genetic systems. They conduct searches aimed at providing an optimal solution for a given evaluation in a given problem. The genetic algorithm deals with simultaneously multiple solutions and makes use of the fitness functions values in obtaining the solutions. While solving the problem a solution string is used. The string in this case is coded and is of a finite length over a finite alphabet. The coded strings are the chromosomes. During the computation, each chromosome is considered to be individual. Therefore, a collection of the chromosomes is referred to as a population. It begins with the generation of a given size M. For every given size of the population iteration after generation there are a new generation developed. There are three major operations involved in the creation of a new generation of chromosomes. The operations include selection, reproduction, and mutation. Reproduction is also known as crossover. The newly created generation is then used to generate another population of chromosomes. These chromosomes may have different traits from the initially used parent chromosomes. The knowledge on the initial chromosome may be retained in the population or in a different location that is outside the population. The algorithms are therefore able to give the value established for the chromosomes (Chambers, 2019).

The coded solutions are recorded. The model used is thus referred to as the ELITIST model. While solving a given problem the consideration is placed on the maximizing function that contains a finite set. The chromosomal representation and initial population involve a string in a finite set of a given alphabet being used to represent the chromosome. In this case, the length of the chromosome is represented using the letter L. Therefore, the total number of strings may be represented in the form a^L. Therefore, the fitness function for a given set of strings S is equivalent to the function f. The selection is an artificial version of the natural selection. It is therefore a modification of the Darwinian survival of the fitness theory. It involves individual strings of a given population being replicated in a mating pool. This is done with respect to empirical probability distribution that is dependent of on the fitness function values. It therefore requires one to calculate the fitness value for each chromosome, the total fitness of the population, the probability for selection, as well as the cumulative probability. It is then followed by reproduction. Reproduction involves the exchanging of information between potential strings and therefore leading to the generation of two off springs of the next generation.

The probability of a chromosome taking part in the reproduction is also considered. The reproduction operation is then conducted by having a random generation of the integer position. The generation has to be conducted within the given range of values of the chromosomes.

The selected values or variables undergo replacement with a different pair of values or variables. The operation of reproduction within a given mating pool of a given size is conducted using a given procedure. It involves one randomly choosing a given pair of strings from the given mating pool. This is such that the selected strings belong to a given pair of strings. For the selected pair of strings, a random number of rnd's are generated. The reproduction procedure is then conducted between the two strings and it carried out at a given point and thus is referred to as a single point crossover. The crossover operations in this case may include the multiple point shuffles, shuffle, as well as the uniform crossover (Chambers, 2019).

Mutation is the final process. It is the common random alteration in a character in a position. It is conducted on the character in each chromosome. Mutation is conducted in a given manner which involves a given character in a certain position in the chromosome. One should note that any string can be used in the generation of new strings and maybe denoted using a different character. Various steps are involved in a simple genetic algorithm. It involves the generation of an initial population as well as the calculation of the fitness value. Afterwards the selection operation is conducted. It is then followed by the reproduction operation which is followed by the mutation operation.

The Elitist method is used in most of the genetic algorithm operation. It involves the preservation of the best string within the given population. There are common steps followed during the Elitist model of the Genetic algorithm. It involves the generation of an initial population and the calculation of the fitness value of the individual strings.

Then the best string is then established. A selection is then conducted on the initial population. Afterwards the reproduction process is conducted followed by the mutation operation resulting to the generation of a new population. It is followed by a comparison being made on the fitness values of the individual strings.

The bad string is replaced using another string with a better fitness value as well as a value of S that is significantly minimum (Chambers, 2019).

9.9. GENETIC PARAMETERS

They are among the principles that govern the process of genetic algorithms. It involves the values of unknown variables being determined. However, it is required that these variables should be carefully determined before they are included into the given operations.

9.9.1. Stopping Criterion

In the first iteration, the genetic operations involve it being conducted on a given population and thereby resulting into a new population of strings. The next process of iteration involves the newly generated population undergoing the generation operations and they are subsequently done. They are conducted until an optimal solution is obtained. Commonly there are two stopping criteria used in genetic algorithms. The first case scenario involves the operations being done over a fixed number of iterations. This process requires that the best string is used during the operations. The other case scenario involves the algorithm being terminated if there are no improvements on the fitness values of the string used. This is after the strings are observed for a given number of iterations. In this case, the generated string it used as the optimal one.

There are various processes under the mathematical modeling of the EGA. In this case, strings of a given length L are taken under consideration in a finite alphabet in an aim to represent a given solution. A collection of strings is thus taken as S. The number of strings S is said to be finite and each string consists of a fitness value in terms of fit and therefore there is an existing relationship between them. There are common case scenarios between two strings. In the first case scenario involves the value of the first string being greater than the collection of the second string. The second case involves the collection of the first string being equal to the collection of the second strings while the third case scenario involves the collection of the first string being less than the collection of the second strings. The mathematical modeling of the EGA involves three stages of partitioning (Chambers, 2019).

In the first case, there is the partitioning of strings. It involves the use of a number of elements being used to facilitate an efficient partition of the collection of string into a collection of non-empty subsets. The second partition involves partitioning of the populations. A given population involves a collection of strings (M). In this case, individual strings being derived from S. The population may contain several copies of one or more strings. The given number of copies may be in a population and is useful in defining the type of the population. Therefore, the collection of strings may be as a result of the collection of the given copies. A set is therefore made from a collection of populations that have the same fitness function values.

The third process involves the transitions between two populations. For any given generation the genetic operation leads to the generation of a population. The genetic operations in this case are the selection, mutation, and the crossover. In the operations aim at preserving the best traits of the strings but the genetic operators cannot generate a population from a given variable if a part of a given variable is less than what is expected. This is because the fitness value of the new population is at a least fitness. Therefore, the creation of a new population from a given population is referred to as a transition. It involves the denoting of the transition probability. It is required that a given theorem is followed when. When using the theorem, the resultant value is usually a positive integer. This allows that any given population can be used as a state as of the Markov chain. The probabilities give a representation of the transition probabilities from a given population to a new population. A transition matrix is denoted for use in the Markov chain. In this case, there are some applications that include clustering and classification (Chambers, 2019).

9.9.2. Clustering

First, we need to identify K clusters from our data. In order to partition our dataset S into the K clusters, we need to apply a clustering algorithm. This assumes that a sub-optimal algorithm is available. Also, there is a generic algorithm implementation that should occur. Here there is a string representation that occurs where in this scenario the fitness function represents the objective function. Several experiments are conducted. In one experiment, it involves 10 points being randomly taken. The value of the variable K is determined. Then the optimal value of the objective function is determined by conducting an exhaustive search. Then the generic algorithm is the applied with a maximum number of iterative and it is repeated for five different initial populations. For three data sets, ten points are taken (Kramer, 2017).

Afterwards a selection is conducted by use of a usual selection strategy. It is then followed by a crossover by use of a single point crossover. The crossover is then repeated multiple times until a certain value of K groups is attained or until the limit on the number of the attempted crossovers is attained. Afterwards a child set of the given parents is selected randomly. Then mutation is conducted. In the next experiment, there are a number of points taken from a number of clusters. The genetic algorithms are then applied on the different initial positions. Under classification, we get to discuss the supervised classification. This involves the training samples being provided, the classifier is then designed, the number of the line segments is established as well as the number of the correctly classified points in this case the fitness.

There are various computations that are conducted including the boundary approximation by use of hyper planes, the triangular distribution of points by use of the Bayes-line as well as the GA-lines commonly known as arrows. There is also a theoretical analysis which is conducted under restrained conditions. Here the performance of the genetic classifier tends to approach that of the Bayes classifier. By so doing the values of the hyper lines will be at a minimum. It is important to note that the Bayes classifier is also referred to as the optimum classifier in the case where the class in prior probabilities and the conditional densities are established. There is also the fitness computation which may involve some of the values in the population being misclassified (Kramer, 2017).

When conducting these operations, one has to identify when to stop the Elitist model of the genetic algorithm. There are pointers that assist the operator in making such decision. They include one identifying the minimum stopping time that was essential for the operator. In the case where there is an assumption that there is only one optimal string, the new population will contain M copies of the complementary string S. The value of a variable N has to be determined (N is in the equation that is composed of the stopping time) and after doing so the value of the stopping time can be established. The theoretical stopping time is achieved if the value is relatively large. Also, the genetic algorithm results in the production of good strings that have better properties compared to those in the initial iterations. There is also the term optimistic stopping time which is defined on the basis of an optimistic assumption of the fitness function. The final step involves an average value of the stopping time being determined (Kramer, 2017).

9.10. BEST PRACTICES IN GENETIC ALGORITHM

Genetic algorithms are used in evolutionary computing and are inspired by biological evolution. As we will discuss, we tend to focus more on the projects that have made great use of the genetic algorithm. It therefore will require an individual to have knowledge on the basics of genetic algorithms. It will involve the candidate solutions to a given problem undergo a random initialization and form the first population. Afterwards the individual candidate solutions are given a fitness score that is dependent on how it will be efficient when solving the problems. It is followed by a selection step where by individual candidate solutions with higher chances of survival are used during the operations (Jacobson and Kanber, 2015).

The chosen candidates undergo crossover or mutation that will result to the production of new individuals and therefore the new population. The populations undergo a series of operations until the set criteria are attained. Some of the projects that involved the use of genetic algorithm include when NASA made a space antenna. This made use of genetic algorithm but it required a set of complex requirements to be met after the operations. During the project, they said the practice involved the designing and optimization of antennas by use of hand. This however was limited as it causes a restrain on the ability to generate new and better antenna designs. This is attributed to the fact that it will require a significant domain expertise and it will also require much time as well as it is labor intensive.

The random antennas in this case are represented in the form of a list of operations, including the forward (radius, length) or the rotation angle. In case of such operations, the parameters can be mutated. Also, the fitness score is commonly composed of a combination of a wide beam width in a circularly polarized wave as well as a wide impendence bandwidth. The Knapsack problem is a clear illustration of genetic algorithm's depth in a simpler case of the NASA antenna where the optimization of these problems is NP-hard. This illustrates that there has been no known algorithm that can be used to determine whether a given solution is optimized in a certain polynomial time. In this case, the genetic algorithm is used in handling NP-hard problems and making the approximation of the optimal solution (Chambers, 2019).

A series of steps are followed to ensure a successful generation. It involves the creation of a genetic algorithm that will represent the problem in a way that is appropriate to facilitate the suitable application of genetic operators. For example, Knapsack problem can be represented as a flexible sized array containing item identities. Here the fitness score will be the sum of the value of items in the backpack. In the case where the backpack exceeds the carrying limit, the fitness score will be 0. The second step involves the creation of an initial population. A given variable of backpacks will be used.

They will be filled with random items. This is done until the set weight limit is attained. The third step involves the determination of the fitness score as well as the transition to the next population. It involves two individuals being chosen pseudo-randomly. They should contain a higher fitness score which will therefore result to a higher probability value. The first genetic operation conducted is the crossover which is related to giving birth.

The chosen parents combine and bring about a new individual. In this problem, it may be quite difficult to determine the positions of the parents that were used. This is attributed to the fact that two constraints that have to be met. These are that the backpack should not contain duplicate items. Also, the backpack should not exceed the set weight limit. This operation is then followed by the mutation operation. Here there are three operations that can be conducted. However, the operation to be conducted is randomly chosen and then applied. The mutation operation involves an invalid character in the individual being removed and replaced with a more suitable character. When the new population has been generated, genetic operations are repeated automatically. In the case of the knapsack problem, a single iteration in computed in a millisecond thereby facilitating numerous numbers of repetitions to be done. This guarantees the approximation to the optimal solution (Chambers, 2019).

Convolutional Neural Networks led to an increased interest in evolutionary computing. It involves search engines (SEs), such as Google, writing blogposts that clearly outline the research pertained in this field. It involves various architectures being used with some of them containing immense search spaces. The recent developments also involve the researches conducting studies on new architectures as no architecture has been proven to be optimal. Therefore, evolutionary computing has been used to optimize the architectures by exploring the types, amounts, and the order of the layers in the architecture. The parameters of the layers as well as the global parameters of the architectures include the learning rate and the learning function. These parameters can also be optimized (Chambers, 2019).

The major challenge is computing power needed in optimizing the architectures. The fitness score of the given architecture is established by training and evaluating on the given task. In a basic genetic algorithm, this has to be repeated a number of times. In summary, the evolutionary computation techniques are obtained from natural processes and optimized problems that do not have a clear optimal solution. This has been incorporated in a number of projects and in recent days and has been extensively been used in learning and research. A great demonstration is when students use the evolutionary algorithm to make a target image by using a small base image.

The best practices includes checking the convergence of a genetic algorithm where fitness value change across the generations. It involves calculation of fitness value of individual solutions by conducting a comparison with other candidates. The comparison process in this case is carried out by the human users and therefore, it is an interactive genetic algorithm. This symbolizes that there is no real mathematical function and focus is to reach the steady-state solution of the genetic algorithm. The fitness value is obtained as a result of calculation using the value in the comparison. The fitness value is normalized between 0 and 1. Hence, it will be somewhere between 0 and 1; the best value is 1 and the worst value is 0 (Michalewicz, 2013).

The average fitness value will be 0.5. The individuals with the highest fitness values will be used in production of new individuals of a new generation. When comparison is conducted, the chosen individuals and new individuals will combine to for individuals with a variety of fitness values.

Therefore, the fitness value will be relative to the given generation meaning that it cannot be compared across generations. The best practices in ecology and evolution include making a good selection of the genetic algorithm. Therefore, given the type of the system, one needs to select an appropriate algorithm. Specific guidelines may guide an operator to make the correct choice.

A critical aspect is the strength of the genetic algorithm and helps the operator decide which model should be implemented in the genetic algorithm. Some operators use computer simulation programs to visualize fitness values (Michalewicz, 2013).

9.11. MATHEMATICAL ANALYSIS OF GENETIC AL-GORITHMS

Genetic algorithms may not be suitable for problems which require the exact global optimum. Therefore, genetic algorithms are non-deterministic although there are theories that identify how and why genetic algorithms work in certain idealized settings. When conducting an analysis of the genetic algorithms, the operator must be aware of the search space, schema, and implicit parallelism. Some of the concepts have their theorems that assist in the mathematical analysis (Michalewicz, 2013).

9.11.1. Search Space

When an operator wants to solve a problem involving genetic algorithm, they should look for a solution that will be more suitable compared to other solutions. The space of all possible solutions is referred to as the search space. The given points in the search space indicate the feasible solution. These solutions are usually marked according to its value or how it is fit in solving the problem. Therefore, the operator looks for the solution among the points in the solution and identifies one point in the search space that may be more appropriate in solving the give problems. It may involve one looking for the solution in extremes within the search space.

Using some points, we can solve some problems and obtain other points in the search space. In the case where the problem at hand is complex, a method, such as the hill climbing, tabu search, genetic algorithm and stimulated annealing, can identify the possible solutions. However, these methods may not lead to optimal solutions (Michalewicz, 2013).

9.11.2. Schema

It is a template commonly used in genetic algorithms. It is used in identifying of subset strings that contain similar properties with certain positions in the strings. The plural form is schemata and means cylinder sets. They form the topological space. The length of the schema is defined to be the total number of nodes present in the schema. It is important to note that if the child of a given individual solution matches the schema but does not match itself then the given schema is disrupted.

9.11.3. Implicit Parallelism

This term is used to refer to the genetic algorithms ability to conduct an evaluation on multiple types of the schema pattern either simultaneously or in a parallel manner.

9.11.4. The Schema Theorem

The theorem was developed to solve equations with relation to the genetic algorithm. It seeks out to help operators come up with possible solutions to the given problems. It observed that the best schemas are intended to receive an exponential increase in the number of samples for the successive generations. The theorem gives an illustration of how genetic algorithm works. The schema gives a description of the strings within the search space and is usually composed of the binary alphabet. In discussing the schema theorem, we use a wildcard whereby in this case in defining the length of a schema, it will be the distance between the outermost non-wildcard symbols. The genetic algorithm is able to function this being attributed to the fact that a variety of multiple schema can be processed by use of different few strings (Chambers, 2019).

As an example, the number four can be a representation of six different schemata. In most cases, the genetic algorithms process several schemas than the strings present in the given population. In this case, the implicit parallelism will refer to the genetic algorithms ability to conduct an evaluation on different schema patterns that are either simultaneous or parallel. As the reproduction process is conducted so that the most fit schemata will either increase or decrease in their representation in their stomata. In the most recent research, it was observed that the genetic algorithm will effectively process in n^3 schemata if the population size is n. There is a general formula used to describe the number of schemata at a particular time.

For instance, if we take a scenario where the function m describing the number of schema H in a particular time t as m (H, t), then fitness of this schema becomes m (H, t+1) = m (H, t). The fittest schema is most likely to become part of the new generation while the less fit schemata will have less chances of being part of the new generation. The schemata patterns will still be retained although the individuals undergo a split as the crossover takes place (Chambers, 2019).

9.12. BUILDING BLOCK HYPOTHESIS

Building blocks are crucial components in genetic algorithms and refer to schemata with short defining length composed of bits that work well together. The Goldberg hypothesis states that a short, low order and highly fit schemata are the ones that are sampled, recombined, and afterwards resampled resulting to the formation of strings that have higher fitness potentials.

Though this is positive news, Goldberg was, however, able to discover a major weakness in genetic algorithms. If building blocks were to be formed, there must be presence of low epistasis, also known as the interactions among the genes on the given chromosomes. Hence, if the contribution of the gene to the fitness of the chromosome is dependent on the value of other genes in chromosomes, then there will be high epistasis (Chambers, 2019).

This is a practical case of bats that rely on production of ultra-sonic squeaks and highly specialized hearing to be able to detect echo. Some researchers, however, claim that the genetic algorithm may not be effective in problems where they are mostly required due to the requirement of low epistasis. Therefore, it is required that when encoding the different types of the genetic algorithm problems, Goldberg criteria must be met. They include the principle of meaningful building blocks. This principle requires the user to select a coding in an aim that a short, low-order schemata is relevant to the problem at hand. It should also be relatively unrelated to the schemata that are over the fixed positions.

The second criteria are the minimal alphabets. Here the user selects the smallest alphabet that will facilitate a natural expression of the underlying problem. When both criteria are met then the genetic algorithm will provide an effective way of solving the multiple types of problems. Genetic algorithms are commonly used in finding the global maximum of a given function. In most cases, there is use of graphs that is in view of the schema theory. The graphs may be multiple depending on the number of operations. They at times give an illustration of the subsequent operations in the genetic algorithm (Chambers, 2019).

9.13. RELATED TECHNIQUES IN GENETIC ALGO-RITHM

They are also known as related fields in genetic algorithms. They include the evolutionary algorithms, metaheuristics, optimization, evolutionary computing, and stochastic optimization. The evolutionary algorithm is a sub-field of evolutionary computing. It is composed of evolution strategies which involve evolution of individuals through mutation and discrete recombination. They are designed to solve problems related to a given domain. They use de-randomized self-adaptation to adjust control parameters.

Evolutionary programming entails the population of the solutions that have primary mutations, selection, and arbitrary representation. The self-adaptation is used in adjusting the parameters and may entail other variation operations that include combining of information from several parents. In estimation of the distribution algorithm, it involves the substitution of the traditional reproduction operators using the model-guided operators. These models are learned from the population by using machine learning techniques and may be represented as a probabilistic Graphical model. This model allows the sampling of new solutions or their generation as a result of a guided crossover (Kramer, 2017).

Gene-expression programming makes use of population of computer programs. The complex computer programs in linear chromosomes are simple and have fixed lengths. They are then expressed as expression trees. The computer programs then evolve as a result of the mutation operation process that the chromosomes undergo. It is also as a result of the recombination of the chromosomes to a manner that has similarity to the canonical genetic algorithm. In the special organization of the GEP chromosomes, the genetic modifications may lead to a valid computer program. Genetic programming is a technique in computer programs that involves them being optimized. It makes use of the tree-based internal data structures for the representation of the computer programs to allow adaptation. This is preferred to using list structures that are typical of genetic algorithms.

This brings about the grouping genetic algorithm which is an evolution of the genetic algorithm. Here the focus is on the groups of items different from other case scenarios where the emphasis is places on the individual items. This evolution was generated for the sole purpose of solving complex problems. The complex problems are better known as the clustering problems or the partitioning problems. It involves the set of items being divided into disjoint group of items in an optimal manner. This is achieved by making characteristics of the group of items that will equate to the genes. The problems may include bin picking, clustering, and line balancing. They are all respect to the equal piles as well as the distance measures. When the typical genetic algorithm was used, it resulted to a poor performance. Therefore, if the genes are equal to the groups it would mean that the chromosomes will generally contain variable length and special genetic operators that will allow the manipulation of the entire groups of items (Kramer, 2017).

In the case of bin picking the group genetic algorithm hybridized, the dominance criterion is by far the best technique to be used. Interactive evolutionary algorithms make use of human evaluation. They are applied to domains that are hard to design a certain computational fitness function. This is in the case of music, artistic designs, as well as evolving images. In swarm intelligence that is under the evolutionary computing there is the ant colony optimization that makes use of ants fitted with pheromone model to traverse the solution space as well as establishing the locally productive areas. It is considered as an estimation of the distribution algorithm. Here, a computational method relies on population-based approach. A swarm of the particles move into the search space. The movement is influenced by their positions and by swarm's global position.

This method depends on information sharing among population members. In some problems, this method is more efficient compared to genetic algorithms, especially the problems with continuous variables. The metaheuristic methods use electimize algorithm. This is an algorithm that works by simulates the phenomenon of the electron conductivity as well as the electron flow.

This method has been proven to be more effective in solving NP-hard optimization problems. It provides a higher capacity for searching in the solution space and also identifying the global optimal alternatives. Different from others, this algorithm makes an evaluation on the quality of the values within the solution string. This is done independently (Kramer, 2017).

There is also the memetic algorithm that is also referred to as the hybrid genetic algorithm. It is a population-based method whereby the solutions are subject to the local improvement phases.

These algorithms are different from genes in that they have the capability to adapt themselves. They have proven to be more effective when compared to traditional evolutionary algorithms. The cultural algorithms entail a population component that is almost similar to that of the genetic algorithm. Here the knowledge component is also referred to as the belief space. The differential search (DS) algorithms (DS) are formed as a result of the inspiration of the migration of the super organisms.

9.14. APPLICATIONS OF GENETIC ALGORITHMS

The genetic algorithms have a wide area of application.

9.14.1. Natural Sciences, Computer Science, and Mathematics

Natural sciences, mathematics, and computer science calculate bound states, local density proximity, chemical kinetics, and code-breaking to obtain correct decryption, construction of facial composites of suspects, and weak links, such as the look ahead in artificial creativity.

The principles are also used in data centers, distributed computer network topologies, evolvable hardware, machine learning, and so on (Kramer, 2017).

9.14.2. Earth Sciences

In earth sciences, the genetic algorithm is applied in climatology to estimate the heat flux between the sea ice and the atmosphere. It is also used in designing of water resource systems and groundwater monitoring networks.

9.14.3. Social Sciences

In social science genetic algorithm has been applied in the designing of anti-terrorism systems, linguistic analysis such as grammar induction as well as aspects of natural language processing (NLP) in the case of word sense disambiguation.

9.14.4. Finance and Economics

Here, genetic algorithm has been used in financial mathematics to design sophisticated trading systems, real option valuation, and portfolio valuation. It has also been used in economics where it has been used in the representation of rational agents in economic models and also in agent-based computational economics.

9.14.5. Industry Management and Engineering

Applications of genetic algorithms include airline revenue management, automated designs of mechatronic systems by use of genetic programming, automate design of industrial equipment, automated planning of structural inspection, and so on. Additionally, other noteworthy applications include multidimensional systems, multimodal optimization, multiple criteria production scheduling, mutation testing, rare events analysis, stochastic optimization, wireless sensor networks, parallelization of genetic algorithms and programming through the use of hierarchical decomposition.

9.14.6. Research Issues and Summary

This refers to limitations of genetic algorithms, which include repeated fitness function in the evaluation of complex problems. This is a major hindrance in artificial evolutionary algorithms. Therefore, establishing the optimal solution to the complex high dimensional multimodal problems will require that relatively expensive fitness functions being used in the evaluations. The real-world problems including structural optimization problems may require that a large amount of time being used to complete the entire simulation. In this case the typical optimization methods cannot handle such types of problems and it may therefore it may require one to forgo the evaluation and employ the use of a more suitable fitness that will be computationally efficient. It is important that amalgamation of approximate models be conducted as it produces promising approaches which using genetic algorithms in solving complex real-world problems (Kramer, 2017).

The other limitation is that genetic algorithms usually do not scale well with complexity. This is a case scenario that involves the number of elements undergoing mutation being relatively large therefore resulting to an exponential increase in the size of the search space. This makes it quite difficult to use the technique when solving problems such as designing an engine, plane, or a house. It will therefore require the problem to be broken down into the simplest form of the representation of the problem. It will involve the use of the evolutionary algorithms being used in encoding designs for the fan blades in place of engines. The building shapes being made instead of detailed construction plans while airfoils being produced instead of entire aircraft designs. The other problem in terms of complexity may be how to safe guard the parts that have evolved and used in representing good simulations from more destructive mutation more so when their fitness assessment will need them to combine well with other part.

When coming up with a suitable solution in comparison to other solutions may result to stopping criteria that may not be clear in the problems. In multiple problems, the genetic algorithms tend to converge towards a local optima or arbitrary points. This is a deviation as it is required to tend to converge towards the global optimum of the problem. This implies that it lacks the ability to sacrifice short term fitness for it to gain long term fitness. The probability of this occurring is dependent on the shape of the fitness landscape. This means that certain problems may give off an easy ascent that is toward the global optimum while for others it makes it easier for the function to obtain the local optima. The problem may increase as a result of the use of different fitness functions, increasing the mutation rate or by use of selection techniques that retain the diverse population of solutions. The No Free Lunch Theorem has proved that there is no general solution to this underlying problem (Kramer, 2017).

In order to maintain the diversity, the techniques the technique used is the niche penalty which involves a group of individuals that have a suitable similarity having a penalty being added to it. This will cause a reduction in the representation of the group in subsequent generations allowing the less similar individuals to be retained in the population. This method may not be effective as it is dependent on the landscape of the problem. Another technique that may be applied involves the replacement of parts of the population with randomly generated individuals. This is done when most of the population has similarity with each other. Diversity is crucial in genetic algorithms as well as genetic programming. This is attributed to the fact that reproduction in a homogenous population may not yield to new solutions. In the case of evolutionary programming and strategies, diversity is not of much essence as more emphasis is placed on the mutation operation.

The operation of a dynamic set of data may prove to be quite difficult. This is because genomes tend to converge early towards solutions that may no longer be valid for later data. This has led to a variety of methods being proposed as a remedy. It involves increasing the genetic diversity in a way as well as preventing the early convergence. Prevention is done either by increasing the probability of mutation when the solution quality decreases or by introducing newly randomly generated elements into the gene pool occasionally. The increasing of the probability of mutation in the case of a drop in the quality of the solution is referred to as triggered hyper-mutation. Evolutionary programming and evolution strategies may be implemented by use of the comma strategy. This involves the parents not being maintained while the newly selected parents are selected from offspring. This method is mostly effective when used in solving dynamic problems (Kramer, 2017).

Another limitation is that genetic algorithms are not able to effectively solve problems that have fitness measure as their single measure. This will mean that there will be no method for converging on the solution. It will involve a random search why may result to a solution within a short time as a genetic algorithm. But if the solution provides the failure or prosperity of the trial giving a variety of the results. The ratio of the prosperity to failure gives of an appropriate fitness measure. In the case of specified optimization problems, other algorithms may prove to be more efficient when compared to the genetic algorithms. This is measured in terms of the speed of convergence. The other alternative complementary algorithms include evolutionary programming, evolution strategies, Gaussian adaptation, and swarm intelligence, hill climbing and stimulated annealing. These are used alongside methods that are based on integer linear programming.

The appropriateness of the genetic algorithm depends on the amount of knowledge of the underlying problem. If there is much knowledge on the solution, then there will be appropriate solutions availed to solve it.

CHAPTER

10

Combinational Optimization

CONTENTS

10.1. INTRODUCTION

In the scope of operations investigation, practical mathematics and the theoretical computer discipline, combinatorial optimization is a theme that that is made up of finding a most favorable object from a finite position of the objects. In countless such crises, comprehensive search is not biddable. It functions on the area of those optimization problems whereby the location of the reasonable resolution is the disconnected or are even competent of being summarized to disconnected, and whereby the main objective is to discover the best result. A number of these common crises that consists of the combinatorial optimization can be the travelling salesman crises, the minimum straddling tree dilemma, plus the knapsack dilemma. The combinatorial optimization this is a topic of numerical optimization which is connected to the operations study, the algorithm hypothesis, and the computational convolution theory. This has vital applications in a number of fields, such as the artificial intellectual, the machine knowledge, the auction hypothesis, and the software manufacturing.

Various types of research text bear in mind the detached optimization that are to be consist up of the numeral programming together with the combinatorial optimization which in turn are made up of the optimization crises which deal with the graph organization, even though all of these subjects have intimately intertwined the research text. It frequently involves the decisive way to capably allocate the income implemented to discover the solutions to the numerical problems. The applications of combinatorial optimization consist of the:

- Logistics which usually is the comprehensive organization and the execution of a difficult procedures. In a universal business sense, while logistics is the organization of the course of things among different points of the origin and the spot of the expenditure to meet the supplies of the customers or the companies. The resources dealt with in the logistics can consist of tangible merchandise like the materials, tools, and the supplies, also the food and other unpreserved things. The logistics of the physical things generally include the incorporation of the information current, the resources handling, the invention, the wrapping, the record, the transportation, in warehousing, and more frequently the security. In military discipline, logistics is alarmed with preserving of the army provided lines at the similar instance as disturbing those of the rival, ever since the armed force exclusive of the resources and the transportation are defenseless. In the military logistics which was already experienced in the ancient globe and as the modern armed which have an important need for the logistics answers, the sophisticated implementations have been created. In the military logistics, the logistics officials have deal with how and at what time to move the resources to the positions which they are required.

- Optimization refers to the sequence of procedures and equipment that ensure the best possible development and distribution. This consists of the optimal assignment of the catalog within the provision chain, which in turn minimizing the operating expenses which consist of the manufacturing expenses, transportation prices, and the distribution expenses. The procedure often consists of the application of the mathematical representation techniques by means of the computer software. The supply sequence optimization is usually considered to be branch of the supply sequence engineering, even though the final is mainly paying attention on the mathematical representation which is based on the methods, while the supply sequence optimization may also be performed by means of the qualitative, organization which is established on the methods.

- Mounting the most excellent airline systems of the spokes and the destinations.

- By creating a verdict on which cabs in a particular fleet to direction to collect up fares.

- By deciding the most advantageous way to transport the packages.

- Figuring out the best distribution of work posts to people.

10.1.1. Methods

There are big amounts of texts on the polynomial-occasion algorithms for particular special groups of the detached optimization; a substantial amount of it is incorporated by the conjecture of linear programming. Several illustrations of the combinatorial optimization crises which fall within this structure are the shortest ways and the shortest-way trees, the current and the circulations, the straddling trees, the matching, and the Metroid dilemmas.

For the NP-whole discrete optimization dilemmas, the existing research text consists of the subsequent areas:

- The polynomial-occasion exactly solvable particular cases of the crises at offered;
- The algorithms that works well on the unsystematic example for the TSP;
- The rough calculation algorithms that operate in the polynomial occasion and come across an explanation that is very close to the most favorable; and
- Tackling the actual world examples that happen in practice and they do not necessarily demonstrate the most awful-case performance inherent in the NP-whole problems for instances such as the TSP examples with tens of the thousands of the nodes.

The combinatorial optimization crises may be observed as the penetrating for the best excellent elements of several sets of the discrete substance; for that reason, in the principle, whichever sort of exploration algorithm or the metaheuristic can be implemented to tackle them.

The largest part of the universally appropriate approaches is branch-and-the bound approach. This is a precise algorithm that may be stopped anytime to serve as the heuristic branch-and-the. This heuristic implements linear optimization to create the bounds and vibrant programming. On the other hand, the generic hunt algorithms are not certain to discover the optimal answer first, neither are they surefire to run rapidly in the polynomial point in time. Ever since several discrete optimization dilemmas are the NP-whole, for instance as the wandering salesman dilemma this is also anticipated as unless P=NP (Schrijver, 2003).

10.2. INTEGER LINEAR PLANS

An integer indoctrination dilemma is an arithmetic optimization or the viability plan in which several or even all of the required variables are to be the integers. In majority of the settings, the word refers to the numeral linear plan in which the purpose function and the limitation which further than the particular integer limitations are the linear. In the integer plan is the NP-whole. In exacting, the exceptional cases of the 0–1 integer linear plan, in the unknowns are the double, and the only limitations must be pleased, which is one of the 21 Karp's NP-whole dilemmas. If a number of these decision variables are not detached the dilemma is known as varied-integer plan crises (Schrijver, 2003).

10.2.1. Applications

Presently there are two major reasons for implementing the integer variables when modeling the crises as the linear plan are:

- The variables of the integer which are represent the amount which can only be the integer. For instance, it is not likely to construct 3.7 vehicles.

- The variables of the integer which are stand for the decisions for example whether to take account of a boundary in a chart and as a result should only obtain on the worth 0 or even 1.

These particular reflections occur regularly in the practice and as a result, the integer linear plan can be implemented in many request areas, a number of which are for a short time expressed as below.

10.2.2. Production Preparation

The varied integer programming has a number of applications in the industrial manufacturing, which consists of the job-store modeling. One of the major examples occurs in the agricultural production preparation which consists of determining the manufacturing yield for various yields that may be split resources for instance the Land, manual labor, the investment, the planting seeds, the fertilizer, and many others. The possible purpose is to get the most out of the total yields, without going beyond the accessible resources. In a number of scenarios, this may be articulated in terms of the linear agenda, but these variables should be controlled to be integer.

10.2.3. Development

These dilemmas consist of the overhaul and the automobile scheduling in the transportation systems. For instances, a dilemma may consist of the assigning the buses or the subways to their individual directions so that a specific schedule may be achieved, plus also to provide them with efficient drivers. At this time, the binary choice variables point out whether the bus or the subway is allocated to a specific route plus whether the driver is allocated to a specific train or the subway. The nil-one programming procedure has been productively applied to the tackling the project collection problems in which the projects are equally exclusive or their technologically mutually sustaining. It is implemented in a particular case of the integer plans, whereby all the conclusion variables are integers. It may be taken for granted the principles either as the zero or even one.

10.2.4. Telecommunications System

The main aim of these crises is to plan a system of lines to fit so that any predefined positions of the communication supplies are acquired and the whole cost of the system is minimal. This entails the optimizing of mutually the topology of the system alongside with the setting the ability of the diverse lines. In a lot of these cases, the abilities are controlled to be integer amounts. More frequently than not there are, relying on the knowledge implemented the additional limitations that may be representation as the linear discrimination with the integer or the double variables.

10.2.5. Cellular Systems

The duty of the frequency preparation in the GSM mobile systems consists of the distributing accessible frequencies transversely in the aerial so that consumer may be served and the intrusion is the reduced between the masts. This nuisance may be articulated as being the integer linear plan whereby the binary variables designate whether the occurrence is allocated to any particular antenna.

10.3. ALGORITHMS

The inexperienced way to tackle the ILP is to basically remove the limitation that x is the integer, and tackle the equivalent LP which are referred to as the LP relaxation of the particular ILP, and then later surrounding the access points of the explanation to the LP repose. However, not merely might this explanation not be most favorable, it cannot even be possible; with the aim of, it can even defy a number of the constraint (Lawler, 2012).

10.3.1. The Precise Algorithms

When medium A is not completely unimodular, other algorithms that may be implemented to tackle this linear program. One particular group of the algorithms is the splitting plane procedures which normally function by tackling the LP respite and then later adding the linear restriction that operate deviation explanation towards being the integer not including the excluding of any type of the integer possible points. Another group of the algorithms is the deviation of the branch and the bound procedure. For instance, the branch and slice procedure that unites both the branch and the bound and slicing plane procedures. The branch and the bound algorithms have several numbers of rewards over the algorithms that may only implement the cutting planes. The main advantage is so as the algorithms may be completed early and as extensive as at the smallest amount one of the integral explanations has been establish, a possible, even though not necessarily the optimal, explanation may be revisited. Furthermore, LP relaxation may be implemented to provide the worst-case bound for the optimal solution. To conclude, branch-and-bound procedures may be implemented to revisit the multiple optimal explanations (Lawler, 2012).

Lenstra in 1983 illustrated that as soon as the figure of the variables is predetermined, the viability of the integer programming dilemma can be tackled in the polynomial occasion.

10.3.2. Heuristic Procedures

Ever since the numeral linear training is the NP-firm, majority of this problem illustrations are intractable and as a result heuristic procedure must be implemented instead. For instance, the tabu exploration which can be implemented to find for resolutions to the ILPs. To implement the tabu resolution to tackle the ILPs, travels may be described as the incrementing or the decrementing the integer controlled changeable of a possible solution at the same time as keeping all the additional integer-controlled variables steady. The unlimited variables are after that tackled for. The small term recollection can comprise of the beforehand tried answer at the identical occasion as the average-term recollection which may consist of the principles for the integer-controlled variables which have resulted in elevated objective principles which presumptuous the ILP this is a reduction of the crisis. In conclusion, the extended term recollections which can guide the exploration towards the integer principles that previously have not been attempted (Lawler, 2012).

Other heuristic procedures that may be implemented to the ILPs comprise of:

- Hill hiking;
- Replicated annealing;
- Reactive exploration optimization;
- Ant settlement optimization; and
- Hopfield neural systems.

There are other varieties of problem-precise heuristics, such as the k-opt heuristic intended for the wandering salesman dilemma. The difficulty of these heuristic procedures is that if the condition fails to discover an explanation, it should be resolved why this solution cannot be found. Further, it is normally impossible to enumerate how close up to the most advantageous solution which is revisited by these procedures is.

10.4. POLYHEDRAL COMBINATORICS

Polyhedral combinatorics this is a limb of the arithmetic, within which the combinatorics and the distinct geometry, which investigates the dilemmas of counting and the recounting of the features of the curved polyhedra and the higher-dimensional curved polytopes.

The investigation in the polyhedral combinatorics cascade into two separate regions. Mathematicians in this field investigate the combinatorics of the polytopes; for example, they may search for the inequalities that explain the relationships among the figures of the vertices, the limits, and the features of higher sizes in the random polytopes or in the certain significant subclasses of the polytopes, and the investigation other combinatorial features of the polytopes like the connectivity and the diameter which are the figures of the steps that are needed to attain any of the highest point from whichever other highest point. Furthermore, a number of these computer scientists implement the expression polyhedral combinatorics to explain the research into various accurate descriptions of the features of certain exact polytopes in particular the 0–1 polytopes, and whose points are subsets of the hypercube which is occurs from the integer training crises (Paschos, 2012).

10.4.1. Faces and Features as Well as the Vectors

The features of a curved polytope P can be distinct as the crossroads of the P and a congested semi space H like that of the margin of the H which consists of no inner position of the P. The measurement of the countenance is the measurement of this particular hull. The 0-measurement features are the specific vertices themselves, also the 1-measurement faces are known as the boundaries which are the line sections that are joining the pairs of the vertices. Note down that this description also comprises of the faces the unfilled set and the complete polytope P. However, if the P itself has the measurement d, the features of the P with the element $d - 1$ are known as the aspect of P and the features with this particular measurement $d - 2$ are also known as the edges. The features of the p can be partially prearranged by the inclusion, and in turn forming the face web which has its top aspect, P itself also as it's underneath element the unfilled set.

The major tool in the polyhedral combinatorics can be the f-vector of the polytope, this vector whereby the fi is the figure of the i-measurement features of this particular polytope. For illustration, is a dice which has only eight vertices, with twelve limits, also with six aspects, as a result its f-vector are the numbers 8, 12 and 6. The double polytope having an f-vector which has the similar figures in the turnaround order; hence, for example, the normal octahedron, and the double to a dice, normally has the f-vector which is numbers such as 6, 12 and 8. The pattern matrices comprise the f-vectors of the normal polytopes as the diagonal essentials (Paschos, 2012).

10.4.2. Graph Hypothetical Properties

Along with examining the figures of the faces of the polytopes, the researchers have gained knowledge in many other combinatorial of them, which include the imagery of the charts that are acquired from the various vertices and the boundaries of the polytopes also their 1-skeleta.

Balinski theorem testifies that the chart obtained in this particular method from any of the d-measurement curved polytope is the d-pinnacle-associated. In this particular of the three-measurement polyhedra, this particular aspect and the planarity can be implemented to be the precise distinguishing the charts of the polyhedra the Steinitz's theorem testifies that the G is the precise framework of the three-measurement polyhedron but and only if the G is a 3-summit which is linked to the planar diagram.

Blind and Mani-Levitska theorem in 1987 testifies that an individual can renovate the face arrangement of a trouble-free polytope from its diagram. Hence, a particular undirected diagram is an accurate structure of an easy polytope. It is in pointed contrast in the midst of non-simple friendly polytopes whose charts are a whole graph also there may be many dissimilar friendly polytopes for the similar graph.

One more proof of these particular theorem which is supported on the unique submerged orientations was provided by Kalai in 1988, and Friedman in the year 2009 which illustrated how to implement this particular theorem to obtain a polynomial occasion algorithm for the renovating the face patterns of the trouble-free polytopes from their charts. Nevertheless, the testing whether a particular chart or web can be achieved as the appearance lattice of an easy polytope is the corresponding by the polarity to the realization of the simplicial polytopes, which was revealed to be whole for the existential hypothesis of the actual by the Adiprasito and Padrol in 2014 (Paschos, 2012).

In the situation of the simplex procedure for the linear plan, it is significant to appreciate the length of the polytope, the smallest amount of the number of limits needed to acquire any of the apexes by a trail from any other apex. The organization of the linear inequalities of the linear plan that define the aspects of a polytope on behalf of all the feasible resolution to the plan, and the simplex procedures which discover the optimal resolution by following a course in this particular polytope. Hence, the width provides a lesser bound on the figures of the steps this particular procedure entails. The Hirsch assumption, now invalidated, that recommended a tough hurdle on how bulky the diameter could be. The weaker quasi-polynomial they are the upper limits on the width are recognized, as well as the evidence of the Hirsch assumption for the special groups of the polytope (Talbi, 2006).

10.4.3. Computational Properties

Coming to a decision whether the figures of the vertices of a particular polytope is surrounded by several natural figure k this is a computationally complex problem and the absolute for the convolution of the group PP.

10.4.4. Features of the 0–1 Polytopes

It is vital in the situation of the cutting-plane procedures for the numeral programming to be competent to describe the precisely the features of the polytopes that normally have the vertices equivalent to the explanation of the combinatorial optimization tribulations. Frequently, these crises give explanations to solutions that may be able to explain the binary vectors; also, the equivalent polytopes have summit coordinates which are all nil or one.

As an illustration, reflect on the Birkhoff polytope, the group of the $n \times n$ medium that may be formed from the curved combinations of the permutation medium. Homogeneously, its vertices may be consideration of the recounting all the perfect matching's in an absolute bipartite chart, also the linear optimization dilemma on this polytope may be taken to mean as the bipartite smallest amount of weight ideal matching dilemma. The Birkhoff-Neumann theorem testifies that this particular polytope may be illustrated by the two kinds of the linear variation or the equality. Initially, for every matrix cell, here is a restriction that this compartment has a non-unconstructive worth. Subsequently, for every row or article of the medium, in attendance is a drawback that the amounts of the compartment in that line or the column are equivalent to one. The line and the article limitations define the linear subspace of the measurement $n2 - 2n + 1$ which the polytope of Birkhoff lies, also the non-disapproval constraints that describe the appearance of the particular polytope of the Birkhoff contained by that particular subspace. Yet, the polytope of the Birkhoff is remarkable in which a whole account of its features are available. For a number of extra 0–1 polytopes, in attendance are the exponentially several or the wonderful exponentially several of this facets, plus only the partial images of their features are obtainable (Talbi, 2006).

10.4.5. Theoretical Polytope

In the scope of mathematics, a theoretical polytope this is an algebraic somewhat ordered position or the poset which poetries the combinatorial features of an established polytope, excluding not only any of the merely geometric features like the angles, frame duration and many others. A normal geometric polytope that is supposed to be an understanding in some of the actual N-dimensional gap, characteristically the Euclidean, of the equivalent conceptual polytope.

The theoretical definition permits some extra general combinatorial arrangements than the traditional descriptions of the polytope, hence allowing several new substances that normally have no matching part in the traditional hypothesis. The word polytope is a sweeping statement of the polygons and the polyhedra within any particular number of the proportions (Talbi, 2006).

10.4.6. Combinatorial Commutative Algebra

This is a comparatively new and fast developing arithmetical authority. As its name entails, it lies between the junction of two more recognized areas, the commutative algebra, plus the combinatorics, and the regularly used procedures of an individual to tackle with crises that occur in the other. A smaller amount obviously, the polyhedral geometry holds an important part. One of the main milestones was bound assumption for the simplicial areas, established by Melvin Hochster and the Gerald Reisner. Whereas the crises may be put together purely on the geometric requisites, the procedures of this evidence drew on the commutative algebra methods. The autograph theorem in the combinatorial algebra of commutative is the description of the h-vectors of the simplicial polytopes that were assumed in 1970 by McMullen Peter which was known as the g-theorem, it was established in 1979 by Stanley requirement of the situation the algebraic disagreement and by the Billera Louis and Lee W. Carl competence, and also the combinatorial and the geometric building. A main open query was the addition of this description from the simplicial polytopes to the simplicial areas, the g-conjecture that was resoluted in the year 2018 by a person known as Karim Adiprasito (Talbi, 2006).

10.5. INCOMPLETE ENUMERATION PROCEDURES

The incomplete enumeration is obtainable as a technique for the treating large and linear representation. The incomplete enumeration and online optimization attain this goal. Forms of the incomplete enumeration are revealed to be closed-ring constant. The details of an algorithm respond to a computational crisis. For every contribution, the detail algorithm must create the list of all answers, without photocopy, and then later it brings it to a standstill. The presentation of a particular enumeration algorithm is measured in expressions of the occasion required to create the answers, both in expressions of the complete time necessary to produce all the solutions, or in expressions of the maximal hindrance among two uninterrupted answers and in terms of the preprocessing occasion, which is calculated as the occasion before the outputting the initial solution. This particular intricacy may be articulated in expressions of the dimension of the contribution, the dimension of every individual productivity, or the whole size of the position of all outputs, likewise to what is performed with the productivity-sensitive algorithms.

10.5.1. Common Intricacy Classes

Enumeration crises have been investigated in computational intricacy theory and other intricacy classes which have been set up for such particular troubles. An extremely general group is EnumP, which may be checkered in the polynomial instance in the contribution and productivity. Officially, for these types troubles, there have to be obliged to exist the algorithm A that takes as the involvement the dilemma input x, this candidate productivity y, which tackles the decision crises of whether the y is the right output for the particular contribution x, in the polynomial occasion in the x and the y. For example, this group consists of all the problems that add up to the enumerating of the witnesses of a particular dilemma in the group NP (Talbi, 2006).

Other groups that already been distinct consists of the subsequent. In the particular case of the crises that are as well in the EnumP, these tribulations are prearranged from the smallest amount to the most specific one:

- The productivity polynomial, this particular group of crises whose whole output may be computed in the polynomial occasion.

- Incremental polynomial moment in time, this class of crises where, all i, and the i-th productivity which may be produced in the polynomial occasion in the contribution size and in the figure i.

- Polynomial interruption, the group of dilemmas where the interruption among the two uninterrupted outputs is the polynomial in the particular contribution and which is self-governing from the productivity.

- Strongly polynomial interruption, this group of problems where the interruption before each productivity is the polynomial in the dimension of this particular output and which is self-governing from the contribution or after the other output. This preprocessing is usually understood to be the polynomial.

- Constant impediment, this particular group of problems where the impediment before both outputs is the constant, for example the sovereign from the contribution and the productivity. The preprocessing stage is usually understood to be the polynomial in the participation.

10.5.2. Common Methods

- Backtracking is the simplest method to enumerate all the solutions by systematically searching for the break. However, backtracking still cannot give the best guarantees regarding the interruption. For instance, a turn back algorithm can spend an extended time exploring sections of that space.

- Flashlight exploration: This particular method improves on backtracking by searching the space of all the possible answers by tackling the dilemma of whether the present partial resolution can be an incomplete resolution. And if they respond is no, then the specific algorithm may immediately be backtracked to stay away from wasting moment in time, making it easier to explain the assurance on the interruption among any two absolute solutions. In exacting, this method which applies fit to the self-reducible crises.

- Closing under the set procedures: If we might desire to enumerate the put out of place union of the two positions, then we might tackle the crisis by the enumerating the initial set and later the subsequent set. Moreover, if the combination is the none displaced but the locate may be detailed in the sorted arrangement, then the details may be performed in the corresponding on both of the sets at the identical occasion as eliminating the photocopy on the fly. In addition, if the amalgamation is not dislodged and both of the sets are not arranged then photocopy may be eradicated at the expenditure of the higher recollection usage, for instance, implementing the hash table. The same as the Cartesian of the two positions may be itemized efficiently by the enumerating of one position and the combination of each consequence with all consequences acquired when itemizing the succeeding step.

10.5.3. Illustrations of the Enumeration Tribulations

The highest point of enumeration tribulations is linear variation and we should enumerate the vertices of the polytope. This trouble is connected to the monotone idealization which is linked to various applications in the database hypothesis and the graph hypothesis. Enumerating the respond to a particular catalog query, for example the conjunctive inquiry or the inquiry expressed in the monadic subsequent-arrangement. There has been classification in the database hypothesis of which the conjunctive uncertainty would be enumerated with the linear preprocessing and the steady delay. The crisis of the enumerating maximal groups in a contribution graph, for example, with Bron-Kerbosch algorithm. A catalog all the elements of the organization like the matroids and the greedoids. A number of these problems on the grid, for example, the enumerating of the self-governing sets, routes, and cuts, and many others. Enumerating the pleasing assignments of the demonstrations of the Boolean purpose, for instance, the Boolean rule which is written in the conjunctive usual form or the disjunctive usual appearance, the binary verdict diagram like the OBDD, or the Boolean route in the restricted groups which are learnt in the knowledge collection, a good example is the negative normal shape (Talbi, 2006).

10.5.4. Association to the Computability Hypothesis

The conception of the enumeration algorithms is as well implemented in the area of the computability hypothesis to describe various high difficulty classes like the RE, the group of all the recursively enumerable crisis. This is the group of sets with which there subsist an enumeration algorithm which will create all the elements of the position: the specific algorithm can run perpetually if the given set is never-ending, but every answer should be shaped by the algorithm subsequent to a limited occasion.

10.6. LINEAR TRAINING

The linear training, also known as the linear optimization, achieves the excellent outcome. This type of linear programming is also referred to as the mathematical optimization and its goal is to optimize the linear objective function. It leads to an feasible area in a curved polytope, that is a set of the distinct as the juncture of the finitely several half places, all of which is later distinct by a linear variation. Its idea function is the actual-valued affine the linear purpose that is defined on this specific polyhedron. The linear training algorithm discovers the point in the specific polytope whereby this purpose has the negligible or the prime value but if only that peak exists.

10.6.1. Applications of the Linear Training

Linear training is extensively implemented in the area of optimization for the several grounds. Majority of the practical crisis in the operations study may be articulated as the linear programming crisis. The sure special cases of the linear programming, like the network course problems and the multicommodity course of problems are measured by being significant enough to contain the generated greatly research on the particular algorithms for their particular elucidation. The figures of the algorithms for several other categories of the optimization troubles perform by tackling the linear training problems as the sub-dilemmas. In the olden times, thoughts from the linear plans have greatly stimulated majority of the innermost concepts of the optimization conjecture, for example the duality, the putrefaction, and the significance of the convexity and its oversimplification. Similarly, the linear training was heavily implemented in the before time the arrangement of the microeconomics which it is at present being utilized in the company administration for example the preparation, the manufacture, the shipping, the knowledge and any other concern. Even though the present management problems are ever-altering, majority of the companies should like to be make best use of the profits and the minimize values within the limited income. Consequently, majority of the problems may be described as the linear training tribulations (Schrijver, 2003).

10.6.2. The Presumption Behind the Survival of the Optimal Resolution

Geometrically, the particular linear controls describe the feasible state that is the curved polyhedron. The linear role is a turned in function, which entails that every restricted minimum is the global least; correspondingly, to a linear purpose is a hollow function that entails that every restricted maximum is a comprehensive maximum. The most favorable solution required does not subsist, for two causes. Initially, if the limitations are contradictory, then is no possible solution that exists.

10.6.3. The Most Favorable Vertices and Emission of the Polyhedra

Otherwise, if a possible solution subsists and if the limitation set is delimited, then the most favorable value is constantly attained on the edge of the control set, by the utmost principle for the curved functions this is achieved by the then again, by the smallest amount of the principle for the bowl-shaped functions given that the linear operations are either turned in and bowl-shaped.

Nonetheless, a number of these problems have divergent optimal results; for instance, the predicament of discovering a feasible way out to a structure of the linear variation is a linear training problem in that the objective purpose is the nil function which is, the unvarying function which is taking the importance of zero universally. For this achievability the predicament with the nil-function for its intention-function, if they are double distinct mixtures, then all the turned in mishmash of the resolution is the way out (Schrijver, 2003).

The vertices of all the polytope are also known as the critical feasible explanation. The explanation for this particular option of name is as understand. Accede to d denote the figure of the variables.

Then the essential theorem of the linear discrimination implies for the feasible troubles that for all the vertex xx of the linear plan feasible area, there subsist a set of the d or even fewer the inequality limitation which are from the linear plan like that, as soon as we treat those d limitations as the equalities, the exceptional solution is the x*. By this means, we may study these particular vertices by methods of the looking at some assured subsets of the position of all the constraints in a disconnected set, to a certain extent than the variety of the linear programming solutions.

This theory brings about the simplex algorithm for the tackling of the linear programs.

10.7. CRUCIAL SUBSTITUTE OF THE ALGORITHMS

10.7.1. Simplex Algorithm of the Dantzig

The simplex algorithm was created by Dantzig George in 1947. It tackles the linear programming problems by the building of a feasible way out at a pinnacle of the polytope and then later walking along a course on the boundaries of the polytope to the vertices with the non-diminishing values of the idea function until the optimum is achieved for certain. In majority of the practical crisis, stalling arises: as the majority of the pivots are created with no augment in the intent purpose. In the uncommon practical dilemmas, the usual description of the simplex algorithm can point of fact the series. To keep away from the sequence, the researchers created new revolving rules (Schrijver, 2003).

When put into practice, the simplex algorithm is to a certain extent efficient and may be assured to discover the global best possible if certain safety measures against the cycling are put in use. The simplex algorithm which has been demonstrated to tackle the random tribulations efficiently, for example in a cubic figure of steps, which are parallel to its performance on the practical tribulations (Schrijver, 2003).

Nonetheless, the simplex algorithms have deprived worst-casing behavior, Minty, and Klee erected a family of the linear training problems that which the simple procedures obtain a figure of the ladder of exponential in the difficulty dimension. In reality, for some occasion it was not acknowledged whether the linear plan problem was able to be tackled in the polynomial occasion for instance the complexity group P.

10.7.2. Evaluation of the Interior-Position Techniques and the Simplex Algorithms

The modern estimation is that the particular efficiencies of high-quality implementations of the simplex-foundation methods and the interior position methods that are related for the routine functions of the linear plan. Conversely, for the specific kinds of the linear programming dilemmas, it can be that a lone type of the solver is more enhanced than any more on occasion much superior, in that the configuration of the explanations that are generated by the inner point procedures versus the simplex-foundation procedures which are significantly unusual with the prop up to the position of dynamic variables being classically less significant for the final one (Lawler, 2012).

10.7.3. Bowed Optimization

Bowed optimization is a subdivision of the geometric optimization that investigates the predicament of the minimizing of the bowed functions over the bowed sets. Majority of these classes of the bowed optimization crisis's that admit the polynomial-occasion algorithms, where the geometric optimization is in the common NP-rigid.

The bowed optimization has been implemented in a wide collection of disciplines, like the routine control structure, evaluation, and the signal dispensation, infrastructure, and arrangement, electronic circuit devise, the statistics analysis and the representation, economics, information the optimal tentative design, and the structural optimization, whereby the rough calculation impression has demonstrated to be efficient. With current advancements in the computing and the optimization algorithms, the bowed programming is virtually as undemanding as the linear programming (Schrijver, 2003).

10.7.4. Vibrant Programming

The vibrant programming is mutually a mathematical optimization procedure and a computer programming technique. This technique was created by Bellman Richard in the year 1950s and has been implemented in numerous areas, from the aerospace manufacturing to the economics. In all the mutually contexts it describes to the simplifying of a complicated crises by the breaking it loosely into simpler small-crises in a recursive approach. Notwithstanding the reality that some decision crises cannot be performed apart from this way, verdict that span a number of points in occasion do frequently break separately recursively. Similarly, in the computer discipline, if a predicament can be tackled optimally by the breaking it into small-crises and then recursively discovering the optimal keys to the particular sub-difficulties, then it is whispered to have the most favorable base. If the particular sub-problems may be nested recursively within the larger troubles, so that the vibrant programming techniques are appropriate, then there is a link flanked by the worth of the superior crises and the worth of the dub sub-crises. In that optimization text, this link is dubbed as the Bellman solution (Lawler, 2012).

10.7.5. The Effort-Productivity Models

In the scope of investments, the effort-productivity mock-up is a quantitative financial mock-up that corresponds to the interdependencies flanked by the different zones of a national financial system or the different area of economies. Wassily Leontief in the year 1906–1999 is ascribed with emergent of this kind of scrutiny and later he earned the Nobel trophy in finances for his advance of this particular model.

10.7.6. The Linear-Incomplete Programming

In the mathematical optimization, the linear-incomplete programming is an oversimplification of the linear training. While the intention utility in a linear plan is a linear task, the intent of the task in a linear-incomplete program is a relative amount of the double linear tasks. The linear plan may be considered as an extraordinary case of the linear-incomplete plan in which that denominator is the unvarying function lone.

10.7.7. Mathematical Optimization

Mathematical optimization then again spelled as the optimization or the arithmetic programming which is the selection of the most excellent component which has looked upon to several criteria from which a number of set of the existing options. Optimization crises of species arise in all the quantitative branches of learning from the computer knowledge and the engineering to operations delve into and the economics, and the progress of the solution procedures which has always been of concern in arithmetic for centuries.

Within the simplest case, the optimization predicament consists of the maximizing or the diminishing of an actual function by the methodically selection of the involvement values from within the allowed position and the computing of the worth of the task.

The oversimplification of the optimization and the procedures to any other formulations which comprise a huge area of the practical mathematics. More usually,

optimization consists of discovering the best accessible values of several objective tasks given a distinct domain or even the input, together with a range of different category of the intent tasks and the different categories of the domains (Lawler, 2012).

10.7.8. The Non-Linear Training

In the field of mathematics, the nonlinear training is the actual process of tackling the optimization crises where a quantity of the limitation or the goal function is the non-linear. The optimization dilemma is one of the reckoning of the extrema, the maxima, the minima or the still points of any objective tasks over a particular set of the mysterious actual variables and the restricted to the fulfillment of the structure of the equalities and the discrimination, that are collectively expressed as the limitation. This is the sub-area of the mathematical optimization that pacts with the predicaments that are not linear.

The emblematic of the non-bowed quandary is that of the optimizing shipping costs by the assortment from a particular set of the transportation techniques, one or several of which the exhibit of the financial system of scale, with an assortment of the connectivity and the ability of the constraints. A good instance would be the gasoline product shipping given a particular assortment or the combination of the pipeline, the banister tanker, the highway tanker, the stream barge, or even the coastal tankship. Due to the economic consignment size, the value functions can have the discontinuities in the accumulation to the smooth transformations (Lawler, 2012).

In the investigational science, several of the simple content analysis like the fitting of a continuum with a computation of the climax of the known position and the shape but its unidentified magnitude which may be performed with the linear procedures, but in common these particular predicaments, in addition, are the nonlinear. Classically, one encloses a theoretical representation of the structure under the investigation with the variable boundaries in it and the representation of the trial or testing, which can moreover have the unknown edges. An individual tries to discover the most excellent on top form the numerically. Within this particular case, we should determine meticulousness of the result.

10.7.9. The Slanting Metroid

This is a numerical structure that summaries the features of the directed diagram, the vector structure above the ordered areas, and the hyperplane planning more than the ordered areas. In evaluation, a regular for example non-slanting matroid synopsis the confidence of the features that are frequent both to in the grids, that are not essentially intended for, and to the preparations of the vectors that are greater than areas, that are not inevitably ordered.

All the slanting matroids have a basic matroid. Consequently, results on the regular matroids that may be applied to the slanting matroids. Nevertheless, the opposite is counterfeit; several of this matroids may not become the slanting matroid by the formalization of the underlying organization for instance of the trail or the sovereign set. The characteristic stuck between the matroids and the slanting matroids is later conversed further (Talbi, 2006).

The matroids are regularly useful in the region like the dimension premise and the algorithms. Since of a slanting matroid's enclosure of the extra details regarding the slanting nature of a given arrangement, its effectiveness extends more into the several fields which consists of the geometry and the optimization.

10.7.10. The Shadow Worth

The shadow worth is a economic value that is assigned to at that time unknowable or the complex-to-estimate prices in the nonexistence of the accurate market charge. It is founded on the enthusiasm to disburse the standard a bulky quantity of the accurate evaluation of the worth of a good or the examination is what the citizens are enthusiastic to bestow up in classification to get it. The shadow worth is regularly estimated based on the assured assumptions, also it is the biased and the somewhat imprecise.

The basis of these overheads is usually values that are exterior to a particular market or a disinclination to recalculate the method to report for the marginal construction. For instance, think about a firm that previously has an industrial unit that is full of the apparatus and the personnel (Talbi, 2006).

10.8. NUMERAL PROGRAMMING

This is the most powerful method for solving problems which consist of a mixture of unremitting and the separate activities, particularly those linking the scheduling. Unlike the Linear Programming, the numeral programming cannot purely be considered as the black box. Dilemmas should be particularly vigilant and the analyst should investigate with the numeral program code to discover the best strategy to be implemented. This particular item searches what the numeral program can performed and give details why several approaches to the articulating of the crises which are greatly more successful than the rest. The numeral program is the most excellent suitable method, but the very initial subject that should be tackled is whether the numeral program is an appropriate technique for the solving the crises. In a number of the compliments, the decisive factor is much comparable to those for the choosing whether the crises are acquiescent to the numeral program. Which is, there should be the:

- Several potentially tolerable explanations;
- Several ways of the evaluating the superiority of the alternative explanations; and
- A number of this interconnectedness among the unpredictable basics of the structure.

Generally speaking, the lesser the detachment that is needed to transfer from the numeral program the most favorable to arrive at the integer answers, the most probable that the numeral program will be an appropriate to the method to discovering the best, and the most probably the best, answers. Therefore, the numeral program is the best at tackling the crises which consists of the rounding of the numeral program resolution. This is more often than not true of the crises in which a comparatively small quantity of the decision which the variables should be the integer. It as well as applies to the crises whereby the numeral variables are the partially-continuous or the receiving integer values which are bigger than 1. Numerous problems consist of the special prearranged sets are as well relatively simple to tackle, but majority are not. The numeral program is much lesser when the best where there is an important combinatorial factors, for instance, wherever a figure of the amalgamation of the items should be selected and the values plus the viability of the mixture are further a purpose of the amalgamation than of the constituent items. The Travelling Salesman crises are a typical case in point. The dilemma is to discover the shortest course for visiting a set of positions. This is more difficult to tackle because the distance from end to end of a course is basically a purpose of the series of points appointed. The figure of these particular sequences of the positions raises as the n the factorial of the n, whereby the n is the digit of the points. The Travelling Salesman crises have been the matter of most of these investigations. Somewhat unpredictably, numeral programs are capable of delivering fast and precise solutions. They also demonstrate that they have found the most favorable solution. Regrettably, the numeral programs cannot tackle other crises in combinatorial areas (Schrijver, 2003).

10.8.1. Cutting Stock Crises

A comparable process is implemented to solve the so-called cutting-reserve crises. The process works out if any obtainable stock can meet specific dimensions. Such particular crises may be an individual-dimensional which is slitting within an unremitting roll of paper, the carpet or the layer stock for example into various tubes of the variety of widths or the double-dimensional which is cutting detailed shapes from various pieces of metal or the plastic.

Dynamic feature generation can solve these crises. There are is a massive figure of the possible critical models which should be implemented. A group of candidate models are created whereby in general these might be those with the least consumption and the numeral program crises which are tackled to discover that amalgamation of the cutting models which gathers the demand at the least amount of cost (Schrijver, 2003).

In most cases, the crises will later be tackled to an integer most favorable by implementing the existing group of the cutting models. In other instances, the subsequently stage can be an external worth routine which discovers to recognize other cutting models which should have been implemented in the numeral program explanation if they have been obtainable. These are supplementary to the dilemma and it is re-tackled. This procedure is repeated and to conclude the dilemma is tackled to an integer most favorable by implementing the augmented position of the cutting prototypes.

10.8.2. Aircrew Preparation

The aircrew preparation problem can be solved successfully using column invention methods. Each particular voyage in an airline's schedule must be equipped with the suitable aircrew. There are difficult rules for the operational hours of the different categories of personnel and these determine the total expenditure of an airline. The problem is to find out the least amount of resources that are necessary for the airline operation (Schrijver, 2003).

This is solved by generating rows which represent the possible trips and merging them into huge numeral programs. Such particular medium is among the file major in the regular use and can exceed by 100,000 files and ranks. In case readers mull over that cost reduction is dehumanizing, it is later given an account that the crews like better the optimized to-do list because they diminish the time depleted hanging around the airdrome waiting for the subsequently flight.

10.8.3. Connection of the Decisions

The fundamental complexity of discovering solutions leads to theoretical consequences. These discard the light on what is being performed on and assisting to guide us towards the formulations of the numeral program crises which are most likely to perform. The central crises in the integer plan occur from the juncture of the decisions. In other terms, one can make existence hard for the numeral program code whereby some movement arises from the intersection of two or more decisions, each of which is represented by a separate decision variable. If one implements a sole decision uneven to correspond to the combination of the decisions, the tribulations disappear.

This is exactly the approach espoused with the wounding stock crisis. The conclusion variables which have been implemented embed the rigid part of the crisis. The cutting design is adapted as stated and the verdict is followed by only how countless times to reproduce that design. With the travelling salesman crisis, the complexity occurs because the verdict of the variables each correspond to only a minute part of the whole set of the decisions whose juncture determines the value of the course (Lawler, 2012).

10.8.4. A Machine Development Example

The consequence of the various formulations may be observed with another illustration. This is a piece of a preparation problem from the flexible developing system. It is alarmed with choosing when all the figures of the tasks would take position.

Such a specific crisis can be tackled approximately by the impressive structure of occasion periods and by implementing the binary verdict variables which are preferably in the Special Controlled Sets of category 1, for whether a particular task begins at the commencement of a time era. If the occasion periods would be picked such that every particular task acquires a whole figure of time eras, this could acquiesce the optimum explanation.

Nevertheless, it cares for not to be feasible to implement such excellent time eras. A variety of approaches may be in use to prevail over this. Majority of these consist of the approximating the crisis. As effects the best explanation to the fairly accurate problem cannot be tackle the actual problem or, even if it does, it cannot be the most excellent solution to the actual problem. On the other hand, such specific advances may be very successful and they may be probably the paramount way to solve such crisis. If one needs to tackle the actual problem precisely we need to implement the verdict variables which correspond to the precise time when every particular task was established. Such a specific formulation procures for eternally to tackle this is observed on a number of computers (Lawler, 2012).

Bibliography

1. Akhgar, B., (2009). *ICCS 2007: Proceedings of the 15th International Workshops on Conceptual Structures* (pp. 3–94). Berlin: Springer Science & Business Media.

2. Aumasson, J. P., (2017). *Serious Cryptography: A Practical Introduction to Modern Encryption* (p. 312). California: No Starch Press.

3. Basu, S. K., (2013). *Design Methods and Analysis of Algorithms* (pp. 1–83). New Delhi: PHI Learning Pvt. Ltd.

4. Buchmann, J., (2004). *Introduction to Cryptography* (p. 338). Berlin: Springer Science & Business Media.

5. Calude, C., (2011). *Theories of Computational Complexity* (pp. 1–87). London: Elsevier.

6. Chambers, L. D., (2019). *The Practical Handbook of Genetic Algorithms: New Frontiers,* (Vol. 2, pp. 5–93). Florida: CRC Press.

7. Cohen, H., (2013). *A Course in Computational Algebraic Number Theory* (pp. 1–45). Berlin: Springer Science & Business Media.

8. Dave, P. H., (2007). *Design and Analysis of Algorithms* (pp. 3–64). New Delhi: Pearson Education India.

9. Dooley, J. F., (2018). *History of Cryptography and Cryptanalysis: Codes, Ciphers, and Their Algorithms* (pp. 1–86). Berlin: Springer.

10. Erciyes, K. (2013). *Distributed Graph Algorithms for Computer Networks* (pp. 1–9). Berlin: Springer Science & Business Media.

11. Erciyes, K., (2018). *Guide to Graph Algorithms: Sequential, Parallel, and Distributed* (pp. 3–77). Berlin: Springer.

12. Gebali, F., (2011). *Algorithms and Parallel Computing* (pp. 29–69). New Jersey: John Wiley & Sons.

13. Goldreich, O., (2010). *P, NP, and NP-Completeness: The Basics of Computational Complexity* (pp. 1–74). London: Cambridge University Press.

14. Jungnickel, D., (2013). *Graphs, Networks, and Algorithms* (pp. 1–63). Berlin: Springer Science & Business Media.

15. Kabat, M. R., (2013). *Design and Analysis of Algorithms* (pp. 1–66). New Delhi: PHI Learning Pvt. Ltd.

16. Karl, H. H., & Arnd, M., (2007). *Parallel Algorithms and Cluster Computing: Implementations, Algorithms, and Applications* (pp. 3–86). Berlin: Springer Science & Business Media.

17. Ko, K., (2012). *Complexity Theory of Real Functions* (pp. 1–71). Berlin: Springer Science & Business Media.

18. Kontoghiorghes, E., (2000). *Parallel Algorithms for Linear Models: Numerical Methods and Estimation Problems* (pp. 1–75). Berlin: Springer Science & Business Media.

19. Kozen, D. C., (2006). *Theory of Computation* (pp. 3–90). Berlin: Springer Science & Business Media.

20. Kramer, O., (2017). *Genetic Algorithm Essentials* (pp. 1–90). Berlin: Springer.

21. Lau, H. T., (2006). *A Java Library of Graph Algorithms and Optimization* (pp. 3–89). Florida: CRC Press.

22. Lawler, E., (2012). *Combinatorial Optimization: Networks and Matroids* (p. 400). Massachusetts: Courier Corporation.

23. Lee, J., & Burak, K., (2015). *Genetic Algorithms in Java Basics* (pp. 21–105). New York: Apress.

24. Lolli, G., (2011). *Recursion Theory and Computational Complexity: Lectures given at a Summer School of the Centro Internazionale Matematico Estivo (C.I.M.E.) Held in Bressanone (Bolzano), Italy,*

June 14–23, 1979 (pp. 7–101). Berlin: Springer Science & Business Media.

25. Mandloi, B. S., (2018). *Design and Analysis of Algorithms: DAA* (p. 135). New Delhi: Bhupendra Singh Mandloi.

26. Michalewicz, Z., (2013). *Genetic Algorithms + Data Structures = Evolution Programs* (pp. 13–53). Berlin: Springer Science & Business Media.

27. Mishra, B., (2013). *Algorithmic Algebra* (pp. 1–71). Berlin: Springer Science & Business Media.

28. Paschos, V. T., (2012). *Concepts of Combinatorial Optimization* (p. 368). New Jersey: John Wiley & Sons.

29. Paschos, V. T., (2013). *Paradigms of Combinatorial Optimization: Problems and New Approaches,* (Vol. 2, p. 678). New Jersey: John Wiley & Sons.

30. Puntambekar, A. A., (2010). *Design and Analysis of Algorithms* (p. 376). New Delhi: Technical Publications.

31. Roosta, S. H., (2012). *Parallel Processing and Parallel Algorithms: Theory and Computation* (pp. 1–83). Berlin: Springer Science & Business Media.

32. Rubinstein-Salzedo, S., (2018). *Cryptography* (pp. 2–99). Berlin: Springer.

33. Sayood, K., (2006). *Introduction to Data Compression* (pp. 1–41). Netherlands: Elsevier.

34. Schrijver, A., (2003). *Combinatorial Optimization: Polyhedra and Efficiency* (Vol. 1, p. 1881). Berlin: Springer Science & Business Media.

35. Sirmacek, B., (2018). *Graph Theory: Advanced Algorithms and Applications* (p. 194). Berlin: BoD-Books on Demand.

36. Talbi, E. G., (2006). *Parallel Combinatorial Optimization* (pp. 1–53). New Jersey: John Wiley & Sons.

37. Valiente, G., (2013). *Algorithms on Trees and Graphs* (pp. 1–54). Berlin: Springer Science & Business Media.

38. Vasconcelos, W., (2004). *Computational Methods in Commutative Algebra and Algebraic Geometry* (pp. 7–104). Berlin: Springer Science & Business Media.

39. Wayner, P., (2000). *Compression Algorithms for Real Programmers*

(pp. 636). Massachusetts: Morgan Kaufmann.

40. Wegener, I., (2005). *Complexity Theory: Exploring the Limits of Efficient Algorithms* (pp. 11–77). Berlin: Springer Science & Business Media.

41. Winkler, F., (2012). *Polynomial Algorithms in Computer Algebra* (pp. 1–82). Berlin: Springer Science & Business Media.

42. Zelkowitz, M., (2005). *Advances in Computers: Parallel, Distributed, and Pervasive Computing* (pp. 1–35). Netherlands: Elsevier.

INDEX

Printed in the United States
By Bookmasters